I HAD TO SURVIVE

I HAD TO SURVIVE

How a Plane Crash in the Andes
Helped Me to Save Lives

Dr. Roberto Canessa and Pablo Vierci

Translated by Carlos Frías

Constable • London

CONSTABLE

First published in the US in 2016 by Atria Books, an imprint of Simon & Schuster, Inc.

This edition published in Great Britain in 2016 by Constable

3 5 7 9 10 8 6 4 2

Interior design by Kyoko Watanabe
Map on p. 291 by Rossana Barone (graphic design), courtesy of Jörg P.A. Thomsen
(Director of the Andes Museum 1972)

Printed in Great Britain by Clays Ltd, St Ives plc

Papers used by Constable are from well-managed forests
and other sustainable forests

MIX
Paper from
responsible sources
FSC® C104740

Constable
is an imprint of
Little, Brown Book Group
Carmelite House
50 Victoria Embankment
London EC4Y 0DZ

An Hachette UK Company
www.hachette.co.uk

www.littlebrown.co.uk

To those who are suffering
and don't yet realize there is hope.

ROBERTO CANESSA

To Roberto, an inspiration to all of us.

PABLO VIERCI

I HAD TO SURVIVE

Part One

Part One

Chapter 1

Where is the line between life and death?

Through the screen of an ultrasound machine, I study the heart of a child about to be born. I take my time, watching the tiny hands and feet on the monitor, feeling as if we're communicating somehow through the screen. I'm fascinated at this life that will soon be among us—and at this heart that will have to be repaired in order for the child to survive.

One moment I'm gazing at the ultrasound screen, and the next I'm staring out the window of the crumpled fuselage of a plane, scanning the horizon to see if my friends will return alive from their test hikes. Ever since we escaped from the plane crash in the Andes mountains on December 22, 1972, after being lost for more than two months, I have asked myself a litany of questions, which is constantly changing. Foremost among them: What do you do when all the odds seem stacked against you?

I turn to the pregnant mother, who is lying on a gurney on the second floor of the Hospital Italiano in Montevideo, Uruguay. What is the best way to tell her that the child in her womb has developed in utero lacking the most important chamber of her heart? Until just a few years ago, newborns with these kinds of congenital heart defects, who came into the world stricken through no fault of their own, would die shortly after birth. Their only mark on the world would be a brief agony followed by a lasting trauma for their families. Fortunately, however, medicine took a crucial step forward, and this mother, Azucena, with the look of consternation on her face, can now have hope. There is a long, arduous journey ahead for this woman and her baby daughter, as well as for her husband and their two other children. It is an uncharted path as precarious as the one I made through the Andes. My friends and I were lucky enough to emerge from those mountains finally and reach the verdant valley of Los Maitenes. That's where I'm trying to lead these children, into their own verdant valley, although I carry the burden of knowing that not all of them will survive the journey.

This is my dilemma as a doctor. I find myself teetering between life and death as I watch this baby, whose mother has already named her Maria del Rosario. She can live for now, tethered to the placenta in her mother's womb, but what is to be done afterward? Should I propose a series of long, drawn-out surgeries so that she has a chance at living? And will it be worth all the risks and costs involved? I'm sometimes overwhelmed at the similarities between our predicaments.

When we finally left the fuselage to trek across the peaks and chasms leading to that valley in Chile, we encountered a vast no-man's-land. It's almost impossible to remain alive in that weather, at thirty below, without any gear and after having lost nearly seventy pounds. It was impossible, everyone assumed, to trek more than fifty miles from east to west directly over the Andes, because no one in our weakened physical state would be able to withstand the rigors. We could have chosen to remain in that uterine fuselage, safe, until it, too, became inhospitable when we ran out of the only nourishment that was keeping us alive, the lifeless bodies of our friends. Just as the infant gets nourishment from the mother, we were able to do so from our friends, the most precious thing we had in that world. Should we stay or should we go? Remain huddled or press forward? The only equipment we had to help us on our journey was a sleeping bag we cobbled together out of insulation from the pipes of the plane's heating system, stitched with copper wire. It looked like something plucked from a landfill.

This child, still a fetus, still connected to her source of nourishment, can survive a little longer, just as we did in the fuselage. But one day, as with us, the cord will have to be cut if she is to live, because we are in a race against time. I was the last one to decide to venture out, and that's why this recurring image has remained with me, intense and haunting. When should we cut the cord? When should we subject ourselves to the ordeal of attempting to cross the hostile mountain range? I knew that a hasty decision to trek across the mountains carried great risk, just as premature labor does for these children with congenital heart defects.

It took me a lot of deliberation to make my choice. There were simply too many factors, but I knew we were down to our last chance. Nando Parrado understood my doubts because he was wary as well, although he couldn't say this out loud for fear of letting down the rest of the survivors of the plane crash. With each person who died, we all died a little bit, too. It wasn't until Gustavo Zerbino told me that one of the bravest of our friends, Numa Turcatti, had died, that I decided it was time to go. It was time to leave the safety of the fuselage, to be born with a heart that wasn't ready for the outside world. One of my friends, Arturo Nogueira, who'd had both of his legs broken in the crash and eventually perished, told me, "You're so lucky, Roberto, that you can walk for the rest of us." Otherwise he might have been the one here today, in my place.

I was nineteen years old, a second-year medical student, a rugby player, and Lauri Surraco was my girlfriend when our plane crashed into the mountain that October 13, 1972. Those seventy days on the mountain were literally a crash course in the medicine of catastrophes, of survival, where the spark for my vocation would become a roaring flame. It was the most brutal of laboratories, where we were the guinea pigs—and we all knew it. In that sinister proving ground, I gained a new perspective on medicine: To be healed meant simply to survive. Nothing I learned since could compare with that ignoble birth.

In the hospitals where I've worked, some of my colleagues have criticized me, behind my back and to my face, for being domineering, impetuous, for flouting the rules or going beyond what's considered proper conduct—something my companions on the mountain accused me of at times as well. But patients don't care about the social mores of a medical corporation; they come to a hospital and then go home, no longer subject to its rules. My ways are the ways of the mountains. Hard, implacable, steeled over the anvil of an unrelenting wilderness in which only one thing matters: the fight to stay alive.

Chapter 2

When I close my eyes, I often travel through time and space to find myself back in the Valley of Tears on the day of the crash. Until that moment, my friends and I had been living in a predictable universe. Then, all of a sudden, there was a tear in the expectations of our lives—and we were left adrift in an eternal limbo where time neither begins nor ends.

It was 3:29 p.m. on October 13, 1972. When I looked out of the plane window, I was surprised to see the peaks of the Andes so close to the wings of our Fairchild FH-227D. Our rugby team, from Stella Maris–Christian Brothers, had chartered the forty-five-passenger turboprop from Uruguay's air force to carry the players, alumni, and fans to a match in Chile.

Suddenly, I felt the plane drop into a pocket of turbulence. Then another. The plane tried to pull up and gain altitude. Although the pilot had the engines at full thrust, they simply were not powerful enough. A moment later, there was a sinister sound as a wing was lost to the mountaintop. This was followed by a shattering explosion, the sound of crumpling metal, and a spinning descent.

We were tossed around as if in a hurricane. I was stunned, dizzy, as the plane made impact and tumbled amid deafening explosions, sliding down the side of the mountain at what felt like supersonic speed. I was gripped by the realization that our plane had crashed into the Andes—and that I was going to die. No one walked away from an accident like this, man and machine, limbs and steel, twisted and smashed. I held on to my seat so fiercely that I tore off chunks of fabric with my bare hands as my insides were jolted about. I bowed my head, ready for the final blow that would send me into oblivion. *What will it be like to die? Will I gasp for air, lose my sight? Will the world go dark? How much pain can I tolerate? Will I have to watch my limbs be torn from my body? Will I be aware until the final moment of my death? When will I finally lose consciousness?*

We quickly came to a violent stop, and my seat, to which I was still belted, ripped away from its moorings and plowed into the seat in front of mine, a chain reaction that didn't end until our rows of seats were piled up against the cockpit. *But I'm still breathing.* I started to think that maybe this was death, because I couldn't believe I was still alive. I hadn't yet realized that death would come for us in small doses, bit by bit.

I passed out for what seemed like seconds. When I came to, I couldn't quite grasp what had happened. I was having trouble seeing and was dizzy and in pain, but I couldn't seem to pinpoint what hurt. I heard disoriented moans and groans and breathed in the pungent fumes of jet fuel. Looking behind me, I saw the body of the plane was wide open. I couldn't believe my eyes: The fuselage had been torn apart and the tail section was missing. There were mountains all around us where the rest of the plane should have been, and a blizzard was whipping aside everything in its path, lashing us with the cold. Heads and hands started to move in the chairs that had been strewn about, torn free of their bolts. Flaco Vazquez, who was in the seat across the aisle from me, looked at me for help. He was pale, confused, in shock. . . . Someone behind me removed the tangle of seats and metal that was pinning me in. I turned around to see Gustavo Zerbino. He looked at me as if to say: *You're alive!*

Wordlessly, we asked ourselves: *Now what? Where do we begin?* But it was Carlitos Paez, another friend, who, still in shock, finally managed to speak, saying only, "Canessa, this is a disaster, isn't it?"

I looked over and realized Flaco Vazquez's leg was injured, and we had to stop the bleeding. There wasn't a moment to lose. The instinct to act kicked in, helping me to take my first steps. It wasn't that I had no doubts; it was just that there wasn't any time for them.

As I started to move about, I stumbled over something—or rather, someone: Alvaro Mangino, who was lying under his seat, trapped by twisted steel. Gustavo lifted the seat and I dragged Alvaro out. His right leg had been pinned under metal, and when I freed him, I could see that his leg was broken. I told Alvaro to concentrate on anything else, and then quickly, I set the break. Tears ran down Alvaro's cheeks, but he didn't so much as grunt. I wrapped his leg tightly in a piece of torn shirt that Gustavo handed me. That would have to do until we could find something better to make a splint.

We continued our search through the wreckage. The next person we came upon was the heavyset Enrique Platero. He pointed down at his body, as if it were someone else's, to show us a piece of metal jammed into his stomach. How deep, we had no idea. Gustavo told him to turn away, and he dislodged the metal, which came out with a piece of peritoneal fat. I tucked it back inside and bandaged it over with a rugby jersey. "Thank you," Platero said.

The cold was immediately everywhere. Instead of the 75 degrees it had been inside the cabin, it was now 10 below, and we were surrounded by blustery snow and ice. We opened luggage in search of jackets and sweaters, as well as T-shirts that we could use as bandages.

I saw our team captain, Marcelo Perez del Castillo, followed by a few others who were all helping the survivors. We tried to clear a path in a cabin riddled with twisted, razor-sharp shrapnel that was pinning in many other passengers, who began to stir like shadows from another world. A short distance away, Gustavo joined Daniel Fernandez and Moncho Sabella, who were trying to speak with the agonized copilot about what had happened—and what was going to happen next.

"This one's alive. . . . This one's dead," Gustavo noted as we moved about the ruptured cabin, and he reached down to check the pulse of a third. We bandaged one, consoled another . . .

God, I'm exhausted. Why is it so hard to breathe? I looked toward the back of the plane, through the gaping maw where a snowy universe was visible, a world indifferent to the terror and plight around us. For the first time, I asked myself, *Where the hell are we? Could we have crashed this far up the mountain? How could a plane, filled with fuel, crash into a mountain ridge and not totally explode?* I looked out and saw my best friend, Bobby François, sitting on a piece of luggage in the snow, shaking his head and muttering over and over, "We're doomed."

Before I knew it, darkness began to fall. Almost immediately, it became completely black. We used a lighter to see, all the while fearing that we might ignite the jet fuel that permeated everything around us. Three more lighters flicked on, their flames whipping and fading in the dark ruptured cabin as the freezing gusts battered us.

The air was so thin at this altitude that I was completely exhausted. My hands were covered in the blood of the dying and the dead. I found a corner where I could rest without stumbling over the injured, the mutilated, or the corpses. The net that delineated the luggage compartment, near the flight deck, was supported by two aluminum bars, forming a kind of hammock. When I got there, I realized someone else had had the same idea, someone I had never met, Coche Inciarte. We huddled together, shivering in the darkness, and lay down to sleep. I closed my eyes and tried to use all my senses. At first, I thought how unlucky I was. But then, as I moved my tired muscles and felt my body respond to each of my brain's commands, I felt exactly the opposite: No one on earth was luckier, and for that, I should be eternally grateful.

Chapter 3

My mother was a brave, beautiful woman, but she had a quirk: She stuttered when she was nervous. However, that never stopped her. On the contrary, it seemed to make her more determined, more audacious, and impervious to criticism or embarrassment when she knew she was right. I never actually noticed her stutter.

My father's family, meanwhile—all Genoese descendants who held Italian citizenship—was focused on medicine. My great grandfather was a prominent member of the medical academy, and my father was a highly regarded professor of cardiology at the medical school.

Although Papa was elegant and dapper, Mama never worried about dressing her sons like well-off people. My father's sober disposition was the yin to my mother's yang, and I think that's why they got along so well for so many years. They complemented each other, which made for a rare home life for me and my siblings, a place where no two days were alike. They ended up raising four completely different children.

My mother's family was huge and loving. Since my grandfather had died at an early age and my mother's sisters didn't yet have children of their own, I was the beloved baby boy in a family of doting aunts in their thirties. My mother had asked my father if she could name me after her late father, and so I was named Roberto Jorge.

My family believed in the free, secular, and mandatory education that Jose Pedro Varela had established in 1876 in Uruguay—the first Latin American country to have such a system—and so education was like a religion in my home. Teachers and professors were among the most important people in society. Education was so central to our lives that my mother took in an orphan boy and fostered him for years just to ensure that he would graduate.

Since I was the only boy in such a large family, they loved to spoil me. They gave me too many liberties, and I became wild and mischievous. My aunts exposed me to all kinds of art and music. Throughout my childhood, I wrote poetry they loved to read aloud or have me read aloud, mixed in with some of the famous poets such as Gustavo Adolfo Becquer, Antonio Machado, and Jorge Manrique. One of my uncles jokingly called me "Satan's spawn" because I was such a rascal. And one of my aunts gave me a horse, Alfin, for me to burn off some of my pent-up energy. And so the son of a well-to-do doctor and college professor began riding through the streets of the manicured neighborhood in tattered clothing and on horseback.

Everyone assumed I would go on to do well in school, which was the highest calling in my family, but school turned out to be my first big challenge. Everyone figured that my natural brightness would carry me far, but my free spirit clashed with the Irish Christian Brothers of the 1950s and 1960s. I may have been hardheaded thanks to my aunts' spoiling me, but the Brothers more than matched my stubbornness. I kept banging my head up against that ceiling because I didn't want to acknowledge that there were rules I had to respect.

Going to school was like being in the military, or in jail. I'd often end up in fights. But the Brothers were never intimidated by my rebelliousness. For the Brothers, to whom attitude was always more important than academic achievements, dealing with me was like trying to break a wild mustang. I had the hardest time trying to figure out my new surroundings.

The Brothers told my mother that clearly I was different from all the other boys, but that they wouldn't deviate from their teaching method. That fair-but-tough upbringing was as much a part of their trademark as their great rugby teams were. The only reason they didn't expel me, as they had so many others, was because amid all the havoc I'd wrought, I had never lied. Just one little white lie, they told her, and they'd kick my butt right to the curb. They checked in with all my teachers frequently, but I never committed the one transgression they wouldn't tolerate.

I learned the mores of this new society the hard way. And the Brothers started to understand me as well. By the time I was fourteen or fifteen, they gave me the honor of naming me leader of Iona House, one of the groups our school was divided into for intramural sports and academic competitions, as well as group prefect. I was perplexed as to why, when it came time to pick a leader, they had chosen the most undisciplined, troublesome boy among us. I asked Brother Brendan Wall, who had become my friend, why they had picked me. "Who better to deal with the knuckleheads than a retired knucklehead? Takes one to know one," he told me.

By the time I was sixteen, I'd started to come into my own in school and prepared to enter college, where I intended to study medicine. Meanwhile, I got better at rugby every day as my body began to develop. I worked out tirelessly, and soon I left behind a scrawny physique to earn my nickname, "Muscles." Since I loved to make individual plays, I was moved from my position of half scrum to wing, where I could take the ball and make a play all on my own—which fit my personality. And in 1971, I was named to the Uruguayan national rugby team.

One of the unique things throughout my childhood was that my parents would let my siblings and me spend the weekends at the small family farm of Elena Bielli, who worked as our nanny during the week. She was a humble farmer from Las Piedras, on the outskirts of Montevideo. My siblings got homesick sometimes, but

I never did. I immediately adapted to the place, which felt rustic and mysterious to us and which fascinated me. The farmers tilled the soil with an ox, grew vegetables, made wine from their very own vineyard, and raised pigs, which they sometimes butchered for meat and homemade sausage. I jumped right in like one of the farmworkers, because here, at Elena's house, our roles were reversed: She was the boss, and we were the workers. I'd arrive neat and clean, and a little while later, I would be helping butcher pigs and stuff sausages, my clothes stained with blood and guts like a military field medic. When they dropped us off at the farm, I could see my mother turning in her seat as the car drove off, my father looking back at us through his dark sunglasses in the rearview mirror.

In a way, I was a cross between all my backgrounds: my father's dignified professorial family; my mother's loving, free-spirited, humanistic family; and Elena Bielli's humble, hardworking farm family.

There's a reason why I wasn't much for following society's conventions: It's something I learned from my mother. She wasn't much for following the rules, and, without saying a word, she taught me to do the same.

One day, when I was a boy, years before Armstrong, Collins, and Aldrin landed on the moon in 1969, my mother was chatting with me in my room. "Roberto," she told me, "even if you decide to go to the moon, you can count on me to pack your bag." The day I watched Armstrong actually set foot on the moon, I looked at my mother, who was sitting next to me, completely enthralled. *Maybe she wasn't kidding.*

There was a time when my parents were still dating that the professor of clinical medicine failed my father on an exam, unjustly my mother thought, and she went to pound on the teacher's door for an explanation. That episode caused my father equal parts admiration and worry. At first they complemented each other. But in time, that kind of behavior wore down the bond between them, until the day my father left her, fracturing our home.

My mother was not only fearless, she also had no filter. Thoughts became actions, with no stopping point in between. It was with this indefatigable determination and certainty that she loved and supported me, her firstborn son. It was with that drive and determination that she taught me to swim upstream, so to speak, in turbulent waters. "Don't be afraid, Roberto. Fear is a fantasy. Rise above it and watch as it disappears." It was that drive I kept with me on the mountain and have carried with me all the days of my life. After I returned from the Andes, she would stop by every day so that she could watch me up close, to make sure she wouldn't lose me again.

Her unconditional love and support were so strong that they erased my fears. I lost the fear of failure. I became brave enough to face life head-on, because I knew she was much braver. "Never hold on to any bitterness," she would say, as she called my father's new wife, who was also a doctor, to ask for medicine when she needed it for her four children.

She didn't use her strong nature to hurt or be domineering but to express her point of view, however odd it might be—even if she had to deliver it through syncopated speech. Some might think that those who stutter do so because they're hesitant and unsure about what they want to say. My mother taught me it's the other way around. She was so steadfast in her point of view that her body was trying to physically temper her delivery, a sputtering torrent of emotion that left me both stunned and in awe of what came thundering out. It was my mother, finally, who prepared me to understand and confront the mountain.

Chapter 4

The first night seemed to last forever. I woke up startled amid a nightmare. I looked around: The fuselage was frosted over, and everything near the open end was covered in ice. The area toward the front of the cabin had been mostly sheltered from the snow. The light of the overcast morning took forever in coming, and when the first rays finally fell on the battered plane, I could barely believe my eyes. Only then did Coche Inciarte see my face: He stared at me bewildered, as if he'd seen a ghost. A frigid night of moans and wails had aged us in a matter of hours.

What survived of the fuselage lay on its side in the snow with eight cabin windows turned to the sky, five pressed against the ice below. The plane evidently had broken apart before it hit the ground at an angle. Loose cables and wires were dangling from the ceiling. I headed outside to face an overwhelming sight, a vast amphitheater of open space stretching to the east (Argentina) and an intractable U-shaped wall of mountains hemming us in on the west. There was no time to feel sorry for myself.

I began my morning rounds with Gustavo Zerbino at my side. Several had died overnight. Some, such as Enrique Platero, remained stable, while others, such as Nando's sister, Susana, had only gotten worse. Nando, who we had feared dead, remained in a coma.

Our first task that morning was to remove the bodies from the fuselage. As opposed to the previous night, when the surrounding snow had been powdery soft (our friend Carlos Valeta had taken a misstep and sunk in over his head), the ground was now packed and frozen. Jagged black rocks and chunks of airplane wreckage covered the terrain.

Some of the bodies were stiff, and it took three of us to drag them out with straps fashioned from airplane seat belts. The goal was to stabilize the seriously injured until help arrived. That second day, we were under the illusion that it was a miracle we had survived, and since we believed that we had crashed much farther down the mountain than we actually had, we firmly believed our rescue was imminent. It kept us from being overwhelmed with panic after a hysterical night, during which the darkness was filled with desperate screams and groans. Before he died, the copilot, Dante Lagurara, the only crew member from the pilot cabin that had survived, said the Chileans knew we had passed Curico and were in the Chilean foot-hills, which he thought would be the key to our rescue. The plane's altimeter read only 7,000 feet—a figure we later learned was wrong, a result of the needle going haywire after the impact.

Marcelo Perez del Castillo got a group together to round up whatever food and useful items we could find. But we found only a scarce amount of food. The mores of our snowy society began to develop. We rationed the found provisions equally, and there were no disputes over a jacket or shirt or pants anyone might find while searching the wreckage.

We had to remain calm; if we panicked, we were dead. Everyone moved languidly due to the altitude. Whatever aches or regrets any of us felt, we kept to ourselves. The worst was behind us, we told ourselves. We needed to stay positive for those who were seriously injured, to give them hope. They were our responsibility, and we refused to disappoint or abandon them.

Marcelo and his group arranged the empty baggage that we

found into the shape of an enormous cross so that our rescuers might see us from high above. We scratched out an S.O.S. into the snow with our feet. But to our astonishment, shattering our expectations, no one came for us. With nightfall, we returned to the fuselage to await another frigid evening, hoping that this one would be less brutal after we'd built a wall of suitcases over the opening.

The next morning we clearly heard a jet flying high overhead. Almost immediately afterward, a prop plane followed it, even higher than the first. Each of us swore we saw the first plane dip its wing, a clear message that it had seen us—a sign that we should get ourselves ready, that a blessed rescue was finally on the way. We were sure of it. An hour later, when we heard the distant buzzing of a small, twin-engine airplane, we were convinced that it, too, was part of the rescue—the plane was scanning the ground below, sending coordinates back to base about the location of the wreckage, the debris field, and the tiny moving dots that were us, the survivors.

We jumped and screamed and cried because we'd been found— we were saved. Our main concern in that fleeting moment of euphoria was how we would explain what had happened to the families of the deceased. Little did we know that before long, some of us would be counted among the dead.

Despite all our predictions, despite the signals that the planes had so clearly sent us, help did not arrive that day. There were no more hopeful signs, no charitable drops of food or warm clothing. And so began the series of questions without answers: Why? Where are we? When are they coming? What did we do wrong? We lied to ourselves again, to buy some time, to let ourselves down easily so that we didn't go insane. It's not an easy rescue, we told ourselves; they'll need helicopters, or possibly they've already set off on foot with mules; it's only a matter of time before we'll see them come over the least treacherous mountains to the northeast.

When dusk arrived, we trudged back inside the plane. Another fearsome night awaited us.

On day three, we heard the buzzing of airplanes again, but to our surprise, they were no longer overhead. The search had moved on to another area. We discovered a commercial airplane flight path high overhead, from a world that was going on without us—and which we were no longer a part of. I began to pray that some guiding hand would lift my pleas to the planes overhead, and miraculously, they would send down help. Even to this day, whenever I fly over a mountain range, I feel that very emotion and ask God to bless the shepherds below, sleeping in caves as they tend their flocks.

We didn't know what was taking so long but remained convinced that help was on the way. What could those planes be searching for so far away from us? Maybe the rest of the broken Fairchild? The crash site? The tail section that ended up God knows where? We remained in limbo.

Gradually, as the days passed, the fractured cabin ceased to be the wreckage of a plane that had had a destination—and a destiny. It was now a wretched refuge amid a hostile mountain. The fuselage and those of us huddled inside were no longer of this world. The twenty-seven of us—which would soon become nineteen . . . and then sixteen—were strangers now, beings from another dimension. We could not imagine in those first desperate days that our shelter would soon become a tomb.

Chapter 5

Roberto's Father: Juan Carlos Canessa

At 7:00 p.m. on October 13, 1972, I was driving down the road in Montevideo, near the Rio de la Plata, when I heard a radio report that they believed a Uruguayan plane had gone down in the Andes mountains. Minutes later, they revealed the details that it had been on its way to Santiago, Chile, but had never arrived. My hands began to shake. But since Roberto and his friends had been traveling the day before, on October 12, I stopped the car and sighed with a mixture of fright and relief. They dodged a bullet—*we* dodged a bullet! Thank God, Roberto just barely missed crashing into the Andes!

But when I pulled up to our house in Carrasco, the mayhem on the sidewalk made my heart sink. A nervous crowd had formed. It suddenly reminded me of a wake. I parked in the driveway and got out, and when I stared into their faces, that was when it hit me: Roberto was on that plane. *How could it be, if they left yesterday?* I did the math, tried to will the days to be wrong, when someone said, "They laid over for the night in Mendoza because of bad weather." The words were like a physical blow to my chest, what I always heard a heart attack felt like. I knew I was too young for a heart attack, but it was exactly what's described in the medical journals when someone suffers overwhelmingly joyous or painful news too intense for the heart to withstand.

The next day, on October 14, I flew to Chile with Luis Surraco, the father of my son's girlfriend, because we wanted to be part of the search team. But they wouldn't let us on the flights. The Chilean search and rescue team was in charge of the mission, and there was no room for relatives on the planes. I returned to Montevideo, but when they still hadn't been found five days later, I flew back to Santiago. I posted myself outside the home of the president of the republic, Salvador Allende, because apparently the best helicopter for the task was assigned to his administration. But I wasn't able to get them to loan it.

I returned to Montevideo empty-handed. Without my son.

Time passed in a constant nightmare. I don't remember what was real or imagined. But what I do know is that on October 23, the Chilean search and rescue team abandoned its search.

Chapter 6

In the midst of October storms in the Andes, which sometimes kept us trapped in the fuselage for up to twenty-four hours at a time, the death toll began to mount. It took a new victim every few days and exacted a toll on the survivors, who began to see that dying was much easier than clinging to life in this frozen Andean field hospital that was the wreckage of our plane.

Our group began to transform into a single organism, including those who could barely move for lack of oxygen or serious injuries. We would gravitate around the best ideas, just as humans might have done to survive at the beginning of time. Each one of us contributed in his own way, selflessly and without ego, so that our efforts grew exponentially. In a way, we were like a rugby team unable to substitute players; when a man went down, it only forced us to extract that much more strength from each individual. Everything else we might have brought with us from the outside world—selfishness, vanity, dishonor, greed—was forgotten in this frozen world.

Nando Parrado had a severe cerebral edema, which might have killed him, but a fortunate accident proved the best treatment imaginable: He spent one night with his head against the ice. And ice, as it turns out, is not only the world's most abundant medical provision but is also the best remedy for edemas and pain relief, which the field of medicine wouldn't begin using widely as such until twenty years later.

The first thing that struck Fito Strauch in those early days was the problem of thirst: Although we were surrounded by snow, attempting to drink it irritated our gums and made our tongues and throats swell. The method he discovered for melting the snow was as simple as it was ingenious. He set a thin layer of ice on a sheet of aluminum from the back part of the seats, twisted it into a funnel out in the sun, and let it drain into a bottle.

We took apart the seats and lay the cushions over the cold metal below us. I pulled off their thick turquoise fabric and used electrical wiring to sew them into blankets. With the leftover squares, we made mittens and caps.

Women's perfume became disinfectant, razor blades scalpels. Rugby jerseys became bandages.

Fito worried that the glare off the snow would eventually lead to snow blindness, so he fashioned several pairs of sunglasses out of the sunshield we found in the cockpit. Since it was impossible to walk outside after midday without sinking waist-deep in snow, Fito strapped a pair of seat cushions to his feet with seat belts to use as makeshift snowshoes.

We developed a rotation for sleeping in the more comfortable parts of the fuselage and eventually fashioned a sleeping bag for our expeditions. That heat would mean the difference between life and death.

Our team, whose average age was twenty, grew into a family, with all the unconditional attachments that link mothers and fathers, sons and daughters, grandparents, aunts, and uncles.

I can still see them: Gustavo Nicolich and Fito Strauch rebuilding the cross out of luggage every morning after it had been covered with snow; Alvaro Mangino and Arturo Nogueira running the water production; me, taking care of Vasco Echavarren's injuries; Daniel Fernandez massaging Bobby François's feet so they wouldn't freeze;

Coche Inciarte telling stories to hearten the two youngest members of our group; Roy Harley organizing the inside of the fuselage to keep it habitable; Carlitos Paez entranced with a glow-in-the-dark statuette of the Virgin Mary and the rosary he had found; and Gustavo Zerbino storing in a small suitcase the documents, medallions, crucifixes, and watches of those who had died.

Each of us performed a vital function to sustain this delicate balance, like the various organs of the human body. Our common goal was to survive, to overcome nature's inherent desire to destroy us, to break us apart, to transform us into what we rightly should have been up there on that frigid mountain: ice. Sometimes we advanced; other times we retreated into the shell of our fuselage. There was a delicate dance between the organic and the inorganic.

The power we had initially bestowed on our captain, Marcelo, eventually passed to the three Strauch cousins—Fito Strauch, Daniel Fernandez Strauch, and Eduardo Strauch—after Marcelo died in an avalanche. With that power came the respect of the other survivors, who treated the three like tribal elders even though they were only a few years older than the rest of the group. The cousins didn't make all the decisions but rather would give their approval. They led the group, but they listened to the others' ideas.

While we had imbued them with moral authority and the power to render justice, it was not surprising that at times individuals questioned their decisions. On other occasions, unjustified complaints would arise among us, because the group required escape valves to maintain its balance. The scapegoats were strong enough to withstand this occasional pressure, to help alleviate the group's tension. But we had to be careful; we knew the group's stability relied on regulating this dynamic. And so we came to this sort of equilibrium, the homeostasis of a desperate group, the seesaw between justice and catharsis.

In that erratic and precarious society, my role was to play every role. I asked the cousins to allow me to use my outside-the-box thinking that had often earned me the title of "unbearable" in the civilized world. It was time to proverbially jump back on the untamed horse of my childhood, to push things to the limit, even though it might come off as bold or reckless or even disrespectful. The cousins, in their wisdom, agreed that this kind of thinking could be favorable to the group.

Our story became world famous because of how we survived: by eating those who had died. It was, by far, our most eccentric idea, one that was simultaneously simple and audacious, and perhaps inconceivable. But we had felt the sensation of our bodies consuming themselves just to remain alive, the feeling of total and complete starvation, where merely standing up was enough to make us dizzy and pass out from hunger. We experienced that primitive instinct of true hunger—and perhaps what wild animals feel. It's something innate, irrational. It was a young man with his mouth stained blue after trying to eat the synthetic leather of luggage that, in modern times, is no longer made from actual hides. Hunger demands, above all else, to be satisfied.

When my son Hilario was four, his kindergarten classmates came up to him and said, "Did you know your dad ate his friends?" And, as if it were the most ordinary question in the world, Hilario sat them down and said, "Yes, let me tell you how it happened." When he finished telling his story, their hunger had been satisfied.

When we finally resorted to the cadavers to survive, we thought we had gone mad, or that we had become savages. But later, we realized that it was the only sane thing to do—although the outside world might always carry a kernel of suspicion that we had, indeed, gone insane.

The decision to nourish ourselves with the bodies—Fito Strauch, Gustavo Zerbino, Daniel Maspons, and I would be the first to make the incisions—would be the last definitive step in our transformation. The final goodbye to innocence. We were pushing the limits of our fear. I knew the protein in the bodies could help us survive.

And I also knew that if we delayed our decision any longer, we would become too weak to recover from starvation. We couldn't wait forever, or our bodies would be so far gone that the effects would be irreversible. But at the same time, what if a miracle occurred in time to avoid this transgression? Never had the consequences of time seemed so gruesome.

Ultimately, we must face these critical moments on our own. I will never forget that first incision, when each man was alone with his conscience on that infinite mountaintop, on a day colder and grayer than any before it or since. The four of us, with a razor blade or a shard of glass in hand, carefully cut the clothing off a body whose face we could not bear to look at. We lay the thin strips of frozen flesh aside on a piece of sheet metal. Each of us consumed his piece when he could finally bring himself to.

Javier Methol prayed to God for enlightenment and said that God responded that it was like a holy communion. Javier recited the New Testament verses to us, straight from memory from John 6:54 and Matthew 26:26: "He who eats of my flesh and drinks of my blood will have eternal life, and I will resurrect him on the last day. Take and eat, this is my body."

In turn, my God had become dissociated into two personalities. There was the God of the outside world, the one of the Ten Commandments, who ordered that we not steal or lie. But my God of the mountain was different. While I prayed to him for eternal life, I also begged him to allow me to stay on earth just a little bit longer. He was the God I prayed would help me make it across the mountain range, the one to whom I made promises I have yet to keep: that if he saved me, I would go to church every day at 7:00 a.m. after having the most succulent breakfast imaginable at 6:00. Because true hunger is atrocious, beastly, instinctive, primordial—and the God of the mountain witnessed the groaning of my insides. So while I promised to honor him, he saw me and knew I had lost the ability to lie or to conceal my overwhelming starvation.

So I prayed to my mountain God about whether I could eat my friends. Because without his consent, I felt I would be violating their memory, that I would be stealing their souls. What's worse, I could not ask their permission. But a rational and loving solution to the question that had haunted me emerged to quell my fears and fill me with serenity. While we were still alive, those of us who were willing said out loud that if we died, the rest could use our bodies to survive. And for me, it was an honor to say that if my heart stopped beating, my arms and legs and muscles could still be a part of our mission to get off that mountain, and that it could always be said that Roberto died trying to make that goal a reality. That was our greatest invention in the Andes: a generous death.

I cannot help but associate that event, using a dead body to continue living, with something that would be realized the world over in the coming decades: organ and tissue transplants. We broke the taboo, and in a way, the world broke it along with us in the years to come as what was once thought bizarre became a new way to respect and honor the dead.

For us, taking this leap was a final break, and the consequences were irreversible: We were never the same.

Saying "You're the ones who saved yourselves by eating your dead," is too much an oversimplification. We offered our bodies up to one another so that in some way, we might all walk off that mountain together. Besides staving off starvation, it bought us time. When it was clear that the search had been called off, we knew we had to turn to eating the dead to survive. It became a tool, as critical as sleeping huddled together for warmth or rigging that sleeping bag. As critical as organizing a new flawed and fragile society. As critical as daring to hike off that mountain.

What was at first taboo simply became another part of our struggle, like using our minds and our courage to do what was necessary to stay alive. Plan A, waiting for help, had failed. The world of the living evidently had carved our tombstones—and we were on our own. Against that backdrop, where there was no help in sight and adversity continued to mount, our deceased friends became nourishment. Plan B became doing whatever was necessary to get back home.

A day later, on October 23, 1972, ten days after the accident, as we were scanning our tiny Spica transistor radio for news about where the search was centered, only to learn that it had been called off, another memory from my home in Montevideo filled the airwaves and resounded all around us: the tango "Volver" (Return) by Carlos Gardel and Alfredo Le Pera. My heart shuddered. *Was he singing directly to me?* "I imagine the flickering of the lights that in the distance will be marking my return," he sings.

Both Gardel and Le Pera had died in a plane crash in the Andes thirty-seven years earlier in Medellin, Colombia.

"To live . . . with the soul clutched to a sweet memory that I cry once again."

Was he singing to me about the lights marking my return? Was he talking about the twinkling lights in the snow all around us, the way the sun played over the angles on this mountaintop? Was he saying that twenty years were nothing, that I had to cling to the memories of those things that would make me cry tears of joy again?

Now, more than forty years later, when the snows of time have silvered my own temples, I feel once again as I did that morning in the Andes when I shuddered at hearing those words.

Chapter 7

As a teenager, I had been wild and romantic, all at once. Or maybe I was just a wild child until something changed when I was fourteen. Shortly after I met Lauri for the first time, she asked me to help her bury her dead pet hamsters. Somehow in that role as gravedigger, with a pair of tiny animal corpses in my hands, I also became her spiritual adviser and confidant. I wasn't grossed out at handling the tiny bodies because, as Lauri had said, I was a beast myself. Yet there was something about me, she said, in the way I could handle her dead rodents and yet still talk to her about the sadness she felt at losing her pets. That's the reason she kept talking to me. I grew from a boy to a young man in those next few months.

Our conversations went on and on, as one topic segued into the next, and we found that we thought and felt the same way about many things. "Maybe you're not such a savage. Maybe you're even a little romantic," she told me one day. We've spent the past forty years talking that way.

I began to be a little less of a wild child. A few months earlier, an aunt had given me a horse. I had yearned for a horse so long that when I went to the train station to pick it up, I immediately named it "Alfin"—after the Spanish phrase "al fin," meaning "at last." Right there in the station, in the center of the city, I put on its saddle and rode it all the way home to Carrasco through the morning traffic. We would spend all day together and take long rides along the beach at sunset, following the tide's ebb and flow.

Eventually I started to feel a new emotion—shame. Shame at the way I let Alfin clip-clop over neighbors' gardens or tear up people's lawns. One day when I tied him to a sprinkler spigot and he got spooked at a loud noise, he tore off down the road dragging forty feet of plumbing behind him. I became ashamed at being such a rambunctious student. I wanted to be *more*—more disciplined and less rebellious—and I decided I wanted to go to medical school when I turned eighteen. I began by training my horse to be less feral—and Lauri started training me. Although neither my horse nor I would ever change who we were, we became on friendlier terms with the world around us.

Years later, when Lauri and I were dating, and I was getting ready to leave for Chile to play rugby in October 1972, Lauri called me and said, "I left a letter for you inside my mailbox." I picked it up and kept it with me for the entire time on the mountain. I still carry it with me to this day.

I used to go camping with Lauri's family. It was just one of the many things we had in common: We loved being outdoors, in nature, and we always felt at ease there. One day, we had set up camp near the Don Esteban River, about 125 miles from Montevideo. While we were pitching the final tent, I noticed my future father-in-law, the doctor Luis Surraco, carefully studying the roof of one of the tents. "What are you looking at, doctor?" I asked. We had left behind one of the poles for the tent I was supposed to sleep in and would somehow have to make two poles do the job of three. Dr. Surraco just stared up at the roof in thought. Suddenly, he had it. He took apart one of the telescopic poles, whittled a tree branch with his hunting knife, and inserted it into the top. The tent stood perfectly.

I did exactly the same thing when I had to finagle hanging beds for the injured passengers inside the fuselage. Using the telescopic poles in the aircraft stairs and the net I'd slept on that first night with Coche Inciarte, I rigged several hammocks that hung from the luggage racks. They held until the very last injured passenger died.

Everything was in short supply on the mountain, but we did have several important strengths: We were a group with a lot in common, a team that had played rugby together, a sport that requires discipline, effort, and the cooperation of every player to work together for the sake of the team. Most of us had known one another for years. We had been ingrained with the same religion and taught by the strict Irish Christian Brothers at Stella Maris, who prized a tough, stringent, altruistic brand of education. My long and curious relationship with the Brothers formed part of my arsenal for staying alive.

I remained friends with many of them, who now live and reside on the fourth floor of the Cardinal Newman School in the Boulogne neighborhood of Buenos Aires. They always joke that my parents ought to have paid double what the other kids' parents paid because the Brothers always had to keep me after class for two-hour detentions. And I always got in trouble for the same thing: acting out in class. At first, I'd do my detention indoors, performing chores or reciting prayers or working on extra math problems on the blackboard. But the Brothers eventually realized this wasn't helping straighten out my feral, independent personality. So instead they let me remain outside for my detention. They couldn't get over the fact that I was always in a good mood and that after my detention was up, I'd ask for a ball to play rugby out on the field for another couple of hours. In all that extra time—which I'd use to perfect my penalty kicks—I developed a closer relationship with the Brothers, especially once they started joining me out on the pitch. Their lives were lived against the grain, too—far from their homes, their friends, their loved ones.

I'd often noticed them looking down at me from their third-story window, as if trying to figure me out. When it got dark, I'd saddle my horse—which I tied to the fence on the back rugby fields during school—and ride home to 1726 Espinola Street. I'd let my horse graze on the field next to my house.

Except for the horse, I became that boy again in the Andes. I threw out all the norms and focused on coming up with practical solutions to help ease as many people's suffering as best I could. That's how I became the mountain doctor.

Lauri's letter, which I took with me the night of October 11, 1972, reads: "I love you very much and am enchanted that you're both a romantic and a savage all at once. I think we're a lot alike. Oh, and don't forget to take the sweater I knitted for you to Chile."

On my nineteenth birthday, eight months before the crash, Lauri had given me a sweater she'd made herself, one so thick and heavy that I figured I'd never get the chance to use it in the mild Uruguayan winters.

"Well, I do like it," I'd told her. "But why did you make it so thick?"

"It's rustic and strong like you. And don't worry about it being too thick. I know you're going to need it one day," she had said.

It wasn't until eight months later that I recalled the conversation we'd had in front of her house in Carrasco. We were two young kids who had just turned nineteen arguing over the kind of cold neither of us had ever experienced. At that moment, we had no idea what we were talking about. But it's clear that we were both preparing for what lay ahead.

The moment the wing of our Fairchild FH-227D clipped the top of the mountain to the south of the Valley of Tears—the name of the place where the accident happened—I stopped believing in chance. Thanks in part to the warm red sweater my girlfriend had knitted for me, I was able to survive in the days after the crash. Wearing that sweater, I returned to the land of the living, and I still have it to this day.

Chapter 8

We matured fast, too fast, up in the Andes, although we had only recently left behind our adolescence. We soon learned that failure was only the operating cost of success. Our first forays out on the mountain were to try to determine where we were. It was frightening not knowing what might await us beyond the peaks to the north and the south or the wall of ice to the west. The only open landscape lay to the east, toward Argentina, where the land extended over a series of mountains culminating (we would later learn) with the volcano Sosneado, which blocked our view of what was beyond it. We were in the middle of an ice box whose walls kept us from guessing where we might have crashed because we couldn't judge distances.

We decided to take exploratory hikes, which would allow us to temper our bodies and minds against this new reality. Instead of lying down like lambs, licking our wounds, we felt emboldened like lions. Although we were starving, frozen, and gasping for air because of the altitude, we set out to overcome that wall of ice. I participated in the first hike and all the final ones. Many of the others who did the same died.

Each hike accomplished two things: It kept our spirits up and it taught us something. Those of us who attempted to scale our snowy surroundings learned valuable lessons, as did those who stayed behind huddled in the fuselage, even if it was just whether the hikers could make it back alive. When they delayed in returning, I waited for them outside for hours, trying to see if I could spot them on the horizon. When the cold was too great, I watched from one of the windows of the fuselage.

Our first hike took place on the fourth day after the accident. Fito Strauch, Numa Turcatti, Carlitos Paez, and I set out. We didn't hike too far, because Fito thought it was too dangerous. We were surrounded by soft snow that was God knows how many yards deep; we could easily disappear down a sinkhole, as Carlos Valeta had on the day of the crash.

What we learned was that we were in a much more inaccessible area than we had ever imagined. Our snowy society would have to come together to get through this, because any other society was too far away.

Our second trek occurred on our eleventh day on the mountain, one day after Roy Harley and Gustavo Nicolich fixed the small Spica radio and we learned that the search for survivors had been called off. By that time, we had all begun eating the bodies, and that hike was perhaps the most desperate—and the rashest. Gustavo Zerbino, Numa Turcatti, and Daniel Maspons each set out with their shoes wrapped in nylon or using our innovated snowshoes. Numa and Daniel would die shortly thereafter.

They hiked south toward the place where the plane had first hit the rocky peaks that had sawed the fuselage in half. They would soon come across a trail of bodies and human remains, a propeller, shards of twisted metal. They pressed ahead, against their better judgment, to try to find the tail section and whatever else might be helpful. But as night fell, there was no time to hike back. In their desperation, they had not been thinking clearly and had miscalculated the distance and hour of the day. They had to sleep outdoors in the 30-below temperature without the necessary clothing, and they nearly froze to death. The only thing they found was an infinite vista of snow and ice, probably the worst thing any of them could have seen at that time.

Numa Turcatti returned with the look of death in his eyes, believing that we would never escape this wintry trap. Gustavo had lost his improvised sun visor during the trek and had become snow blind. Or perhaps his mind just didn't want to look at any more of this world. I think that may have been what saved him. He hadn't seen what was at the end, and when he made it back to the fuselage, I bandaged his swollen red eyes with strips of a torn rugby jersey. He said he felt sand and needles in his eyes, and his teeth had gotten so loose from the beginning stages of frostbite that I had to chew up the frozen bits of meat before feeding it to him. After that hike, Daniel Maspons, a close friend and classmate, lost the vigor and vitality that he exuded and had once spread to the rest of the group. He died six days later in the most sinister episode in our odyssey: the avalanche.

We would massage their feet for hours over the next few days to try to relieve the pain of their near-frostbite.

We didn't strike out again until November 5, after the avalanche, when Tintin Vizintin, Carlitos Paez, and Roy Harley headed out on another fateful trip in which the three of them nearly died. Carlitos and Roy returned in terrible shape. Only Tintin would join Nando and me on the final attempt to escape the Andes.

I had paid close attention to how the previous groups had returned from their hikes. My role at the moment was to tend to their injuries from that trial by ice. I observed carefully which parts of the human body seemed the most easily injured and which were heartier in this cold. I tried to figure out what mistakes they had made, what we were doing wrong—and where, in that freezing death, salvation might be lying in wait.

The number of volunteers, those who felt that they needed to try it for themselves, soon waned. As domineering as I can be, I'm not the kind of person to offer himself up as a guinea pig. But I finally realized that I had to be the one to make the final push and that perhaps salvation was not completely impossible, just highly improbable.

I started going out on scouting missions. Those left behind in the fuselage suffered a particular kind of misery; ours was a different, nomadic brand. We became outsiders to the group—even though we knew they still relied on us to be their eyes and ears, their arms and legs, and their hope. But they had their own challenges in staying alive—and sane. Those left inside became explorers of their own minds, entering new regions of consciousness to keep from going insane.

To be part of this group you had to have the physical, psychological, and spiritual fortitude, and I felt I did. Or you had to be like Nando and have a desperate need to flee this place. He could not bear to be trapped in the fuselage when the time might come that his own mother and sister would become food for the rest of us, his mother having died in the crash and his sister eight days later. But on the day he and I left the fuselage for good, he told Fito and the rest of the survivors that if their lives depended on it, they could indeed take that desperate step.

It was curious how being among the group that hiked afforded us certain privileges. We were allotted more food, better clothing, and a choice spot to sleep in the fuselage. We were even freed of several chores as we trained for the long hike, although I still kept up my duties. In the end, these freedoms felt like ephemeral vanities that disappeared into the thin mountain air once we began our trek up the San Hilario Sierra. The higher you climbed, the smaller and humbler you became, as hikers hugged one another for warmth to survive another night in the Andes. Whatever privileges you might have had, the mountain stripped them away with impunity.

Leaving the plane, venturing out a little farther each time, meant stretching our umbilical cord, knowing that one day it would finally snap. We were like tiny satellites spinning into the eternal cosmos, drifting farther away from the sun each time, hoping to find warmth in some other place in the Milky Way.

Chapter 9

Toward the end of October, it snowed for days and the world seemed cloaked in gray. Time vanished, or rather, we seemed caught in a place where time meandered at its own pace. That period, the worst of all, began with the avalanche on the night of Sunday, October 29, sixteen days after the accident. Those days stood on their own, under their own wintry sky, apart from the rest of our time on the mountain.

We had huddled inside the fuselage early that day, at four in the afternoon. It had snowed nonstop in the days before, and we had already heard the rumble of avalanches in the distance. But to us, the idea of being caught in an avalanche was as alien as it had once been to believe we could be involved in a plane crash: It was something that would happen somewhere else, because we'd already had our share of bad luck.

It was my turn in the rotation to sleep in the best part of the fuselage, near the cockpit, away from the opening, alongside Daniel Maspons. Suddenly, we heard a rumble, and then there was a flash like a signal flare. I was smacked in the chest by a wall of ice and snow that instantly became as hard as cement as it enveloped me. It was hard to understand exactly what was happening because I was quickly turning into stone. I pissed in my pants, and for a second I was surprised by this suddenly agreeable warm feeling between my legs. When you're dying, you think about few precious things.

Just before passing out for good, forever—I knew what it felt like because I'd already passed out once; for how long, I can't even guess—Roy Harley's face popped up in front of mine. He dug the snow away from my mouth, and I gasped. With the oxygen, just as in the moments after the crash, came the frenetic desire to breathe, to survive. They dug out my arms, and I pulled myself up from my grave, shivering, still trying to figure out what had happened. I tried to get my bearings as time seemed to have stopped. I fell to my hands and knees, stunned. And I was surprised to find my heart still beating. Everything felt incongruous, unreal. We were suffocating and we were soaked. In the tiny pocket of space, plunged in darkness, we had barely any air to breathe. Shadows resurrected all around us, rising from their icy tombs, but there was no room to stand. So they remained with their heads hunched over, like other-worldly creatures, their heads pressed against the roof of the plane. Others who had managed to shake off their bewilderment started digging through the compact snow with their bare hands to find other stirring shadows. *Move, Canessa, move!* I told myself, and then, in a flash I remembered: Daniel had been right next to me. I clawed desperately at the icy snow, scraping it with my nails. I wanted to tear away the ice with my teeth like a wild animal. I dug and dug until I uncovered the face of my friend, my dear friend Daniel Maspons, who had survived the initial crash without a scratch on him, who had set out on the most dangerous and desperate of hikes over the mountains trying to find a way out. I swept the snow away from his face and out of his mouth, and I leaned in to listen for his breath. But there was only silence. My friend was dead. The briefest thought flickered through my mind: *Daniel, my friend, you can finally rest in peace.*

I continued digging until I fell over from exhaustion. I took one breath, two breaths, and continued digging. One person emerged and then another. Some gasped for breath again, others did not. All around me, I noticed those who were digging finally stopped, one at a time, utterly exhausted. Methol sobbed over the body of his wife. Someone else began to count aloud until they summed up the final tally: "Eighteen and eight."

On the night of the avalanche, the worst night of my life, we lost eight of our friends along with everything we'd managed to construct—the clothes on our backs, the ponchos we'd fashioned out of the airplane seats, everything. We were soaked down to our socks and shoes. And we didn't know how long the oxygen in this tiny capsule we'd carved out would last.

Because we were running out of oxygen, some of us began to dig a hole to the outside, hoping to push through one of the tubes we had used to make the hammocks. We eventually managed to do so, up through the cockpit, which was pitched upward and closer to the surface.

I hesitated to even move again. But I found myself clinging to the remote possibility that I might yet survive this. I decided that I needed to know what other pitfalls this mountain had planned for us, to find out what it was that would eventually kill me—because until now, death had been a series of false alarms.

By the bursts of flickering lighters that sputtered for lack of oxygen, we looked around at one another over the passing hours, the reality of our situation dawning on us: We were entombed in an icy sarcophagus God knows how many feet under snow. We had no food, not even the frozen bodies we were relying on to stay alive. Everyone was waiting for someone to do something. Or for no one to do anything else and just let the end come. That's when I steeled myself to do what needed to be done: to use one of the bodies. I knew that if I didn't take this step, it would have been the end of us, because the reality of our situation was paralyzing. I had done things that I never imagined I would have to do in my darkest nightmares. I think that studying medicine helped me to act like a surgeon, who manages to set aside his emotions while opening up a warm body and excising an organ. And so we took yet another step in the descent toward our ultimate indignity: to eat the body of the person lying next to us. Each of us would have to be stained with this blood if we were to keep the seed of life from withering. Perhaps we could be like life-giving wheat, which falls to the ground and can bring forth new seeds in death, new life. Ours could be a fruitful death. It's what I would have wanted out of my own death.

Teaching by example wasn't just one way to accomplish this; it was the only way. Although at that moment I didn't want to teach anyone anything, I took action unconsciously. As always, we were left with two finite choices: surrender or act. Quit or forge ahead. Our icy tomb left room for nothing else.

Our view through the airplane's windows was gone. We were left literally and figuratively in the dark.

And so, we learned to wait without despairing. During the next two days, we celebrated two birthdays underground—for Numa Turcatti and Carlitos Paez—with a pair of cakes shaped out of hardened snow.

Our group had changed again. Because, in a way, on the night of the avalanche, we all died and rose again. Trapped inside that damp prison of the fuselage, with its lack of oxygen and its awful metallic smell, we were like a small chrysalis encapsulating life. Like an unborn child with a heart condition, floating in a womb, the possibility of survival still very much in doubt.

Chapter 10

After being buried for three days, we finally managed to dig our way up to the cockpit. We sat back in the captain's chair, kicked out the front windshield, and dug ourselves the rest of the way up to the surface. Coche Inciarte was the first to make it out. He remembers watching us emerge, pulling our way out of the ground into the eternal snow, as if the mountain had given birth to us.

After the grueling work of digging the fuselage out of the snow, we concentrated on preparing the hikers for another long trek. This was another part of our new society, in which some sacrificed the best of what they had—a warmer coat, a better spot in the plane, a piece of frozen meat—for those of us who were trying to get physically prepared for this dangerous journey. Whereas these hikes had initially been more like reconnaissance missions, now they became necessary trips for survival; treks to reach the outside world or die trying. That made selecting those who would make the attempt all the more important.

I carefully weighed our options to ensure our meager strengths would yield the maximum results. As we neared December, I knew that success depended on several factors: how many hours of sun we could get and whether we could avoid a blinding blizzard. I felt that this was a one-way trip, and if we failed, we would never be able to return to the fuselage. Our goal was to make it or die trying. Every time I thought about what lay ahead, the notion kept popping into my mind: Quit now or press forward?

Although Nando insisted that we hike west in a straight line toward the Pacific, no matter what our maps told him to the contrary, we eventually convinced him to go east toward Argentina. I felt that there was no good way to scale the wall of ice to the west and that the only rational idea—if any idea could be considered rational at this point—was to avoid that obstacle at all costs.

Nando, Tintin, and I left on November 17 at 8:00 a.m. on a hike that we had figured would take three or four days. Leaving behind the relative silence of the fuselage, we entered a universe of different sounds: the crunch of snow under our boots, the rhythm of our quickened breathing, and, from time to time, the rumble of nearby avalanches. We started out at a calm but brisk pace because we assumed that the tallest peak, the volcano Sosneado, was two or three days away. But our greatest challenge was the crucial question of whether we could resist sleeping at night out in the open, despite all the heavy coats we had brought with us.

On the way, we found traces of plane wreckage that we were surprised to see had traveled that far. And we couldn't believe our eyes when we happened upon the unexpected: the tail section of the Fairchild. From a distance, it took me a minute to figure out what it was. The tail was missing its rudders, but amazingly it was lying perfectly upright, as if the rest were simply buried beneath the snow. I stood stunned for a moment. It was the first new thing we had seen in thirty-six days on the mountain, the first thing that connected us to our old lives. It was from that other world, the one where men built and destroyed things like airplanes. When we reached it, we spread our hands over it incredulously. There was the galley, with scraps of food, including a pair of frozen empanadas we'd brought on board when the plane laid over in Mendoza on October 12 because of bad weather. Scavenging among the sections destroyed on impact, I opened a compartment and found the plane's batteries. It felt like a miracle. I was overcome when I found them undamaged and intact. When I touched both poles with a loose cable, they sparked. Although the plan had been to hike east, it seemed like a sign to rethink our plan, because this could be our chance at a shortcut. Like us, the batteries were still alive. In the tail section, I found my luggage, which was like stumbling upon the person I used to be. It was redolent with the smell of my home and of a life before all this.

We spent that night in the tail section, delaying our concerns over sleeping outside. Thanks to the batteries, we were able to hook up a few lights and power a radio aboard the plane. We now had an outpost in case our expedition east failed and we had to turn back to the fuselage. Gustavo Zerbino, Numa Turcatti, and Daniel Maspons had taught us what having to spend a night outdoors, unprepared, could do to a man. It remained to be seen how anyone could last a second night outdoors.

I turned my attention to fixing the plane's radio with the same zeal that Nando had when he had initially insisted we go west. The prospect of fixing the radio, which was designed to call for help during a crisis, seemed closer, less abstract, than heading off into the infinite whiteness and likely ending up frozen to death. I had to put myself in the shoes of the engineer who had built it. Salvation seemed so close and yet so incredibly far. One misconnected cable would make all the difference. Making things more difficult, of course, was the fact that none of us knew anything about radios, VHF, super VHF, or any of these signals that can travel hundreds of miles to reach an airplane flying at 10,000 feet. As curious as I was about how things worked, I regretted never having met anyone in my short nineteen years who knew how to fix a radio. I knew that someone with even the most rudimentary knowledge of electronics, even a hobbyist, would know how to get it to work.

The next day, even as my legs carried me east when we continued our hike toward what I felt was certain death, my mind kept going back to the tail section of the airplane.

There was no one right answer for anything we tried on the mountain. Had we kept heading east down the valley after spending the next night sleeping outdoors, we might have reached some kind of destination. If we managed to steer clear of any chasms, blizzards, or avalanches, we might have been able to skirt the volcano and arrive in the Atuel river basin and maybe stumble across some abandoned hostel or even an Argentine police outpost.

Instead, after digging a trench in the snow when we attempted to sleep outdoors that second night, we ended up like Zerbino, Turcatti, and Maspons. It didn't matter that we had three times the warm layers or that we built a makeshift tent with blankets. We nearly froze to death as we slept huddled together, pounding our arms and legs to keep the blood flowing throughout a sinister eternal darkness. That night, we learned the limits of the best-prepared of us: one night out in the cold. None of us had any doubt that sleeping a second night outdoors meant death.

At 9:00 the next morning, the sun melted the frost that had covered us overnight. After a sleepless night, with our clothing as stiff as our aching muscles, more dead than alive and prematurely aged, we began the slow, arduous hike back to the tail section.

While we rested there for the hike back to the fuselage, I spent hours studying the batteries. I carefully removed each cell, one by one, as delicately as if they were made of crystal. I looked over all the buttons and connections. They all looked undamaged, especially when I compared them to my memory of the trashed radio back in the fuselage. If my passion for the heart grew after the avalanche, then my passion for repairing devices strengthened at the thought of how connecting cables meant reconnecting lives. The two came together on that mountain, because the heart, after all, is the most perfect machine.

Chapter 11

On November 22, we returned to the fuselage. It had been five days since the passengers of the plane saw us leave in exactly the same condition, except we came back with one crucial discovery: We had found the tail section. And in it we had found coats, cigarettes, a bottle of rum, a kilo of sugar, half-eaten empanadas from Mendoza, and (we left it for last) the batteries. Since they were so heavy, we decided we couldn't bring them with us. Instead, we would have to take the broken radio to the batteries. Roy, a first-year engineering student, guessed that he would be part of the plan, since he was the unofficial engineer of the group. A few months earlier, he had fixed some audio equipment for his cousin, and he was the one who had gotten the small transistor radio working, two feats that made him our chief engineer the way my two years of medical school had made me the chief surgeon. That's how it was in our snow society; we were exaggerated versions of ourselves. Necessity had forced us to be more than what we actually were.

At the same time, I believed (though I kept it to myself) that even if we failed to fix the radio, it would buy us time to let the temperature warm just enough to thaw certain areas of the mountain range and allow our improbable hike to the west. Because the eastern route had unequivocally been ruled out.

I convinced Nando and Tintin to let me try to fix the radio by promising that if I failed, we would head west on our next attempt, toward Chile and the Pacific.

On November 23, Roy, Nando, and I dislodged the radio from the fuselage's cockpit, careful not to sever a single one of the countless wires or lose any of the transistors. The next day, we took the shattered pieces of a radio that looked as if it had been found in a salvage yard and loaded them on a sled made out of a Samsonite bag before heading back toward the tail section. We moved heaven and earth to try to fix that radio. Roy, Nando, Tintin, and I worked nonstop for three days to strip the wire ends and splice them to the batteries. And then we spent another three days trying to tune it to a frequency. But all we ever heard back was a garbled, hissing static that never turned into words.

We were so close. We even managed to broadcast a shortwave signal. The plane had VHF and super VHF. VHF is linear, and if a plane had passed overhead and we had seen each other, we might have been able to communicate. Sometimes a signal could bounce off the clouds and reach some far-off location. We had everything we needed to make the VHF work: the plane's tuner, correctly coded cables, antenna, and battery. But we never managed to get the super VHF to work so that we could communicate over long distances. Even though the cable connections were correct—all the wires were clearly labeled—we hadn't connected the high-voltage transformer, a black box covered in oil that had come loose during the crash and ended up near the fuselage. We never knew what that black box was for. (It was explained to me years later.) As I scoured the area around the wreckage trying to find things we could use, I'd see that black box dripping in oil among the other pieces of twisted metal. I racked my brain wondering how we might use it. Little did I know that it was the key to our salvation.

After three days of listening to static—which sounded more like a funeral march—we admitted we didn't have the knowledge to make it work. We were missing one tiny piece of information. We were so close, and we had all the parts. If only we had had an instruction manual.

On November 29, we spent our last night in the tail section. The winds had picked up, and we were afraid the whole section might go tumbling down the valley with us in it. Nando was so nervous he barely let me rest. "If you're going to move that much, you might as well sleep outside," he grumbled.

All in all, despite our failure with the radio, the strategy did pay off. Not only had we bought ourselves some time, but it was in the tail section that we discovered the source of warmth that would save our lives: the insulating fabric we would use to make our sleeping bag.

Surrounding the heating pipes, Tintin found material that was made out of two waterproof fabrics with insulation pressed between them. He was surprised at how durable it was. He cut off a small piece. "Look, this would be great to make vests out of," he said. We wrapped snow inside the fabric and noticed that the water didn't leak through the other side. Since the night we almost froze to death, we had been on the lookout for a way to make a sleeping bag that would allow us to survive the night sleeping outdoors.

When we returned to face our disappointed friends in the fuselage on November 30, we announced that we had a surprise, pointing at the bag as if there might be an airplane inside. When we opened it up, everyone asked what that bundle of frayed fabric was.

"This is what's going to allow us to spend a night outside," Tintin said. It was heat, the key to life on the mountain.

After the avalanche, we had taken the fact that we were still alive as a positive sign and had pressed forward. Now, after our failure with the radio, we were placing all our hopes in this insulating fabric. We were as excited as if we had found a rescue plane in that tail section. And we were so ecstatic that when we tried to explain it to the others after returning from six days of failure, they looked at us as if we were crazy. Many watched the three Strauch cousins for their reaction, but they kept an even keel—which meant they still had hope. They knew our efforts were the only thing keeping desperation and death at bay. Whether the new fabric was the answer was another matter. But that wasn't important. The point was that we still had something to believe in, to hope for. Some people say, "If there's life, there's hope." But for us, it was the opposite: "If there's hope, there's life."

Chapter 12

We were all a part of the escape plan, but three of us had to make the trek: Nando, Tintin, and I. Three days after leaving, it would be just Nando and I. I say we "had to" because I was never quite sure I wanted to make this hike.

In our last days in the fuselage, we had decided on the route. While we had chosen the most difficult course, walking out was the only certainty we had left in our situation. Everything else was completely unknown. There would be no rescue, no radio—nothing. We had only our own two feet. Distance was no longer measured in yards or miles, but in steps. Steps hindered by a mountain range and extreme exhaustion.

Just looking at our position on the map was enough to fill us with dread. The Andes mountains extend from Panama in the north to Cape Horn in the south, a distance of nearly 4,500 miles. By our estimation, with a margin of error of 30 miles (in reality, it was much more), we were somewhere in an arid region on the Argentine side of the mountains, which would mean some 250,000 to 300,000 steps through a desolate wasteland. The thought of finally making it out of the Andean region only to face a barren desert devoid of crops or humans was too depressing. But it was possible to walk directly to the west. From the map we had on the plane, we estimated the distance to the foothills could be no more than 40 miles (about 100,000 steps). The map showed the mountain range was about 75 miles across, and since we calculated that we were closer to the Pacific than we actually were, we figured we were 35 miles away at most. We would have to walk those 35 miles through a mountain range, at a temperature of minus 20 degrees Fahrenheit, with the lethal Andean winds blistering our skin, and without appropriate clothing, gear, nutrition, or knowledge of the terrain.

We would follow the sun, and if we could not see the sun, we would use the compass from the airplane to direct our path.

With the help of Arturo Nogueira, who was the best at analyzing the aeronautical maps, we could clearly imagine the inhabitants of the towns on the other side of that gigantic wall of ice, Chimbarongo, La Rufina, and Puente Negro. Our most optimistic guess put us between just 6 and 10 miles from those towns. But we couldn't understand why, if they were so close, did the area where we were seem so inhospitable? Much farther east on the map we noticed some immeasurable altitudes at which we never imagined we could actually be—Tinguiririca, Sosneado, Palomo, El Brujo. But that turned out to be exactly where we had crashed.

We never actually reached Chimbarongo, La Rufina, or Puente Negro, but those three names still resonate in my memory because they were the anchors we clung to, the hope that sustained us. When I closed my eyes, I imagined one of those towns as the oasis where we would finally regain contact with civilization. I pictured tiny mountain towns, where farm animals grazed upon a resplendent green valley, and chickens ran around small stone houses. We would approach them cautiously so as not to frighten them with our fearsome visages and body odor, which we could not smell but rightfully suspected. We would stumble upon some frightened farmer and say something like, "We were in a plane crash in the mountains, and we need your help." Or we might invert the phrase: "We need your help; we've been in a plane crash." And if they didn't believe us, we would bring along cash to. buy a horse and supplies—just to complete our pipe dreams.

But just like that, we would awaken to our nightmare. We were dead men, spirits who no longer existed in the world of the living. If we held out hope of returning to that world that had turned its back on us and left us for dead, a part of us wondered whether people would welcome us back. Perhaps none of this would be over until we found ourselves knocking on the doors of our own homes. At the same time, the thought of reaching a farmer's house and having him open his home to us was the most seductive scene we could imagine. I'd share this fantasy with Nando, who would build on the illusion, adding characters and colors. Meanwhile, resting just a few feet away in the fuselage, Tintin would watch us dispassionately as he prepared himself psychologically for what lay ahead.

"Farmers are good, working-class people," I would say, recalling my nanny Elena Bielli and her family's farm, where I had spent many weekends as a child. In the warm evenings, she would take me by the hand, and we would go outside to pray to the moon to ease her sorrows.

I spent the two days before we struck out studying the enormous wall of ice we were about to scale. I'd scrutinize its details, section by section, trying to determine the best path across it. Before, I had spent my days imagining what was on the other side, but now I concerned myself with more pressing matters: actually charting a course to whatever lay on the other side. We would try to imagine the rock outcroppings, the peaks, the drops, the twists and turns, and the narrow gorges. We decided to attack it head-on, hiking directly west over the tallest part because it was also the shortest route.

Tintin was calm and ready to go whenever he was ordered to. Nando, on the other hand, who had appeared restless to get going, harbored the same fears I did, though he didn't show it. We balanced each other out. I was the brake to his locomotive speeding full steam ahead.

But our prospects looked grim. All you had to do was look at the variables such as the wildly changing weather, the scarcity of food, and, ultimately, the biggest unknown: how long the injured survivors in the fuselage could hold out. You could almost measure their life expectancy by gauging the irregularity of their breathing and the look in their eyes, whose color would fade as life drained from their bodies.

I made my decision about leaving quite coldly, looking only at the variables. And I'm sure I've never seemed more intolerable to my friends because of it. First off, I decided I wouldn't venture out if I wasn't convinced that our newly constructed sleeping bag could safely keep the three of us warm in that rugged terrain. Secondly, I insisted we delay our departure as much as possible to allow for a late December trek. We couldn't wait for it to get too warm, because that would allow for the spread of infection, which I had managed to keep in check because of the cold weather. Plus, if I stalled, perhaps it would buy time for some unforeseen miracle to appear, as the batteries and the tail section of the plane had.

One of those unexpected events happened, though it wasn't enough. On December 8, four days before we were to set out, we heard surprising news over our Spica transistor radio. For the first time since October 23, the Uruguayan Air Force (whose plane had gotten us in this mess in the first place) had outfitted an old World War II Douglas C-47 airplane to reinitiate the search for us. It was set to leave Montevideo on December 10 at 7:00 a.m. Even if it turned out to be only a mission to recover our bodies, it meant they hadn't forgotten about us! Again, I was filled with doubt about striking out with this kind of news on the way, but I kept it to myself for fear my hesitation would affect the others. I asked myself whether now, with better weather, they might have a better chance of finding us than back in October.

On December 11, as I was calculating how long it would take them to begin searching the foothills once again, the dream of the C-47 coming to our rescue shattered when Gustavo Zerbino came to speak with me privately.

"Numa is dead. And in a couple of days, Roy will be, too. If we keep waiting, we're all going to die," he said.

I knew then that we couldn't delay our trek any longer. Numa Turcatti's death had started a countdown to the moment when we set out on our final expedition. No one had fought harder than Numa to stay alive. And if he had succumbed, then it was only a matter of time before we all followed suit. That C-47 was fool's gold, a specter from another dimension, one that gave us hope only to have it dashed by the foul stench of death. Our two dimensions would not overlap. If we were to survive this tragedy, it was up to us.

Although I concluded that any of the outside world's efforts to save us were destined to fail, the thought of that C-47 was still a beacon for me throughout my final trek. It was a symbol that someone was still tugging, however futilely, at the other end of the rope. We were on our own, adrift in the cosmos, but we had not been forgotten. There were other forces at work that would not let us fade into oblivion.

Forty years after the Uruguayan Air Force C-47 reinitiated the search for our plane, on December 10, 2012, I noticed a peaceful-looking elderly woman in the waiting room outside my office on the second floor of the Hospital Italiano in Montevideo. When I asked my assistant Hilda who she was, she said, "She wants to talk to you but wouldn't say why."

"I want to give you this," the woman said flatly as she handed me some old folders.

I opened them to find several handwritten pages.

"I'm Lili Faira de Terra, widow of Flight Colonel Ruben Terra," she said. "He wrote this exactly forty years ago. He wanted you to have it and to do with it as you see fit. Your father was on that plane with my husband."

When I started leafing through the report of the former Flight Major Ruben Terra, my heart began to pound. Right around that time, in December 2012, I'd set out to chronicle my journey across the Andes, step by step, something I had never done before. One of the crucial factors during that trek was the C-47 that was looking for us. We could hear it. We could feel it. Although we never managed to catch sight of it, we could hear its engines buzzing, the sound echoing amid the mountain peaks, sounding real and imaginary at the same time.

Sometimes it felt as if we were delirious. But how could we not hear them? They had spent thirty hours flying overheard, searching for us. All these years later, Major Ruben Terra had finally arrived to tell us what was happening in the air at the time that we were trekking across the mountains. At different altitudes in the Andes, we were both searching for each other.

I started reading the report, which Lili Faira said no one had read until then. The major's handwriting was clear and firm. I immediately recognized all the characters: Ruben Terra, who had retired as a colonel and later died at age sixty in 1999; his copilot, Captain Eduardo Lepere; my father, Juan Carlos Canessa; Roy Harley, Sr.; Gustavo Nicolich, Sr.; Carlitos Paez's father, the artist Carlos Paez Vilaro; Raul Rodriguez Escalada, an expert pilot and a friend of my family's; and the plane's crew.

Although I never met that flight's commanders, my father had related the story of that fateful journey a handful of times. Every time he told it, he was flooded with memories and emotions, and I could tell it was a strain for him to relive it, possibly because it had been such a frustrating and futile experience. I always felt that it had been rock bottom for him. I think the fact that we appeared shortly thereafter allowed him to bury that memory, and with it all the anxiety and pain that the brave crew must have experienced during that uncertain search for their loved ones.

The one thing I was never able to tell my father was that I never considered that mission a failure. It was the impetus I needed to withstand and carry on. The people on that flight had to overcome their own adversities, and yet they never hesitated. We were both flying blind: we not knowing where we were, and they not knowing we were still alive.

Chapter 13

Flight Major Ruben Terra

On October 13, 1972, the Uruguayan Air Force Fairchild FH-227D (FAU 571) departed Mendoza en route to Santiago, Chile, through the Southern Pass (Malargue–Curico) since the Cristo Pass was an instruments-only flight (closed). The captain of the Fairchild, Julio Cesar Ferradas, reported in at Chilecito after Malargue, and then at Planchon, according to the records provided to the Uruguayan Air Force by Santiago's Central Control. Inexplicably, eight minutes before, he reports in at Curico when he was actually passing Planchon (today Ankon).

After three minutes, from Curico, which was actually Planchon, he erroneously changed course to 006 degrees north and commenced a descent from 18,000 feet to 10,000 feet to check in at Angostura.

What happened? They had begun to descend into the middle of the Andes mountains, and three minutes after having reported in at Curico with a heading of 006 degrees north, Santiago's flight control asked FAU 571 its altitude. And suddenly, Ferradas's calm voice becomes a scream, and he manages only to yell, "ONE FIVE ZERO!" Two minutes later, Santiago control checks back in, but Fairchild FH-227D does not respond. At that altitude—that is,

15,000 feet—the plane is below the Tinguiririca volcano, which is 15,400 feet high, below Sosneado at 17,024 feet, below El Palomo at 15,912 feet, and below Cerro del Brujo, which looks like a line of jagged teeth at 16,000 feet, as we can see from visual flight chart OACI Mount Aconcagua (1436).

So at the moment when Ferradas yells "ONE FIVE ZERO!" or 15,000 feet, three minutes after reporting at Curico, we believe his right wing made contact with the mountain range near Tinguiririca and came apart, followed by the left wing, which sheared off from the fuselage, which slid along the hillside for some 1,800 meters until coming to a stop. The flight was declared "ALERFA" by Chilean air traffic control, a term used to signify there is uncertainty about the safety of a flight and that sets out regulations for the time frame of a search.

In these cases, Chile's aerial search and rescue team begins a ten-day search to find the distressed aircraft. During that time, one hundred three unsuccessful flight missions were conducted using Chilean, Argentine, and Uruguayan aircraft, and the Chilean Air Force ended the operation on October 23.

Nearly two months after the accident, in which all forty-five passengers were considered dead, a second mission is ordered to locate the downed aircraft, now that the mountain has begun to thaw and the prospects of finding it are better.

And this is where I step in as a character, to narrate my experiences during a mission I understood was both difficult and risky. However, I was sure that it was possible to find the aircraft and that we would indeed find it.

The Air Force General Command ordered the mission be fulfilled by the No. 3 Squadron (Transport), which had a staff of sixteen assigned to a C-47 and one AT (photography) to be commanded by me.

I chose a team composed of the best and most experienced Andes mountains experts. I picked myself (besides, I enjoyed the challenge), along with another commander, the pilot Captain Eduardo Lepere; Captain Hugo Spinatelli; First Lieutenant Waldemar Burgueño, a rescue expert; radio operator Miguel Boyan; and Technical Sergeant Luis Paredes. We readied the C-47 FAU 508 and FAU 519 as a backup: Engines, altitude tests, heat systems, oxygen, cameras, altimeter correctors were all go. We were set for a December 8 mission.

To our mission, we added the parents and one friend of the accident victims: Mr. Harley, Dr. Canessa, Mr. Paez Vilaro, Mr. Nicolich, and Mr. Rodriguez Escalada, who would accompany us as passengers.

I had studied every detail of Flight 571, and I marked the place where I thought we would find the downed aircraft on a photocopy of OACI map No. 1, based on the flight data recording from Santiago's control center and on the flight time and speed.

A copy of the map that indicated the location where I deduced the flight had gone down remained at Squadron No. 3 in Montevideo, and, upon our return, we confirmed that was exactly the location where FAU 571 had gone down.

The mission would last ten days in total, unless the Uruguayan Air Force ordered otherwise.

We set out for Santiago on December 10, 1972, with a technical stopover in Mendoza. But over Rio de la Plata, engine number two gave out and forced us to make an emergency landing in El Palomar. This was the first of several setbacks. Why El Palomar? We were trying to avoid the heavy traffic of Aeroparque or Buenos Aires's Ezeiza, which would set us back further.

With a new motor in place, we left El Palomar for Moron that very night to fill up with eight hundred gallons of fuel (which would allow us to fly for eight straight hours) and go on to Santiago. We reached Mendoza-Uspallata and continued on to Juncal using the El Cristo flight path (using VFR or visual flight rules, not flying by instruments). We kept the impressive Aconcagua mountain, at a height of 23,035 feet, to our right, and made our way south to

Santiago. But just as we were passing over the immense Cristo canyon, engine number two, the same engine we had replaced the day before, backfired several times, forcing us to throttle down.

During those uncertain moments when one of our engines was sputtering over the Andes mountains, I thought back on one of the many poems by French aviator and author Antoine de Saint-Exupéry, who had so often flown over these very mountains. During emergencies like the ones we experienced, Saint-Exupéry clung to the Virgin Mary, protector of all aviators, whom he believed was always with us.

Flying in a C-47 amid the monstrous backdrop of that mountain range instills both respect and fear in a man when there's a problem or an emergency.

The planes Saint-Exupéry flew during World War II were piston-style engines like ours, and it was in one of those planes that he disappeared while flying from Sicily to Nazi-occupied Marseille during a mission for the Allies. He was never found.

Eventually, we arrived in Santiago safely.

Chapter 14

Juan Carlos Canessa, Roberto's Father

Fifty days after the Chilean rescue team had abandoned the first search, when the winter snows finally began to thaw, the Uruguayan Air Force mounted another rescue mission. It was impossible, ludicrous to think he might still be alive, but there was no doubt I was going to be on that airplane. The family needed it. If Roberto had been around, he would have told me himself, "Dad, you have to go!"

The air force had outfitted a twin-engine C-47 for the search; the Chileans had only smaller four-engine DC-6s.

The C-47 seemed neither big nor small. The mission seemed neither dangerous nor easy. The fact was I was indifferent about everything. I had been anesthetized by pain. Life was a shade of gray.

We arrived in Santiago after a turbulent flight. The search and rescue chief, Commander Jorge Massa, told me, "Of the thirty-four flights that have crashed in the Andes, there has never been a single survivor. It's hopeless, Dr. Canessa. You're a physician; try to understand." He added that just a month earlier, an American plane—the leaders in advanced technology—had gone down, and it had not been found, either.

We began flying over the mountain range from Planchon, flying north to south. From the first day, we knew it would be a difficult search. The plane was tossed around, and we couldn't distinguish anything on the ground. It was especially rough going between the days of December 11 and 21, which, by a strange coincidence, were the days that Nando and my son were hiking across the mountains.

Chapter 15

I spent the night of December 11 staring up at the sky, listening intently. *Where is that damned C-47 that supposedly set out to find our lost Fairchild FH-227D? Where is it searching for us? Is it going to miss us yet again? Is it going to be like the fruitless October search all over again? Did anyone consider that the digits of this flight number 508 and our ill-fated flight 571 both add up to the unlucky number 13?* There was one more fact that played over in my mind. The rescue plane was supposed to be carrying a team of experts—and some relatives of the crash victims. Was my father—the doctor, the pragmatist, the scientist—on that plane, holding out hope for what might lie over the next mountain, the way we had when we set out over the Andes?

As soon as I'd said I was ready to leave the next day, on December 12, I immediately regretted it. But there was no turning back. A team of people busily started making the final preparations for our journey. I felt like a man condemned to death, hoping against hope for something—anything—to stay his execution.

I had managed to rest on some nights in the fuselage, but on others I had been unable to because of the cold, the discomfort, and the fear. At times, I would pass out from sheer exhaustion. The night before we set out for good I was unable to close my eyes given the terror of having to scale that wall of ice.

Chapter 16

DAY 1: DECEMBER 12

With the first rays of dawn, we said goodbye to our thirteen friends in the Valley of Tears. Carlitos handed Nando one of the booties his mother, Eugenia, who had died in the crash, had bought in Mendoza for her newborn baby nephew. "I'll keep the other one, because I know that soon enough these two will be reunited," he said with startling conviction.

Javier Methol took me by the shoulders. This man, who had lost his wife in the avalanche and had four children waiting back in Montevideo, told me: "Roberto, I'm positive that you're going to make it."

He said it with such profound certainty that I knew he believed in me much more than I believed in myself.

We left at 7:00 a.m. to take advantage of the firm snow, which was still covered in a layer of ice. I carried the sleeping bag and a rugby sock stuffed with our food. I was wearing a jacket, three wool pullovers, including the one from Lauri, and three pairs of jeans, one over the other, which I could wear together because I had lost so much weight. I brought along a case with scissors, a needle and thread, women's makeup which we wore as sunblock, and the plane's compass. Nando carried a backpack and was wearing as many shirts

69

and pants as I was, over a pair of women's thermal underwear. Tintin carried the biggest load and was also wearing three layers of clothes. Additionally, we had each strung over our backs a pair of cushions to use as snowshoes, a metal walking stick, and a length of rope.

I wondered where Javier Methol got his confidence from as I began hiking west. It reminded me of my own mother's blind eternal faith, and it had made me stop and stare into his eyes for a few moments longer, to see if he knew something I didn't. Because up here, we had all developed a kind of seismic radar, sensing unseen changes in the world around us.

Within a hundred feet of setting out on the edge of the glacier, I decided to use a tactic that I employed for the entire trek. I would give myself small, attainable goals to help me keep pushing forward. It could be just reaching that next boulder, that next cliff, that next rock formation, and focusing only on that small goal and nothing else. I couldn't plan out long stretches, much less envision the end of the journey. Instead, I focused on the here and now, what was feasible, and each achievement buoyed my spirit.

As we moved along the terrain, the changing light clarified the land's features. One peak would be revealed to be a series of peaks, the lights and shadows of the mountain playing tricks on the eye.

While the snow was still firm, we were able to scale what felt like many meters up the first slope, crossing it diagonally at first so that we could eventually take it head-on. But when I looked up, it felt like I was walking in place, as if we hadn't moved at all, because that rock formation just over the rise, which looked like a two-hour walk, took half a day to reach in reality. That's why I focused on short-term goals. Soon, we would focus on counting our mere paces, eking out stretches of thirty-three steps at a time. Gashes in the snow where avalanches had broken loose acted as markers as we forged ahead. And soon, the first rays of golden light broke over the land.

Although the landscape fooled us into thinking we were barely moving at all, the fuselage became another marker as it appeared smaller and smaller in the distance. Our friends watched us from afar as we climbed. I turned around occasionally to watch them until they were shadowy pinpricks, tiny black ants moving along a snowy white canvas, losing their shape in the distance. It's no wonder that the planes couldn't see us. We were invisible! Finally, I could no longer see our friends, and I felt a quick rush of anxiety as the umbilical cord that was keeping us alive was severed at last. We now had to fend for ourselves, far from the warmth of our mother, the broken fuselage in the snowy valley.

Around midday, the snow became soft and slushy, forcing us to put on our makeshift snowshoes. Since there was no clear path over this wall of ice, I suggested that we split up to find the easiest way through. I asked Nando to spread out a few meters away and walk a parallel course higher on the mountain. Tintin stayed down below with me. But we realized Nando's path was filled with loose rocks, and soon small boulders began tumbling down the hill, barely missing our heads. So I yelled up to Nando to join us and we continued on, single file, with smaller rocks skipping down the mountain beneath us.

When our path became impeded and we were unable to zigzag up the mountain, we had to scale the icy wall, digging our feet in and pressing our bodies close to the mountainside. The mountain grew steeper with each step, and we began scaling the vertical precipice at a dizzying angle.

By about four in the afternoon, the mountain was mottled with shadows. An icy wind picked up, and every step felt increasingly labored. It took more energy to stand up after each stumble on the ice. Since we hiked in bursts, we got dizzy, and our heads began to pound because of the thin air at that altitude. In those moments I turned to my small goals, telling myself that I'd hike to that next rock, which I couldn't see since it was just over the next rise. But when we reached that peak, we saw that there were only more and more peaks beyond it.

We quickly learned the three different climates we had to endure in the Andes. There was the windless morning cold, which made the snow hard enough to walk on until the sun warmed the land. The snow would then soften around midday, causing us to put on our improvised snowshoes so that we didn't sink in up to our waists, and we'd eventually start sweating because of how much clothing we were wearing. Finally, the sky would cloud over, the sun fading into opacity, and the icy late afternoon winds would begin to blow with piercing gusts that rattled our insides. We felt as if we were wearing nothing at all, because the cold settled into our bones. That was the signal that it was time to stop for the night and test out the biggest unknown: whether the homemade sleeping bag would stave off the Andean freeze. And on that first night, we made a mistake that nearly cost us our lives.

We continued hiking through the afternoon winds and into the early evening's icy blasts. Instead of looking for a place to set up for the night before the evening shadows surrounded us and the icy winds whipped us like a switch, we tried to make the most of the light on our first day. We figured we would be much more tired on the second day. And we thought the trek would take only two days. Three days, at worst. And since we figured we would be more tired with each passing day, we felt it was better to keep hiking. Then the sun disappeared quite suddenly, and we were left only with the light of dusk. Our sweat-soaked clothes began to freeze, and only then did we begin to search for a place to bundle up for the night.

But a campsite proved elusive, as the light dimmed and the wind grew exponentially colder. In my desperation, I considered digging a ditch in the snow as we had on that night when we hiked east. But the ground was too hard, and we barely had the strength to breathe in the oxygen from the thin air. We learned the hard way that none of our trials and errors from the past two months had prepared us for surviving amid the highest peaks. Up here, we had to learn how to remain alive in yet another environment.

Night devoured twilight swiftly, and we could barely see whether we were about to step on firm land or fall into a canyon. *What am I doing here? Where in God's name am I?* I tried to breathe through my mounting desperation, telling myself this was just another marker, another short-term goal I had to cross. I needed to stay calm and keep the faith that God, once again, wouldn't let me down.

I imagined that when I reached the mountaintop, which seemed ever closer yet farther away, I'd see the C-47 searching for us on the other side, so close we could touch it. If its old flickering lights were enough to see it through World War II, I felt certain it would be able to find us now in a time of peace, when the only fight was with nature.

At the same time, I couldn't control the tears of pain from the thought that we'd never live to see it because we were going to die on our first night. Meanwhile, Nando and Tintin called out to me because I had the best eyesight and had had experience camping with my girlfriend's family—something that made me a so-called expert in this new extreme existence of ours. But out here, there was no path, no people to ask for help, no stream flowing languidly through a warm valley. There was only the top of the world, where we were whipped by angry, freezing winds that aimed to sweep us into oblivion. The others yelled at me desperately, but I couldn't or wouldn't hear them. I had to focus all my energy on finding a refuge in the fading light that was ticking down to absolute darkness.

But as always happened when my back was against the wall, instead of shrinking, despair made me fight harder. To stumble in the night was preferable to giving up and awaiting a frozen death. At that moment, when all seemed lost and the world seemed to be extinguished as in the avalanche, I saw it: a clear, windswept area beneath a stone outcropping along the edge of the abyss. A place where we could unroll the sleeping bag and wait out the terrible night. I pointed to it in the last traces of light because I couldn't even manage to form the words. One false move could send us over the edge, but if we managed to huddle together and lie very still, we might just survive the night.

We could barely believe our luck. Nor could we believe it when the wind calmed just as we spread the sleeping bag over our snow-shoe cushions to soften our sleep. The moon rose in the dark sky, illuminating the steep slope we had just scaled, high over the valley where, somewhere down below, the airplane lay. The stars seemed closer, and the silence was so deep we could almost taste it. The one burning question we'd had climbing this icy peak was finally answered: The sleeping bag, though frigid, was providing us enough warmth to breathe and to keep from freezing through. Our crazy invention worked.

Chapter 17

Flight Major Ruben Terra

We began our search on December 11, 1972, trying to fly three to five hours a day, weather permitting. We'd start at Curico, near Los Cerrillos (Santiago, Chile), go into Planchon, then turn toward N 0050, following the path the Fairchild FH-227D was thought to have taken, and finally we'd descend to level 150 between Tinguiririca—Cerro del Brujo to our left, Palomo and Sosneado to our right. We repeated the same flight path every day, flying in circles and figure eights.

But trouble was always lurking right around the corner. In the middle of the mountain range, engine two failed again, backfiring and spewing fuel from the cowl. It was the worst possible spot for something like this to happen. While looking out at the engine, the mechanic, Luis Paredes, yelled out, "Feather the engine or it'll catch fire!"

I tried to eke some power out of that faulty engine, but alas, it was no use. We had to feather it (shut it off and allow the propeller to spin with the least air resistance). Flying into a headwind, I changed course to exit the mountain range through Claro River Valley, which leads to Puente Negro, La Rufina, and Chimbarongo. It takes fifty-eight minutes to reach Los Cerrillos on one engine and losing altitude, but I managed to land on landing strip No. 3 with a tailwind. I hadn't dared to circle back around.

Analyzing it back on the ground, what we should have done was take advantage of the prevailing wind up at the mountain to slip through the Sosneado Valley out to the Argentine side of the Andes and land in Mendoza with little risk. (That was my mistake.)

This was the kind of misfortune that plagued our entire mission. Another was the time when we found what looked like a cross that was clearly man-made on top of the Santa Elena Sierra. We photographed it from all sides and angles—a task that derailed us for two days.

Back in Santiago, Chile's search and rescue headquarters, we studied the photos of a cross with five points at each tip, something someone had gone through the trouble to make perfectly. Convinced that we'd found the aircraft, it was easy for our minds to see the snow forming a tail, a rudder, and a wing with something that looked like an engine. We were sure we'd found it.

Looking back, it was like staring up at the sky and finding shapes in the clouds.

We were all shocked to find something like that in the middle of the mountains, because it meant at least some of the passengers had survived the crash.

Dr. Canessa said, "If my son survived the crash, I'm positive he's still alive," and he suggested that we immediately start dropping provisions with a parachute.

I radioed the Chilean Air Force via VHF for a helicopter, but it turned out the only flight-ready one was being used by President Salvador Allende.

From the Chilean search and rescue headquarters, I called over to Mendoza, Argentina, because the chief there is a friend of mine, and I asked him for help. I told him I needed a jet that could fly low enough to get a better view and still have the power to pull out of there, something our old propeller-powered C-47 couldn't do.

At 9:00 a.m. the next morning, our C-47 circled the site overhead, marking the location for the Argentine Air Force's F-86 Sabre, which made four passes. Over VHF the fighter pilots reported: "It's a weather station with various antennas in a cross-shaped pattern, and a man and a woman waving from inside one of the windows. There is no plane or survivors to be found."

It turned out that a pair of Argentine geologists had set up three days earlier on the mountain to study the season's rainfall and snowdrifts. (We later learned that their installation wasn't far from the actual crash site.) In short, we had lost forty-eight hours over an illusion, the dream that we had found them alive. Instead, we headed back to square one, uncertain and demoralized.

But at this point there was no doubt we were going to find this airplane. It had become an obsession.

Chapter 18

DAYS 2 TO 4: DECEMBER 13 TO 15

After a restless night, day broke and we waited for our shoes and socks to thaw on a nearby rock before continuing our ascent.

We had reached about 14,700 feet. The mountain wall was still nearly a vertical climb as we dug our feet into the cliff face to keep pushing ahead. When we were able to simply hike, we had to stop every few yards to gasp for breath because the air was so thin. Higher up, the glacial winds started earlier in the day, and they were soon chilling us to the bone as they had on our first day. Every stage of our hike seemed unstable, unpredictable.

I stopped for a moment when something caught my eye. There seemed to be two paths cutting east. For a second, I thought it was another mirage or a trick of shadows and light. I took off my improvised sunglasses and rubbed my eyes, but I still saw two parallel paths. *It's some kind of hallucination*, I told myself, and continued climbing. But I kept having this pang of doubt, which helped me focus on something other than my extreme exhaustion and breathlessness. When I looked east again toward Argentina a few hours later, I saw them again, two lines across the mountainside that we hadn't been able to see before because they had been obscured by the other peaks. But there they were now, clearly—and growing farther away.

I didn't say anything at first, but I felt my heart begin to pound. *Those two black lines in the snow look like paths. But they can't be, can they?* I looked for a place to stop so I could study them more carefully from a distance. Nando and Tintin were farther ahead. I could have sworn those two lines looked realer than the other phantom images, but at the same time they were so far away they looked inaccessible. Years later we would learn that the paths led to the Atuel River Sominar sulfur mines. The upper path was for trucks; the lower one, by the river, was for livestock.

I caught up to Nando and Tintin to tell them about it. What to me looked like an exciting new possibility they simply interpreted as another one of the mountain's mind games.

That afternoon we didn't make the same mistake as we had the previous one. Before the sun set, we found a relatively flat rock that was a little bigger than the previous night's, though a little more inclined and treacherous, and rolled out our sleeping bag for the night.

The next morning, our third day hiking, I stayed behind to watch the passage to the east to see if the changing light revealed whether the black lines were actually paths or some kind of geological illusion. Nando and Tintin left the pack with me as they continued on to the summit.

I needed to verify if what I was seeing was real. If there was really a path, we were saved. But if we turned back and it ended up being a mistake, we were doomed. Another impossible decision. I had to be sure—as I had done with the airplane batteries—that one path wasn't more promising than another.

Four hours later, at 2:00 p.m., Tintin returned, completely exhausted. He told me to follow him up the mountain because Nando finally had reached the top.

"What can you see?" I asked anxiously.

"I didn't make it to the top because it was too steep and there were too many loose stones. Nando says you should go up and see for yourself."

That knocked the wind out of my sails. Nando wouldn't have sent me that message if he could see the verdant valleys of Chile. Chimbarongo, La Rufina, Puente Negro . . .

It took me three hours to reach the summit. Nando was standing off to the side, staring silently into the distance. After taking a few steps I could see why: We were at the true summit, seemingly at the top of the world (nearly 17,000 feet), and what lay before us to the west was an infinite number of gigantic snowy peaks disappearing into the horizon. Too much for our diminishing strength. I turned around and saw the same landscape for 360 degrees. I felt an unbearable weight on my shoulders. My legs started to give out, and I nearly fainted as I tried to sit on a rock. *We're dead. Chimbarongo, La Rufina, Puente Negro are ghosts. They're nothing more than mirages on a map, lies told by the World of the Living.*

If Nando was as dispirited as I was, he didn't show it. Or maybe he had already gotten over his desperation and gained a different perspective. Just as I had spent hours looking at the pass to the east, he had been looking west, searching for a place to hang our hopes. And he had noticed two smaller twin peaks that apparently weren't capped with snow.

He pointed to a possible path between the mountains, which formed a sort of Y, with one of the arms leading southwest and the other southeast. I followed his line of sight. It was crazy, but he seemed to be right. There was a sort of Y shape snaking around the mountains, and the two peaks did appear to be thawed at the top. But they were an incredibly long distance away. I nearly said something but realized it was not worth it. Whatever we did, we'd be crossing a virtual galaxy of obstacles, Saturn, Uranus, and Neptune, littered with endless black holes.

One thing was clear: If we took this path west, there would be no turning back. We'd never be able to scale this mountain again. Nando was asking me to burn every bridge and follow him.

When I didn't respond, he asked, "Are you a hundred percent sure about those paths you saw going the other way?"

I shrugged. "I think so," I said.

"We need to do this together," he said.

Down below, while I had been examining the possible eastern pass, I had heard the motors from the C-47 that had resumed the search for us, just as we'd heard over the Spica radio. I told Nando this, and he listened intently but not as if that were even a viable option. Again he asked me to come with him.

It seemed like sheer madness to take on that rocky path. I thought about telling him that we could try the paths down the other way, even though it was impossible to calculate our chances of success or even the immeasurable distance. We could listen for the C-47, signal it with our hands, guide it with our thoughts . . . I was about to tell him.

Just then, I realized that whatever other alternative I posed, I'd have to do it alone. I had convinced them to stay in the tail section to fix the radio, and it had been an abject failure. I had convinced them to wait for a thaw. I couldn't make a journey like this alone.

Nando pressed me for an answer. "Will you come with me?"

He wanted me with him because I had sharp eyesight, because I knew how to read the map, because he said I had good ideas and didn't lose my cool under pressure. Besides, he had the food and I had the sleeping bag. Neither of us could do it alone. Then I remembered something my father had said about not making critical decisions when you're exhausted at the end of the day. It's a recipe for disaster.

"I'll tell you tomorrow," I said finally.

I didn't say it but thought it: *What if we're caught in a deadly blizzard down there?* Better to wipe it from my mind, I told myself, better not to ponder all the terrible things that might beset us.

Nando, ever the pragmatist, had already added another facet to his idea for hiking west toward the twin peaks. He would ask Tintin to return to the fuselage to leave more food and more room in the sleeping bag for us. Plus, if the C-47 did find the crash site, he could tell them about our one-way westward journey.

It wasn't a bad idea.

We hiked back down to the rock where we had spent the night and where Tintin was waiting. We arrived with the last rays of dusk, completely exhausted.

The fourth day of our trek arrived with a resplendent sun. The 20-below overnight cold had cracked the bottle we were using to carry water. Looking out over the endless white snow and the intense blue sky, I felt like the mountains were all at my feet. As if I had a momentary and fleeting dominance over them. Yet I knew Nando was waiting for my answer. Part of me thought about going back to the fragile security of the airplane, where we had survived for the last two months, but how devastating it would be to the survivors on-board. Forging ahead, toward the unknown, felt like a much greater risk, albeit one with a much higher reward.

But the harder decision would be letting Nando go on alone. More than ever, I was convinced we were in this together—till death do us part.

When I told Nando, he couldn't contain his joy. As for Tintin, he was glad to be returning to the airplane because he felt spent from the past two days. And he agreed that since the journey so far had turned out to be much longer than we'd imagined, we should take the extra food rations. That was real teamwork.

At that moment, I reset my focus. For the previous two months, the fuselage had been my homing beacon; now it would be the far-off horizon and the twin peaks without the snowcapped tops. No more half measures. It was all or nothing now.

We had died so many times already; what was one more death? As far as I was concerned, I'd rather die out there in the snow than in the cemetery of the fuselage.

I asked Tintin for his wool cap, we hugged goodbye, and I told him if the C-47 spotted them first, to tell them that we were headed due west.

Before he went sliding tenuously down the mountain on his makeshift snowshoes, Tintin had one final question for me. He wanted to know if the lungs of the remaining corpses were edible; the remaining bits of sustenance were almost gone.

"Every cell, every bit of protein is a source of nourishment," I told him.

As I watched him slide back down the mountain, I realized it wasn't too late for us to turn back. We could still change our minds. But after that moment, it would become a one-way journey. There was a sudden shift in perspective. At first, our major concern had been falling into a chasm or off a cliff or freezing to death; now it was the thought of not being able to turn back.

We briefly took up the conversation of the night before. It had only one positive going for it. But if we couldn't see the fuselage, then the C-47 wouldn't be able to see it, either. It was a tiny, stationary image buried in the snow. On the other hand, we were two dots in motion at the top of the world. Maybe this specially outfitted airplane would find us after all. Little did I know that at that time it was flying at our very altitude.

We spent the remainder of that day, Friday, December 15, 1972, resting on the rock, preparing for the final push. Just before nightfall, we ate bits of meat and fat, took a swig of rum—from the bottle we'd bought in Mendoza, found in the tail section, and saved for this journey—and ate exactly one cubic centimeter of toothpaste before tucking ourselves into the sleeping bag. As the sun cast shadows over the valley to the east, that other option faded in my mind; there was no other choice now. We had to go west. Like two shooting stars in the pitch-black Andes sky.

"Can you imagine how beautiful this would be if we weren't both doomed?" Nando asked.

We fell into a deep silence. We huddled together, not just for warmth, but to fight back the terror of the unknown. We both knew we were likely to die out here, but death wouldn't have such an easy time of it. Because we were ready to fight. With that thought in our minds, along with the peaceful surroundings and the imagined sounds of the C-47's powerful and indestructible engines roaring in the distance on their way toward us, we finally slipped into elusive sleep.

Chapter 19

DAY 5: DECEMBER 16

Before dawn, I tried to open my eyes, but couldn't.

Where am I?

I rubbed away the frost that kept my eyelids from opening. Little by little, it all came back to me: what I'd survived and, more important, what I had yet to survive. I opened my eyes at last and lay stunned for a moment.

We slipped on our nearly frozen rugby cleats and began the task of scaling the mountain. We hiked carefully to the rocky point where we had been two days before, standing on top of the world. Scanning the infinite whiteness, my eyes spotted the twin peaks with the melted summits that Nando had shown me.

After a pause of accumulating awe, we began our descent. We looked for the most adequate path—but there were none. The slope was so steep, the abyss below so incalculable, that it was not fear we felt, but vertigo. Every step seemed cruel and impassible; the void hungered for us just to leap and let go.

We descended slowly, holding on to the protruding stones with all our strength and trying to steady our feet on the rocks jutting out from beneath the snow. During some stretches we slid down the mountain nearly sitting down and tilted back; on others, we clung face-first to the cliff, careful not to let our backpacks (made out of jeans with the leg openings cinched) tip us back. We watched out for each other, always on the alert.

The mountain lay dormant, but when, I wondered, would it start to roar? We didn't dare raise our voices, not even if our exertion had allowed us to speak above a whisper.

Before long, I was exhausted. I began to lose all sensation from the waist down; I could no longer feel my legs. But my mind willed my legs to function.

Soon the angle became less acute, and it allowed us to plot a course.

All of a sudden, I was back home: I was in the garden, watching the trees in their December bloom; from the sidewalk outside, I could see through the walls of my house. There was my mother, my brothers. I remembered the games my brother Conqui and I made up, like the one where we climbed to the top of a tree, tied ourselves to a pulley, and raced to see who could get down first. Everyone said we were crazy. But that was nothing compared to this. I tried to talk to my brothers so they'd keep me company, but when I opened my mouth, they disappeared.

The mountain came to life as the sun grew warmer, and it began to crumble beneath our feet. This side of the slope seemed very different from the other; nothing in the world was built to scale it. Only avalanches dared to tread here.

Conqui, remember when we made a raft out of two barrels and a table over the top so we could cross the lake? It didn't sink and we didn't drown. That wasn't crazy, no. This—this!—is crazy.

We arrived at a cliff made of loose snow, and for a while we just stood there, frozen, stupefied. There was no rocky outcropping to scale, only this mass of loose snow. Every now and then a clump broke off and fell into the abyss—taking the occasional boulder down the mountainside with it. *What now?* Our only hope was to follow the laws of gravity and choose a spot where the snow fell to

Chile, 1971: The Old Christians first division rugby team playing with the Andes in the background. I am on the right with my white headband. In October 1972, we wanted to return to play the same match. (Exequiel Bolumburu)

Airport in Mendoza, October 13, 1972: The last photo taken of the Fairchild 571 — with its commander, Colonel (Aviator) Julio Cesar Ferradas, in front. We had stopped there the day before because rough weather kept us from crossing the mountain range. You can see rainwater underneath the plane here. A few minutes after this photo was taken, we departed en route to Santiago and crashed against the mountains in the middle of the Andes. (Courtesy of Coronel [FAU] Mariano Rodrigo)

Chile, November 1972: Dr Luis Surraco, my girlfriend Lauri's father, searched heaven and earth for me when we were lost. He traversed the Andean foothills on this horse and reached the home of some drovers, who offered to help him. By curious coincidence, one of them was the sister of Sergio Catalan, with whom we would make contact a month and a half later. (Courtesy of the Canessa family)

The Douglas C-47 plane—registered as 508 by the Uruguayan Air Force—in which my father, four other passengers, and the crew, at the command of Major Ruben Terra and Captain Eduardo Lepere, flew over the Andes in search of survivors. This was during practically the same ten days that Nando Parrado and I spent crossing the mountain range on foot. (Fuerza Aerea Uruguaya)

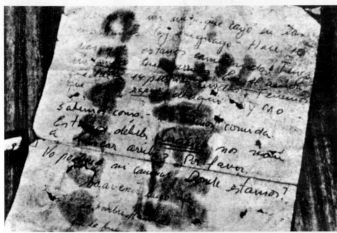

The letter that Nando threw across the San Jose River to Sergio Catalan on the morning of December 21, 1972. (GrupoCOPESA)

Los Maitenes, December 22, 1972: Nando Parrado, Sergio Catalan, and I. There is no glory in our eyes. (*El Pais*, Uruguay)

Los Maitenes, December 22, 1972: With Nando and Sergio Catalan. I remember this moment perfectly: I am focused on the airplane's compass in my hands, which was our guide as we hiked the mountain. (GrupoCOPESA)

Los Maitenes, December 22, 1972: We attempted to exit Los Maitenes on horseback because the dense fog would hinder the helicopters from rescuing our friends who were still in the fuselage. However, shortly after leaving, the fog dissipated and the helicopters intercepted us. (GrupoCOPESA)

San Fernando, December 22, 1972: Survivors Eduardo Strauch, Daniel Fernandez, and I (in the white hat). Two helicopters took us from Los Maitenes in the Andean foothills to San Fernando, where there was a hospital 84.5 miles away from Santiago. (*El Pais*, Uruguay)

San Fernando, December 22, 1972: My arrival at San Fernando. (*El Pais*, Uruguay)

San Fernando, December 23, 1972: In the city of San Fernando, wearing clothes that were a gift from the people there; behind me, wearing sunglasses, is my father. He was a surly man who, those days, could not stop smiling. (*El Pais*, Uruguay)

Hospital in San Fernando, December 23, 1972: Reporters would harass us, but our minds and hearts were elsewhere. (GrupoCOPESA)

Hospital in San Fernando, December 23, 1972: With my parents and Lauri (facing away from the camera). That night I shaved my beard. I wanted to return to life, leave the mountain once and for all, and the beard is what identified us as survivors. The following day, clean-shaven, when they asked me if I was a survivor, I would say no, I was not. (GrupoCOPESA)

Santiago, December 26, 1972: At the San Cristobal Sheraton Hotel with Lauri. Since the light bothered me, my sister, Adriana, lent me her sunglasses. (GrupoCOPESA)

Santiago, December 26, 1972: With Lauri and a reporter at the San Cristobal Sheraton Hotel. (GrupoCOPESA)

Chile, December 28, 1972: Boarding the LAN Chile plane to Montevideo. I was carrying some of the many gifts the Chileans gave us: a typical Chilean sculpture and a rope for rounding up cattle, like the farmers use in the Andes, but much thicker than the ones used for horseback riding in the plains of Uruguay. (GrupoCOPESA)

Montevideo, December 28, 1972: At home with my mother and Lauri, recuperating on the day we returned from Montevideo. (Courtesy of the Canessa family)

Montevideo, December 1972: My mother, Mercedes, my father, Juan Carlos, and my sister, Adriana, in our home in Montevideo, two days after we returned. (Courtesy of the Canessa family)

Aerial view of the Valley of Tears (Valle de las Lagrimas), 2010: Photograph taken at an altitude of 25,000 feet during the same time of year in which we, the survivors, were there. (Daniel Bello, pilot)

The Valley of Tears (Valle de las Lagrimas), January 1973: The last group of survivors was rescued from the Valley of Tears on December 23, 1972. Soon after, in January 1973, the Uruguayan Air Force (Fuerza Aerea Uruguaya, FAU), represented by Captain Enrique Crosa and the Andean Rescue Corps (Cuerpo de Socorro Andino, CSA) of Chile, went to the location to investigate the accident, create a grave, bury the bodies, and burn the fuselage. The following sequence of images was taken on this occasion. (Fuerza Aerea Uruguaya)

The Valley of Tears (Valle de las Lagrimas), January 1973: The gradual thawing of the snow now made the fuselage about five feet higher than when we had been there, with what was left of the airplane practically buried in the snow. (Fuerza Aerea Uruguaya)

The Valley of Tears (Valle de las Lagrimas), January 1973: The rear of the fuselage—which broke away when the right wing detached—where we made a wall of suitcases to keep from freezing. (Fuerza Aerea Uruguaya)

The Valley of Tears (Valle de las Lagrimas), January 1973: The other side of the fuselage, which was eventually buried under so much snow that the windows disappeared. (Fuerza Aerea Uruguaya)

The Valley of Tears (Valle de las Lagrimas), January 1973: The nose of the Fairchild 571, seen from the right-hand side. (Fuerza Aerea Uruguaya)

The Valley of Tears (Valle de las Lagrimas), January 1973: The Fairchild 571, from the front. We never saw it so elevated. (Fuerza Aerea Uruguaya)

April 1973: With the rugby ball under my arm, four months after leaving the Andes. (Courtesy of the Canessa family)

April 1973: After completely recuperating our physical state, Nando Parrado and I returned to playing rugby. In the first match, we wore armbands of mourning on our right arms. (Courtesy of the Canessa family)

Los Maitenes, 1975: In 1988, I returned to the valley of Los Maitenes with my family. When I had first seen it, on December 21, 1972, I believed I had reached paradise. (Roberto Canessa)

Los Maitenes, 1975: In the distance to the right stands one of the two farmers' cabins, where farmer Armando Serda had led us. Sergio Catalan is pictured here with his back to the camera. (Roberto Canessa)

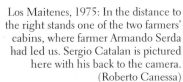

Los Maitenes, 1975: The cabin where we slept: never in my life had I felt so well treated and cared for. (Roberto Canessa)

the lower plateau—without falling all the way down the mountain. It was some strategy: tossing ourselves into the void a little at a time.

"Which way do we go?" Nando asked.

"This way . . ."

We sat back on the cushions we had placed on the snow and began sliding down, forcing a miniature avalanche of snow below us. At first, nothing. We slid down farther, with more force, and suddenly the snow beneath us broke away with us on top. There was an insane free fall, an inexplicable vertigo as we rode an avalanche like feathers in a hurricane. We fell so far and fast we could never turn back. In a breath, we had dropped nearly six hundred feet, riding the snow like a sled. Luckily, no killer boulders dropped along with us. We fell until we hit a small landing, and we quickly turned to the side to let the rest of the avalanche thunder down the precipice without us, its roar echoing all around. Startled and covered in snow, we looked at each other: *Are we OK? We are.* We hadn't been impaled on our metal walking sticks; neither of us was missing a limb. Had we lost our minds? In truth, we'd lost those a long time ago, on the day of the crash. We had only our bodies left.

Nando took off first, but this time it was not just snow beneath us, but sheets of ice. And worse, there was no lower landing. Nando disappeared down the slope toward a bank of either hardened snow or, more likely, snow-covered boulders. He landed with a sickening thud. I looked down, paralyzed with fear.

An entire lifetime passed after the moment I yelled out, "Are you OK?" A thousand ghostly images raced through my mind, the worst of which was the possibility that Nando was dead—and I was all alone. It must have been how Roy Harley felt after the avalanche when he thought he and a handful of injured passengers resting in the hammocks were the only survivors. I figured, at the very least, that Nando had broken an ankle or a leg. What would become of us then? Until that moment, we hadn't considered what we would do if one of us got hurt. Now, at least, we had an answer: One would shoulder the weight of the other until we found a place to rest; one would stay behind with the sleeping bag while the other would seek out help or die trying.

His voice from down below dispelled my macabre thoughts as his head poked through the snow.

"I'm fine! Look!" he said, moving both his arms and legs.

I stared at him for a moment, still in shock.

I had learned a lesson from watching Nando. Instead of sliding down freely, I managed to use the walking stick to slow myself down, digging it deep into the snow like a hand brake.

The mountain's landscape began to change. Soon we came upon an area pockmarked with gorges, and between them were large runs peppered with loose rocks, held in place in the snow as if with pushpins. Sunlight had melted more snow on this side of the slope, revealing more loose earth and rocks beneath. A forty-degree gradient became a sixty-degree drop.

We figured we could do what we'd done with the loose snow, jamming the ground and riding a rocky landslide down like horsemen of the apocalypse. We sat back against the slope, rocking back and forth to make the loose stones break away, and then we were off, sliding down the mountain, holding our arms out for balance until we came to a flat landing below. Then, breathless, we did it all over again.

When we reached the last chute, there were no more loose stones, and our bodies were battered. My outer pair of jeans was worn through with holes; fortunately I had the other two beneath for warmth.

By 4:00 p.m., we were spent. I was nauseated and every part of my stone-ground body hurt. Fog began to roll in, and we searched for a safe place to bed down for the night. But there was none.

As dusk fell, we finally came upon a somewhat flat area that still sloped some twenty degrees. It would have to do. Now we had to figure out how to sleep on this spot, seated with our feet dangling over the abyss. My mind lingered on the chasm, which felt as if it wanted to suck us in.

Instead, I looked out onto the landscape of mountains around us. We were the only things out of place here, completely out of context, intruders in an environment not meant for the living. And unless we could rewrite our destiny, our bones would join this inorganic backdrop.

We tried to lay the sleeping bag over the seat cushions, but it kept sliding down. We tried again, switched sides. Nothing. We'd slowly slide toward the edge. Unless, that is, we put the walking sticks into the ground to act as a barrier. We'd invented so many things by this point that had saved our lives; what was one more? We nailed the aluminum poles into the ground using a rugby cleat as a hammer.

"Ready," I told Nando.

We gingerly slid into the sleeping bag and lay there, perfectly still, a gasp away from hurtling down the side. We intertwined our arms and rested our feet on the poles. And so we managed another kind of invention on the mountain: to sleep practically standing up.

We were tired and frozen, but we slept with one eye open. We could not afford to move our feet, which were crossed over one another to balance on the poles. *What if I fall fast asleep and lose my footing?*

That would have to be a lesson for another day.

Chapter 20

Flight Major Ruben Terra

We went back to our starting point, Tinguiririca, Palomo, Sosneado . . .

But we were so jumpy after everything we'd been through that the slightest fluctuation of the needles from the oil pressure, temperature, or fuel gauges made us nervous—and that was exactly the opposite of what we needed to be, which was calm and collected. Since I was the oldest, it was my job to exude confidence despite what I might be feeling inside. I had to find courage wherever I could. Not to mention that I had to be very watchful, because when C-47 engines fail, they begin showing signs a little at a time through the instruments. I had to make subtle adjustments, throttling back, for instance; otherwise they could fail all at once, those needles rising and falling precipitously.

Days went by. We had dedicated more than thirty hours to the search when, on the last day, December 21, as we were flying over Tinguiririca, Sosneado, Palomo, and El Brujo, trouble paid us another visit. Explosions lit up engine number two again, and fuel began pouring out as we crossed a vast canyon. *No, it can't be!* Paredes, the mechanic, got out of his seat again, yelling up to the cockpit, "Feather the engine or it'll catch fire!" Meanwhile, the radio operator couldn't get the weather report from Mendoza. We couldn't function like this! So we changed direction toward Malargue since we'd be flying with the air currents toward the Argentine side. But the tower reported they had only six hundred meters of runway because the rest was being repaired. No way could we land there, either, much less on one engine! There was no choice but to divert to the tiny San Rafael airport, south of Mendoza. It would take us approximately an hour and thirty minutes to get there on one engine.

The fear of death is something you can feel, something you can almost smell, because sometimes it's right there in front of you, giving off a sensation of anguish and desperation. But it also forces you to keep a cool head, a clear mind. And when you're the commander, you have to project confidence at all times.

We plotted a heading out of the Sosneado Valley as the plane lost altitude, and we were careful not to push engine one as we reached the Argentine foothills. I kept an eye out for a place to land in case engine one failed. But everywhere I looked, there were mountains, peaks, gigantic boulders. . . . There was no doubt that the devil was close at hand if he wasn't already aboard.

We'd been flying for an hour and forty-five minutes when we cleared the last mountain at 10,000 feet. According to the manual, engine one could still fail because of how much weight we were carrying . . . but it didn't. "We're not going to die today!" I yelled out to the rest of the crew.

We landed at San Rafael's Runway 29 with a mix of emotions—anger, nervousness, agitation—over everything that had happened. It was almost impossible to believe we'd been able to survive so many obstacles, although defeat left us with a bitter taste in our mouths.

Chapter 21

DAY 6: DECEMBER 17

By daybreak on day six, we had begun to thaw. I'd barely slept, and whatever time I did drift off, I'd had one eye open.

The snow was hard-packed, and there was no wind. We worked our way down to gorges farther below and set off again over the firm snow. Nando led the way, and I stepped into his footsteps to conserve energy. Every now and then, he stopped to wait for me. He would rest as he waited, but as soon as I caught up to him, there would be no time for me to rest. We had to take advantage of the morning snow.

"What do you think, take the high road or the low road?" he asked.

"The high road."

"You think we can make it?"

"Let's take the high road."

I watched up ahead as Nando stopped suddenly, sat on a nearby rock, and held his right foot with both hands. *Has what I've feared the last two days finally happened? Did he twist his ankle or break a bone? If he's hurt, we're lost.* . . . Even the slightest injury that prevented him from being able to walk would have been a disaster. It was all or nothing. . . . When I reached him, I realized that the sole of his shoe had come loose, nothing more. He secured it with an extra shoelace we were carrying, and we continued on.

I looked up and noticed the clouds. *What if we're caught in a blizzard like the one we barely survived in the fuselage? We're finished.* There were so many possible ways to die it was better to focus on the remote possibility that we'd actually survive. *Keep your head down, keep walking.*

Nando continued out front. That was the strategy we'd devised. From behind, I could get the lay of the land and find the best route, especially since he was nearsighted and my vision was better. He channeled his prodigious strength into blazing a trail. He didn't waste his energy on hesitation; that task fell to me.

The strategy worked, because he couldn't allow himself to think about how desperate he was to reach our destination. There was no end in sight, and if he acted rashly, he'd risk tripping and breaking a leg or twisting an ankle or falling down a gorge. He needed my cautiousness and I needed his brute strength if we were going to overcome the impossible.

Out of the blue, at around 10:00 a.m., I heard the rumbling of an engine drawing near, growing louder and louder as if it were about to fall out of the sky. I looked up but couldn't see anything.

"It's the C-47!" I yelled to Nando, who didn't hear me because he was much farther ahead. "The C-47's here to rescue us, Nando! It's close, I know it!"

––––––––––––

Years later, I would hear all kinds of theories to explain how we had managed to scale the Andes without any gear, while weak, frozen, and nearly starved to death. Some said it was because we were in such good shape as rugby players, that we had already learned to work as a team, that our inexperience with mountain climbing actually made us fearless. But there was only so much that my rugby training could have helped, because I'd lost nearly seventy pounds.

On this sixth day hiking across the mountains, I learned that when you're tiptoeing the line between life and death, you don't despair. You either live or die; you quit or you fight on. When you decide you won't resign yourself to dying, you find a strength you never knew you had, and you push beyond the limits of what you thought was possible. That's how I survived the sixth day. Something came alive inside me, something that went beyond will. There were times when I felt as if I couldn't go any farther, and yet, somehow, my legs kept moving.

The hardest part of the hike was the constantly desolate scenery. We were all alone in this primeval place. The two environments, the one inside the fuselage and this one on the other side of the Andes, were symmetrical in a way. *We need a change of scenery*, I mumbled to myself. We'd nearly managed it when we found the tail section of the plane as we headed east and noticed moisture under rocks, signifying that we were approaching a more temperate zone. But instead of pushing forward, we had gone back to the fuselage so that we could attempt to repair the radio, back to the same suffocating, frozen atmosphere.

Three days ago, we'd had a chance for an escape if we had turned around and headed east toward the lines in the snow that had looked like paths (and in fact were).

At the same time, I, who had considered myself an intruder in these strange lands, now began to identify with them. In the fuselage, we had been twenty-nine survivors after the crash, then nineteen, and eventually sixteen, fighting against nature, which was trying to obliterate us, but instead we had acted as one unit against the mountain.

Once the sight of the plane had faded into the distance, so did some of our ties to our friends. And instead of feeling alien, we began to identify with this rocky, inorganic western zone, which had remained unchanged for aeons. This was where I belonged now. The warmth of the fuselage began to grow cold within me. Human interaction, which I'd cherished so, now belonged to another time, another place. These new surroundings were so overwhelming and omnipresent that the other began to dissolve. At times, I wondered whether it had existed at all.

Between the pressure, the lack of oxygen, and the exhaustion, my heart seemed as if it were nearly beating out of my chest. I'd stop to rest for maybe ten or twenty seconds at a time. And then I'd take another thirty-three steps, huffing like a train.

We walked back in time 20,000 years, to a glacial epoch. And soon we would be nothing but minerals and stone . . .

Now I understood: Nando had been dying to get out of the fuselage; he couldn't stand to be there any longer. He had been suffocated by our society in the snow. He had experienced too much death in his life. He had been in a coma for three days—he'd been dead for all intents and purposes—had sustained a fractured skull, and yet somehow had managed to survive. When he'd awakened from his coma, he'd found his mother dead. His sister had died in his arms on October 21. So his trek was about much more than the terrestrial. The answers he sought were somewhere in the ethereal. His mother, his sister, and half his soul no longer belonged to the realm of the living. We were two lonely, frozen shadows in the snow, and Nando was that much closer to the spectral plane.

The day was fading. I trudged through snow up to my knees as my clothing began to dampen and freeze. We came upon a rock formation where we could wait out the night, and we laid out the sleeping bag.

The only thing that kept my spirits up was the memory of hearing the roar of the C-47 engines overhead. Nando says he never heard them, or he figured they were just hallucinations. The outside world, to him, had ceased to exist. "Those aren't airplane engines— they're avalanches," he said, "and we have to pray to stay clear of them." That afternoon, I'd decided they were engines, and I clung to that belief to sustain me.

Forty years later, the other Douglas C-47 commander, Captain Eduardo Lepere—Major Ruben Terra's fellow airman—told me what they had lived through. In my mind, as they flew overhead with my father aboard, I felt they stretched out a hand to help keep my spirits aloft. Although our fingers never touched, I felt their presence lift my soul.

Chapter 22

Colonel Eduardo Lepere, Copilot

Before beginning the search, Major Ruben Terra and I had agreed we would take turns commanding the mission—although he was the senior officer, with a rank of major, and I was a captain. I knew my way around a C-47. At the time, I had 3,285 flight hours, and about 1,000 of them were in a C-47, which I'd flown since 1968. I'd been a commander since 1970 and a flight instructor since 1971.

Terra wanted in on the mission because he was the squadron chief, and I wanted in because I was the chief of operations. But in fact, we both had much more personal reasons for being invested. Terra had been close friends with Dante Lagurara, the downed Fairchild's copilot. And the Fairchild's navigator, Ramon Martinez, had been a classmate and dear friend of mine.

Although the C-47 was the best search plane in the Uruguayan Air Force fleet, it was not an ideal plane, because its engines had to work at the limit of their capacity. The Andes' altitude affects the engines' climbing strength and performance due to the thin air. At sea level, the C-47 could climb at 700 feet per minute, but at such high altitudes—some 14,000 feet—that number dropped to 100 feet per minute, a real risk when you're climbing over a mountain one moment and dropping into an air pocket the next. The good part was that the plane could stay aloft at a low airspeed, as little as 125 miles per hour, which allowed us to fly low and carefully scan for survivors.

As soon as we arrived in Santiago, we met with the directors of the Chilean Air Force's search and rescue teams, Commanders Carlos Garcia Monasterio and Jorge Massa. The two were experienced pilots who gave us three pieces of advice. First, the winter thaw had come late that year, which would make our search more perilous. Second, if we started our search early, at around 7:00 a.m., we'd be blinded by the sun's glare off the snow. It would make seeing anyone below almost impossible out of the C-47's windows. And third, we would have to wrap up our search by 10:00 a.m. because the heat would cause dangerous turbulence along the mountain range.

On the first day of the mission, we were assigned a young Chilean Air Force lieutenant to pilot the plane, who would take us in through the San Fernando Valley so we wouldn't have to fly south to Curico. But shortly after takeoff, we had a discrepancy in our location. The young lieutenant said we were over the San Fernando Valley, while we believed he was wrong and that we were, in fact, someplace else. He said he flew this airspace every day, and he was so strong in his conviction that eventually we shut our mouths and let him continue on his course. But just a few minutes later, engine two began to fail and backfire, forcing us to reduce thrust and return to the base. On the way back we realized we had been right; we were nowhere near the San Fernando Valley. The lieutenant admitted he had been wrong. If we had continued on that path and the engine had failed just a few minutes later, we wouldn't have been able to pull up, and we would have crashed into the side of the Tinguiririca volcano. That was the inauspicious start to our search for the lost Fairchild.

Just as the search and rescue commanders had told us, we had a very narrow window to search, and the early morning glare was blinding. Some days, we were able to fly in the afternoon. We'd start at 7:00 a.m., return to Santiago at 10:00 a.m., and at 4:00 p.m. we'd be back among the mountains until 7:00 p.m., through the last rays of sunlight.

Canessa said he didn't think his son was alive, except for the day we found the so-called cross, when he had a moment of doubt. For the most part, he would say to us, "I'm searching for him for the sake of my family, but no, I don't think he's alive."

Chapter 23

DAY 7: DECEMBER 18

On day seven, we began to withdraw into ourselves.

After walking for the first few hours, I lost feeling in my legs. Resting against a rock, I removed my rugby cleats and four pairs of socks in order to study my toes.

Our bodies were withering. We were aging at breakneck speed: Every second seemed a year, every day a decade. It was only a matter of time before our organs would begin shutting down, one by one, the body paring down until only the mind and the heart remained. (The heart, always the heart.) *Is this beginning to happen to me?* I'd already seen it happen in the fuselage to those who were dying.

A dark thought crossed my mind: *My body is starting to shut down.* My flesh was white with a greenish tinge. My kidneys must have begun already, because I was not getting enough fluids. And I could see that my toes were starting to turn black from hypothermia.

Since I'd been sleeping on my left side so that I could wrap Nando with my body (because his coat had turned out to be too short), my right side had been bearing the brunt of the cold. It had lost sensation almost entirely. I pressed down along different parts and could feel nothing.

We kept on moving, but I found myself in a different state. I knew that I was nearing the end.

Lauri would have to find another boyfriend. But how would my mother move on? In the fuselage, I'd tried to send my mother telepathic messages that I was still alive, but now there would be no answers for her.

As I felt my body fading, I began sending telepathic messages to Lauri, telling her to move on with her life. I wanted her to be free. I didn't want her to sink into desperation and remain anchored to the impossible instead of embracing a future without me. At the same time, I needed to unburden myself of the responsibility I felt for her feelings. There was no way I could carry that suffering with me, even though I thought about her all the time. I had no strength to spare . . .

As for my father, a practical man who believed in science and reality, I figured he thought I was dead. I didn't know that at times he had glimmers of hope, too, as he flew overhead in the C-47.

By now, we no longer heard the occasional roar of the C-47's engines, and we feared the search had been called off again. Yesterday, we'd heard a plane so close overhead, as if it were headed right toward us, but today there was nothing. Had they crashed, too?

I was so weak that I began to fall regularly, and it would take all my strength to get back on my feet. *We are dying now, I can feel it, one breath at a time.*

I started to think back on my life. I hadn't ever had as good a friend as Nando. The night before, just before falling asleep, whispering so as not to waste any more strength, we'd told each other about all the hopes and dreams we'd had in that other life, in that other world.

I was never as close to any friend as I was to Nando during our trek, nor would I ever be.

Just before 4:00 p.m. on that seventh day of our journey, I told Nando it was time to stop for the night. I didn't know whether there would be a tomorrow for me. My body was cramping, and I could barely stand. My pants were wet, my socks soaked.

Life in the mountains had its own rhythm, its own routine, its own set of savage rules. The day invariably ended at 4:00 p.m., when the sun disappeared behind the western mountains. Life became inhospitable as the icy winds began to surge and the agony of evening descended.

We came across a pair of rock formations that made a sort of shelter.

We stopped and settled in as the temperature began to drop amid the growing shadows.

I looked down at my wrist to see the watch Dr. Nicola had been wearing at the time he was killed in the crash. It was 4:15 p.m.

I sat down among the rocks, a shell of myself.

"You were right to make me stop," Nando said.

We ate bits of meat in silence.

When I set about to stitch up the sleeping bag, as I did every night, since something invariably came loose every day we used it, I noticed something different about our environment. I looked around, and it seemed that some part of the immutable truths about living in the mountains had changed. At first, I wasn't sure what to make of it. It wasn't as overt as an avalanche or rumbling plane engines, but it was nonetheless imposing. I put aside my work with the sleeping bag and stood up to look at the horizon. It had been more than a half hour since we'd stopped—a half hour since the sun should have disappeared behind the mountains, just as it always had before—but not on this night. I looked back down at the watch. Nature seemed all of a sudden to be operating under new rules.

"Nando, look!"

The sun had not yet descended. Orange rays fell warmly over the western-facing valley.

"Nando, how is the sun still lighting up the valley?"

Nando stood up to look at the sky.

"If the sun isn't being blocked, that must mean . . . we're almost out of the mountains!" I stammered. "Over there, where the sun is still shining through—that's the way out!"

Nando continued staring at the landscape with his brow furrowed, reserved, unlike me. He was right to be wary, of course. The next region would pose its own set of unknown challenges. But that was the balance between us; if one of us felt overconfident, the other would be guarded, circumspect. It paid to be judicious, because life had shown us that success never came without a share of suffering and penance.

Despite Nando's mistrust, what this new dogged sun said to me was that we were on the right track. Our reality in the fuselage had given way to a new reality. That was the boost we needed on a day we thought very well could be our last. "Maybe tomorrow," we'd always said. And now, there might actually be a tomorrow.

I followed along with Francisco Nicola's watch, minute by minute, as the sun's rays illuminated the skies past 5:00, 6:00, and even 7:00 p.m. It was our light at the end of the tunnel. Not until 7:12 p.m. did total darkness fall. What a difference that made: It seemed we had traveled across a span of 10,000 years, out of the Ice Age.

Chapter 24

DAY 8: DECEMBER 19

I woke up from a restless sleep to discover that while my body may have felt spent, my mind felt clearer.

"There's much more oxygen down here," I muttered in surprise.

It was something to hold on to: oxygen, the ability to breathe, as we finally descended the mountain.

Nando was up and signaling it was time to go. I looked for the sun among the clouds to orient myself. Soon we were walking again.

As we traveled downward, we realized the snow was giving way to rocky terrain, loose gravel, and even patches of dirt.

A thought cut in: *Maybe my mother will have me back, after all; maybe it's time to recapture Lauri, whom I'd had to abandon 10,000 years ago.*

Up ahead a bit farther, the valley forked into the Y shape we had seen from the mountaintop five days earlier.

Nando picked up his pace, but ahead in the distance, I saw him stop all of a sudden. As I neared him, I could read the anguish on his face. A thunderous noise had stopped him in his tracks. Looking down from the edge of a cliff, we saw a stream coming through the mountain turning into a torrent of water as it flowed down a gorge some one hundred yards below us, heading southwest. We were standing at the birthplace of a river.

"Rapids!" Nando said fearfully.

What to me was a revelation—life-giving water after escaping the Ice Age—was yet another unforeseen obstacle to Nando.

Since we couldn't ford the raging rapids from this point because it would surely drag us under to our deaths, we followed it southwest to see if it became low enough to cross downriver. Our hike along the river proved to be extremely difficult thanks to huge, irregular boulders that we had to scale at different points or divert around. Although the river widened and gained speed as we moved along, we found that we could breathe more easily, recovering some of the oxygen we'd lost so long ago with the crash.

The snow underfoot, which had been slowly disappearing between rocks and dry earth, ended abruptly. The only white we could see now was high up in the distance or in the shadows, so we were able to plot a drier course. I picked up a limestone-like rock to commemorate the change of scenery—and to give to Lauri. I wanted to take her proof of my recovery. A vestige of our tribulations. I tucked it into my jacket pocket, where I could touch it. Every now and then, I took off my glove so I could feel the cold, rocky stone with my fingertips. It allowed me to imagine I was walking toward her, and that she was waiting for me just beyond the bend.

An hour later I stopped suddenly and motioned to Nando, who didn't see me because he was walking in front. I didn't dare yell and scare it off, but six feet ahead of me there was a lizard, staring right at me.

The origins of life were beginning to emerge in their most primitive forms. And there, along with the reptiles, were Nando and I, beings out of time who fell unexpectedly into this ancient realm, disturbing the balance.

At the sight of this other form of life, I was filled with the hope of reaching home again, of seeing Lauri. I wondered whether she was still waiting for me, whether she still wanted me. I turned over the stone in my hand that connected us. Not only would I bring her proof that I had crossed the millennia to find my way back to her—across caverns and glaciers and Dark Ages—but I'd ask her to walk hand in hand with me for the rest of our journey.

Nando made his way back to me when he realized I'd stopped. I couldn't cease staring at this little lizard. I was mesmerized by it. The snow had melted away and taken with it the barrenness of death. There were lizards, water, and, a little farther ahead, flowering purslane. Although it was an arid, desolate place where likely no man had set foot, to me it felt like the gates of paradise.

We continued moving.

There were no guarantees I'd survive, but now I knew I wouldn't end up a frozen rock amid the Ice Age. Maybe this only meant I'd die closer to my civilization, closer to my own time.

The yellowish river we were following, which got its color from the sulfurous volcanic terrain of the mountains, eventually joined another stream of clear water. I later learned that they were in fact called the Amarillo River and the Claro River. We were standing at their confluence.

The river was one hundred feet wide at that point, with nowhere to cross. We backtracked to see whether there was a place where it would be easier to get across, because we could see that between the rocks and the rapids of melting mountain ice, our path was blocked.

We found the narrowest stretch of river with a series of rocks we could hop across. We tied ourselves to opposite ends of a rope, and Nando hopped from rock to rock until he reached the far shore, soaked from the white water crashing onto the boulders. Then it was my turn. I jumped from boulder to boulder until I reached the last one. I felt too weak to make the final leap while wearing the backpack, so I yelled to Nando over the roar of the rapids to yank the rope tied to the backpack as I hurled it toward him. But my throw fell short and the backpack landed in the water. The bottle of rum broke in the fall, infusing our remaining supply of meat with the taste of alcohol and littering the spare socks we were using to cushion the bottle with shards of glass.

We both made it across, but we were soaked and shivering from the icy water. I looked around us and saw brush everywhere, twisted and dried from the wind and cold. It had trunks and stems we could snap off with our hands. Would it be possible to light a fire? We gathered some kindling, and I broke up the twigs into pieces to make a small pile. Then I flicked on Pancho Delgado's Ronson lighter, which we'd carried in our backpack. Soon the spark became a flame, and the flame became a fire. Nando was spellbound.

"Nando, do you realize what we've done? We made fire!"

We rubbed our hands over the flames and got so close it singed our fingertips.

We took out the meat from the rugby sock where we'd kept it and noticed that part of it had turned green and was starting to sour because of the warmer temperature. We ate meat and fat tinged with the taste of rum.

For the first time, we laid out the sleeping bag not over ice and stone, but over a pillowy cushion of vegetation.

I stared into the fire, watching the flames dance. We listened to the crackle as the shadow of the mountain lay behind us, the starry heavens above. It was the first night since October 13 that we did not sleep under the mountain's threat.

Chapter 25

DAY 9: DECEMBER 20

On day nine, just before dawn, we awakened to a stinging all over our bodies.

"What's going on?" Nando asked.

I lifted up my jacket and the three layers of sweaters, and I noticed purple welts all over my body.

"Some kind of red bugs. It's good; it means we're closer to our world," I said.

Although we had been growing weaker each day, we now had the ability to make a fire to keep ourselves warm, so we decided to leave behind our sleeping bag, which every day seemed to weigh more. Since we had gotten used to the freezing snow, now that we were at a lower altitude, the cold didn't bother us. With fire, we could take an evolutionary leap forward, no longer needing scraps from the fuselage to keep us warm.

A half hour later, we found another sign of hope, the first indication of human life: a rusted tin can. I tried to figure out what kind it was just to know it was real. I scraped away the rust to reveal the name "Maggi Soups." I felt as if I could take on the world. I imagined the food that must have been inside and my mouth watered.

I quickly wiped away the thought upon feeling the stab of hunger pangs. I showed Nando the can.

"I don't trust it," Nando said. "Could've fallen from an airplane."

Something had changed about the way I was hiking. I no longer looked over my shoulder for avalanches or landslides, but to the ground for vestiges of human life. An hour later I found a horseshoe. I sat down next to it, amazed, then turned it over in my hands, tracing its shape with my fingers as if it were a relic. It was old and rusted, and further proof that we'd left the Jurassic period and entered the human era, where magnificent objects are made with a hammer and anvil. We had traveled from the Stone Age to the Iron Age.

"You can't toss a horseshoe out of an airplane," I told Nando. "Horses don't fly in airplanes. Only victims and survivors."

A little while later, I could barely believe my eyes when, on the other side of the river, I noticed a patch of far-off trees and next to them two cows.

We each fell back into our roles. Nando was suspicious of anything that might bring hope. Or maybe it was like what happens to cancer patients who struggle so long and hard to survive that when they're told they're cured, they can't believe it.

"You sure they're cows? They're not wild tapirs or something?" he said.

I leaned in and looked closer.

"They're cows, without a doubt," I said. "Skinny mountain cows."

The signs of civilization began to multiply. I felt like a tracker or guide, looking for signs of humanity. Or an archaeologist, looking not for traces of how man lived, but for signs of how we ourselves might yet survive.

Two hours later we came across a path filled with hoofprints from cows, horses, and what seemed like either sheep or goats.

"Nando, look!"

He furrowed his brow.

Still later we saw more cows, as well as trees felled by axes, no doubt the work of men.

"We're going to make it, aren't we?" Nando said with an expression that looked like a smile—something I hadn't seen since before the crash.

Farther along, to our left, we saw another stream flowing down from the mountains, and I realized these two would soon merge and block our path. This serenity would give way to a roar, confronting us with the prospect of having to ford another raging river in our weakened state.

Worse yet, I felt around my pockets for the improvised sunglasses and realized they were gone. I was filled with anxiety because the glare could cause snow blindness as it had to Gustavo Zerbino. Thinking back, I remembered that I'd set them down when I'd stopped to look at the horseshoe at least an hour earlier.

"Nando, I have to go back. I left the glasses."

I retraced my steps but became lost. *Where was that horseshoe? I left it right in the same place. . . .* I tried to find my way back but couldn't for a while: All the rocks and snowdrifts looked the same. When I finally found the horseshoe, right there next to it were the sunglasses. I held them like a precious object, for in that universe, they were my salvation. When I returned, I found Nando resting with his back against a rock, staring east. I'd wasted more than two hours.

Farther along, we came across another trail along the river mottled with hoofprints. The trail opened onto a wide valley, where in the distance, we saw a small herd of horses.

The combination of all these hopeful images had an unexpected effect on me. For the first time since 3:30 p.m. on October 13, the tension in my body began to loosen. Suddenly, I felt painful cramping in my stomach. At first I thought it might have been the meat we ate or the toothpaste we'd consumed for the magnesium after the meat, or perhaps it was simply exhaustion. But later, I came to think it was the release of stress that came from finally being so close to our goal. Maybe my body felt as if I had accomplished my task of plotting our course off the mountain, while Nando's goal was still ahead of him: His journey would not end until he found himself hugging his father. And there was still a long way to go for that moment. Maybe the days he'd spent resting in a coma gave him the extra strength he now needed—strength I no longer had.

We pushed ahead and found an animal pen made of stacked stones and logs.

There was no longer any doubt. Rusted tin cans. A horseshoe. Stacks of chopped wood. And now, a pen made of wire and wood and nails—and maintained by human hands. Boot prints were all around. We had arrived in civilization.

Our original group of forty-five people had been whittled down to sixteen. And now, there was someone new among us, someone we had yet to meet.

Nando set off to find the spot where the livestock might have crossed the river and returned an hour later with bad news: The rivers bracketing us were impossible to cross. I wasn't too alarmed because I knew these men and horses must have crossed somewhere, and not too long ago at that, because their prints were still fresh.

Nando said he'd found the place where the cows slept under a tree, because it was covered in manure. I told him that was probably where they went for shade, not where they slept. He then devised a plan: He would climb the tree and drop a rock on the head of one of the cows when it came to rest so that we could eat. I told him it probably made more sense to slit the tendons of its back legs with our knife, like the early cowboys did. But then it hit me that if we were going to beg for help from whoever owns this cattle, it would probably not be a great idea to pick off one of the herd. No, the best we could do was to milk them.

Amid this absurd conversation about climbing a tree with a rock or attacking a cow in our ridiculously weakened state, I looked over

Nando's shoulder. There, at the very edge of the valley, on the other side of the river, was a moving shadow. The silhouette of a man riding a horse.

A shiver ran down my spine. I rubbed my eyes and looked again. "Nando! A man on horseback!"

I told him to run, that the man was three hundred yards away on the other side of the river, but Nando couldn't see him.

"Just run, Nando, run!"

He charged off toward the edge of the valley, not knowing where he was going, and instead of running in a straight line, he was running all over the place. When I saw he was heading the wrong way and the rider might disappear into the distance, I found enough strength from God knows where to scamper across the rocky, swampy terrain, peppered with thorny rose hip bushes. We arrived practically at the same time, gasping for air, at a spot where the terrain dropped off into a ravine toward the river. On the other side, cloaked by the brush, I saw a boy about ten years old on horseback following the silhouetted rider. He was wearing a floppy cowboy hat as he slowly led a pair of cattle down the mountain.

"There!" I said to Nando, pointing.

We both started yelling, but our screams were drowned out by the roaring river. The rider took a few more steps, stopped—and then turned to look at us. I watched as Nando jumped up and down, screaming the word "airplane" and moving his arms like a plane before finally dropping to his knees and folding his hands in desperate supplication. The rider held perfectly still, as if petrified. The boy had stopped, too, a few paces behind him. *Do they understand us? Are they trying to figure out what we are?* We might easily look like dangerous wild men rather than survivors of an airplane crash.

Nighttime was threatening. The rider gently spurred his horse and began to move again cautiously. The boy did the same. The man was weighing us, measuring us. The entire encounter from opposite

117

sides of the river lasted perhaps five minutes. And then, just before the final rays of sunlight disappeared, the man signaled to us with his hands and yelled a word we managed to hear clearly over the roar of the river: "Tomorrow."

Of all the words to choose, he picked the one we had said so often back in the fuselage. When things were at their worst, there was one phrase we repeated that would give us hope for something better on the horizon: "Maybe tomorrow . . ." Maybe tomorrow something would give. Maybe tomorrow the mountains would just disappear and we'd be back home with our families. Maybe tomorrow we'd find a way out of this hell. Except this time, tomorrow seemed a lot more certain.

Then the rider disappeared into the darkness.

Night came quickly, and so did the cold. I caressed the lighter in my jacket pocket. This was our salvation now. Instead of camping down by the river for the night, we hiked back up about a hundred yards to take shelter under a group of trees.

We gathered up kindling from among the vegetation, which was more substantial than it had been the night before, made a fire, and settled down to think calmly and clearly. The encounter with the man and the boy had rattled us. It felt like an electric current was running through my body. I looked down at my hands: They were trembling.

We sat by the crackling fire. It was not just the two of us anymore; now it was Nando, me, and the anonymous rider who would return the next day.

It was 8:00 p.m. on December 20, 1972. It had been sixty-nine days since the accident.

I looked down at the rugby sock that contained the bits of meat and gristle from our friends, which was starting to rot. *Where am I from? What am I?* The two societies were beginning to clash. I thought that maybe we should bury the remnants there, to enshrine our friends at the gates of paradise.

Years later, on two different occasions, I would search for this very spot. I never found it. But I have continued searching.

Nando suggested we sleep in turns so that we could see the exact moment when the rider returned. I took the first watch. In the distance, I could hear the rushing river. When it was Nando's turn, I tried to wake him, but he was fast asleep. I let him be. Besides, I realized that I couldn't sleep even if I wanted to. My emotions were bubbling over, robbing me of my body's remaining strength.

Chapter 26

Colonel Eduardo Lepere, Copilot

We flew every day until December 21, the day we were set to end our mission, from 7:00 a.m. to 10:00 a.m. and again from 4:00 p.m. to 7:00 p.m. Occasionally, we flew as low as 12,000 feet, even though the peaks around us were 14,000 and 16,000 feet and higher. Generally, we stayed at around 14,000 feet.

Whenever an engine failed, protocol dictated that we reduce thrust and keep flying. On two occasions, the oil pressure dropped when a cylinder cracked. So that the engine wouldn't catch fire, we killed the power and turned the propeller into an angle where it could spin freely while reducing drag. It's what we call feathering the engine. Both times it meant we had to switch out the engine.

Our mission was marked by frustration, beginning with all the problems the plane gave us. Our C-47 was outfitted better than any other plane in the fleet for this kind of work. But even that wasn't enough. No matter what kind of advantage we thought we had, it was always insufficient. Mostly, it was frustrating because our mission failed. An air force aircraft had gone down, and the air force vessel sent to find it didn't succeed.

One day in the middle of our mission, when we realized that our window of time was too narrow to give us any hope of finding them, we decided to stay out past 10:00 a.m., against Massa and Garcia Monasterio's earlier warnings.

We headed toward Cerro del Brujo, a pair of tall peaks with dozens of smaller mountaintops between them, forming a sort of ominous serrated knife. When we were two miles from the Cerro, violent turbulence tossed our plane and we dropped two thousand feet into an air pocket. If we had been over a mountain instead of the valley, we would have been smashed against the peaks. The drop was so sudden and violent that one of the passengers, Rodriguez Escalada, flew out of his seat and gashed his head against the cabin ceiling.

As the winds came over the mountain from the Chilean side, they dropped precipitously over the leeward side, forcing the C-47's powerful 14-cylinder engines to work at maximum power just to keep us aloft. The turbulence was so intense that upon landing, the mechanic, Luis Paredes, asked for a ladder to inspect the wings to make sure they hadn't cracked in the enormous drop.

While Paredes inspected the plane, the rest of us stayed in the cabin, trying to relax. One of the passengers, the artist Paez Vilaro, decided to paint a sun on the door that separated the cabin from the cockpit. When Paredes came back in to tell us the plane had miraculously escaped unscathed, he saw us awed by the painting, which remained in the C-47 until it was decommissioned years later.

Paez Vilaro was like that, able to paint after a fearful incident. The father of Roy Harley was the quiet one. The architect Gustavo Nicolich always carried an extra warm jacket with him. One day he said to me, "Know why I carry it? Because if my son is alive, I want to wrap him up in it."

Days later, after Terra and I got word over the Telex that two survivors had been found, we gave Harley and Nicolich the good news. In all the commotion, however, Nicolich had misplaced the extra jacket for his son. First Lieutenant Burgueño gave him his own flight jacket so that Nicolich could give it to his son.

On December 28, four days after we returned to Montevideo, something happened that I still remember to this day. A man came to the air base and asked to speak to the crew of the C-47. It was Gustavo Nicolich, who had come to return Lieutenant Burgueño's jacket, just days after learning the tragic news that his son was no longer alive to be wrapped in its warmth.

Chapter 27

Juan Carlos Canessa, Roberto's Father

On December 21, after the rescue mission ended in resounding failure, we made preparations to return to Montevideo to spend the holidays with our families and without our missing children. Since we could only manage to get two commercial tickets home, we decided Carlos Paez Vilaro and Raul Rodriguez Escalada should take those seats. The parents of Roy Harley and Gustavo Nicolich and I would fly back on the C-47 with Major Terra, Captain Lepere, and their crew, to whom we were deeply grateful.

As we were flying over the mountains, once again one of the engines started sputtering and spewing black smoke, and the propeller stopped spinning. The commander ordered a crew member to keep an eye on the other engine; if it caught fire, we were doomed. The rest of us monitored the other propeller through the windows, anxiously watching for black smoke and flames. After an unbearably long time, we finally made an emergency landing in San Rafael.

We stumbled off the plane with our legs shaking. The three of us hugged the pilots Ruben Terra and Eduardo Lepere. We didn't know what else to do. The authorities at the tiny airport tried to get us home on a small airplane based there, but they couldn't find a pilot. I finally decided to take a bus to Buenos Aires, which would arrive the next morning. Harley and Nicolich stayed in San Rafael, not sure how they were going to get home.

Chapter 28

DAY 10: DECEMBER 21

Just before sunrise on day ten, I saw a flicker of light on the other side of the river that quickly became a flame and then a blaze. Overwhelmed, I scrambled to wake Nando.

"There he is!"

A bonfire glowed in the twilight of dawn. I tried to stand up, but my body went limp. I could barely lift my head. My entire being was refusing to respond. My potassium level must have been zero.

The rider had lit an enormous fire so that we could see him on the other side of the river.

While I struggled to barely move my head, as though paralyzed, Nando took off toward the fire. When he reached the river, he could see three figures sitting on boulders by the warmth of the fire. It was the man with the hat and the boy from the day before, accompanied by another man. Nearby were three horses. The man with the hat stood up and walked to the edge of the river. Nando tried to yell, but the roar of the river, more than twenty-five yards wide, swallowed his supplications. The man saw he was trying to yell but couldn't understand him. The man took a piece of paper and a small pencil out of his pocket, tied them to a rock, and threw it clear across the river. Nando scrambled over to it, untied the paper, and read: "I've sent a man on his way over to you. Tell me what you want."

Nando scratched out a message on the other side of the paper. "I was in a plane crash in the mountains. I'm Uruguayan. We've been walking for ten days. My friend is injured. There are fourteen other injured survivors back on the plane. We have to get out of here soon and we don't know how. We have no food. We're weak. When are they coming for us? Please, we can't even walk. Where are we?" He did not sign it or identify himself because it was all just too much to explain. Besides, we ourselves barely knew who we were anymore.

Nando tied the note back to the rock and stood at the edge of the river. Then he hurled the stone as hard as he could, worried it might not be enough to reach the other side. But it just made it to the other shore. The man read the note carefully, then looked up and gestured with his hands to calm down, as if to say, *I understand*. Before leaving, he walked back to the horses, took a few loaves of bread and cheese out of a bag, tied them up inside a cloth with a rock, and threw them across the river, which we later learned was the San Jose River, a tributary of the Azufre River.

Nando grabbed the package and rushed back to where I was.

Not only was the man on the other side of the river not suspicious or hostile, as we had feared, but he had thrown us a lifeline of nourishment.

Before we'd left on the trek, Javier Methol, the oldest survivor who was the de facto "treasurer" and "banker" of our group, gave us six hundred dollars to pay whoever found us, in case they were indifferent or hostile. We were wary. After all, we now existed in an aggressive, untrustworthy universe that was constantly trying to exterminate us. It was impossible to imagine whether civilization would welcome people rising from the dead. That's why when the sixteen of us were later reunited, we remained together, traveling first by train to Santiago and then by sea to Montevideo.

Two hours later, as we sat camped under the trees, a rider came into the clearing wearing threadbare clothing and seated on an emaciated horse with a worn harness. Our first extended encounter turned out to be with an Andean farmer, an indigenous Mapuche who knew the secrets of these mountains better than anyone.

Speaking just above a whisper, he told us his name was Armando Serda and the man who'd sent him to help us was Sergio Catalan, who, right after having made contact with Nando, set off for the nearest police outpost—an eight-hour horse ride away. Serda told us he'd thought we were farther up the mountain, near some irrigation ditches he had to fix. He said he was going to do that job now and return in about two hours. He seemed calm and unhurried, as though he were just another survivor of this place.

When he returned, I asked if I could ride his horse because I no longer had any strength to walk. I couldn't get my foot up into the stirrup, and when I tried to mount the horse by grabbing its mane and hopping on, as I'd done my whole life, I didn't even manage to get both feet off the ground. The farmer just stared at me, impassive. I clambered up onto a rock, tried to jump, and ended up slumped across the horse's back. I managed to twist myself into the seat and was winded from the effort. Armando Serda then wordlessly grabbed the reins and set off with Nando at his side.

I looked down and recognized his footprints in the sandy ground. He was wearing sandals with soles made from old truck tires. Those were the same prints I'd seen near the animal pen one day earlier.

As we climbed rugged cliffs and went down slippery gorges, rocks went tumbling down the mountain, but our guide pressed on confidently. We came upon a pair of huge tree trunks that had been laid over fast-moving rapids roaring some twenty feet below. Before I even had a chance to worry, Serda and Nando set out over the logs, pulling the horse behind them. The horse nosed the ground, gingerly trying to find its balance as it moved along. Had I survived a plane crash, an avalanche, and freezing to death on a ten-day hike through the mountains, only to die crossing a perilous wooden bridge on horseback?

Just over the next hill, the scenery changed. We came upon a bright green meadow irrigated by a series of ditches the local farmers used for watering their crops and livestock. The loveliness of this reality surrounding us surpassed the most vivid scenes I'd imagined during all our time in the snow.

Is this paradise, the biblical heaven on earth? I wondered. *Nando, are you sure we didn't die on one of those icy nights in the mountains and this is all a hallucination imagined when the conscious and unconscious minds meet outside the body?*

Two small, rustic cabins poked up from the prairie in the distance. They were simple and beautiful, with thatched roofs, surrounded by roses in full bloom. Off to the side, cows and their calves were grazing in fields so green they seemed almost iridescent. As we approached, another farmer—not quite as lean but with native Andean features—stepped forward and took off his hat in a humble and respectful gesture. Armando Serda introduced him as Enrique Gonzalez.

"Where are we?" Nando asked.

"Los Maitenes," Serda answered.

The horse stopped, and I noticed a fresh farm cheese resting on a nearby table, a cheese made by the *arrieros*, the mule shepherds, which is better the fresher it is eaten, before it dries out. Its aroma piqued my debilitating hunger and flooded my senses. I could smell it from a distance like prey and could think of nothing else.

"May I have a piece?" I asked, pointing to the cheese. I got down from the horse and brought the cheese to my mouth. I took one bite, then another and another, without swallowing the first. I stuffed my mouth voraciously, finally swallowing pieces whole. Nando did the same, and the two farmers watched in disbelief as we ate.

I was like a wild animal, moving cautiously and responding mostly by instinct. Then the aroma of something mesmerizing called to me from behind. I wheeled around to find an iron pot simmering over an outdoor wood-burning fireplace.

Gonzalez noticed the look on my face. As if they had been expecting us, he took the pot off the stove and placed it on the rustic wooden table in front of us, next to a pair of chipped bowls and homemade tin spoons. With a big wooden ladle, he served us steaming, heaping bowls of a bean and noodle stew with chunks of beef, a dish called *porotos con riendas*. We dove in ravenously with spoons, but I fantasized about tipping the entire steaming bowl into my mouth to satiate my crushing hunger, if only the stew weren't so hot. I couldn't eat it fast enough. Next, they brought over loaves of freshly baked bread, and the flavors exploded on my palate. Cheese, beans, beef, bread—I'd never felt such intense and varied ecstasy.

I no longer felt that rumbling in my intestines; it was as if they belonged to a whole other animal. When we had almost devoured our third helping, I looked over and saw the two farmers eating off to the side, eyeing us warily. That's when I realized Nando and I had commandeered not just their places at the table but their meals, while they were eating over a pair of boulders.

I called out to them and asked them to sit with us. I told them it had been more than two months since we'd eaten at a dinner table. I said I wanted more than their food; I wanted their company.

Armando Serda stared at me blankly. And Gonzalez was waiting for Serda to make the first move. I asked them why we weren't eating these delicacies together, while Nando served himself a fourth bowl. But the two men didn't budge.

Nando glanced at me and turned to the shepherds. "He says you should come eat with us, or we'll go over and eat with you," he said clearly.

It took them a minute to make up their minds. By the time they did bring over their half-eaten meals, there was little left in the pot. We peppered them with questions, and they responded with one- and two-word answers, their voices low like ours. They told us, among other things, that they rebuilt the roofs of the huts each spring after the winter snows covered them.

Around six in the evening, Sergio Catalan and ten men from the police outpost arrived on horseback. They were under the command of Sergeant Orlando Menares, a corpulent man with a length of rope looped across his chest. They'd taken two trucks, one filled with men and the other with horses, from San Fernando to the Azufre River bridge, where they had crossed on foot and ridden for two hours to these cabins in Los Maitenes.

It was the first time we saw Sergio Catalan up close. I looked into his eyes and thought, *This is the man who saved us.*

The tone of our gathering changed completely. These carabineros, the state police officers, looked at us in amazement, as if they were the first explorers to reach the Andes. They were voracious for answers. The sergeant unfolded a map on the ground and asked us to point to the crash site with the survivors. We stared at the map and attempted to retrace our journey. We found the river and I traced it back with my finger, past the valley, up into the glacier, into the snow, and up to the mountain at the beginning of time.

"Impossible!" the sergeant said.

But we were emphatic. There was no time to lose; our friends were dying. The sergeant looked us over, trying to decide whether to believe us.

We later learned that Catalan worked on the other side of the river, leasing the land from the owner so that his animals—his cows and sheep—could graze on the tender grasses after the snow melted each spring. Catalan was the shepherd of this flock. He lived with them, knew the mountains well, had learned to take shelter in caverns to keep his flock safe from pumas.

I felt that he was the only one who truly believed us. He understood what it took for an animal and its young to survive here. He told the sergeant that the state police hadn't completely believed him, either, and had called the capital from San Fernando. But after they'd read the letter that Nando had scribbled, and the local chief had vouched for Catalan, they had to admit it was possible. They'd told him to bring Sergeant Menares to us in order to try to find the exact location of the plane as well as to prove that we weren't a hallucination.

The sergeant ordered two of his men to ride to Puente Negro to speak with the San Fernando chief to explain the situation, that we were in fact real, and to ask headquarters in Santiago to dispatch a pair of helicopters.

Puente Negro? Wasn't that one of the locations Arturo Nogueira had shown us on the map back in the fuselage? "Chimbarongo, La Rufina, Puente Negro . . ." I muttered.

The sergeant pointed to the names on the map.

"La Rufina is here, Chimbarongo over there, and this is Puente Negro, the closest outpost," he said.

I studied the names on the map. The sergeant waited for me to say something, but there was nothing left to say.

We were right, Arturo. Except we were off by a ten-day hike.

Sergeant Menares guessed it would take his men six hours to reach Puente Negro on horseback, and since the helicopters would still have to be prepped and couldn't fly into the mountains at night, we would have to wait here until the following day, December 22.

After they gave us coats and more food, we spent the better part of the night answering the carabineros' questions. We recounted parts of our harrowing experience, leaving out the part about food, as we'd agreed to as a group.

Catalan was always just off to the side, within earshot. He was the only one who never asked us a single question.

Chapter 29

Juan Carlos Canessa, Roberto's Father

I had a restless sleep on the ride from Mendoza to Buenos Aires. It was like the long, rambling nightmare that had haunted my dreams since the afternoon of October 13. At 6:00 a.m. the next morning, December 22, I was awakened as the bus started sputtering and ground to a halt just outside of Buenos Aires. A day earlier, our airplane had broken down and we had almost died. Today, the bus broke down. Unbelievable. Several of the passengers stood up, confused. Then the driver popped his head up and called out, "Everyone off. The transmission is busted . . ."

We alighted from the bus unnerved and disoriented. I grabbed my bag from the driver and started walking down the road. I was exhausted and devastated. Morning was coming. In the distance, I could see the black and yellow of a Buenos Aires taxi, and I flagged it down for a ride into the city.

"Good morning," the driver said when I opened the door.

I muttered hello and asked him to take me to the corner of Juncal and Suipacha, across from the Iglesia del Socorro church, where my cousin Carlos Gregorini lived. I had spoken to him the night before by phone from San Rafael and asked him to get me a plane ticket to Montevideo.

"Is there a particular route you'd like me to take?" the driver asked, looking back at me through the rearview mirror.

"Whichever you want," I said.

From those few words he figured out I was Uruguayan.

"You're Uruguayan, right? Did you hear the news?"

The last thing I wanted to do was talk. He kept on by himself.

"They're saying two hikers came down from the mountains. From that plane."

"What plane?"

"The Uruguayan one."

I couldn't understand how this man could know about what had happened to us the night before, how we'd had to come in for an emergency landing in San Rafael, even though it had caused something of a stir locally, and they had tried to get us on that little aircraft home.

In an effort to cut him short, I said, "I was on that flight. We had to make an emergency landing on one engine, but everyone's fine."

"No, not that plane. The other one," he said.

"Which other one?"

"The one with the Uruguayan boys, the one in the Andes."

"I just told you, I was on that plane, I'm Uruguayan and—"

"Didn't you hear the news on the radio?" he interjected.

"No, I haven't heard the radio."

"They're saying on the radio that two men hiked down from the mountain."

I wanted to put this conversation to rest.

"I'm the father of one of the boys whose plane crashed in the Andes. But the incident they're talking about yesterday happened to me, not to the boys. We're the ones who were the survivors. I'm one of them."

"You really don't know, do you?" the driver said, now animated as he looked at me through the rearview mirror. "They found two of the boys who were on the plane with the rugby players!"

"What are you talking about?" I found my voice was rising.

"It's all over the news!" the driver said as he flipped on the radio. "They're even naming the survivors!"

The first word I heard when he turned on the radio was his name. "Roberto Canessa and Fernando Parrado are the two survivors who reached Los Maitenes," the announcer said.

The driver swerved and slammed on the brakes as I broke down and lunged toward the front seat to hug and kiss him, yelling, "That's my son! That's my son!"

The driver and I jumped out of the car and hugged each other. I began to cry and he hugged me tighter, then began to cry just as hard, right there in the middle of the road. I don't remember anything we talked about from that moment until we reached my cousin Gregorini's place; I was floating off somewhere else, crying along with the taxi driver who could barely drive he was crying so hard.

The driver was so moved he wouldn't take my money. When I handed him my wallet so he could take whatever he wanted, he handed it back saying he was in no condition to tell the difference between the bills. When I arrived at my cousin's apartment building, I banged desperately on a door until a woman I didn't recognize opened it.

"What do you want? What's the matter?" she said.

"Where's Gregorini?" I said.

"His apartment's one floor down. What are you, crazy?"

"Yes, yes, I'm crazy!" I said and dashed down the stairs.

My cousin had been waiting for me over at the bus depot because he had already heard the news. His wife came to the door, and he arrived a few minutes later, since my bus had never reached the station. He rushed me to the airport, but instead of heading back to Montevideo, I boarded a flight to Santiago, Chile.

I've thought a lot about that taxi driver, whose name I never learned, the man who gave me my life back just as I had given up.

I remember exactly what he looked like, slightly overweight, with thinning hair, in his fifties. Every time I traveled to Buenos Aires and took a cab, I would check to see whether he was driving. A couple times I took a cab to the place where he had picked me up the day the bus broke down, to see if I might find him. I'd have the cab circle aimlessly—"Go around again," I'd say to the driver, who had no idea whom or what I was looking for. But I never found him. I wanted to pay him back, not just for the trip he never charged me for, but for the warmest, most intense hug I've experienced in all my life.*

Later, I learned that just after I'd left San Rafael, Harley and Nicolich, the remaining family members, had received unbelievable news about a downed Uruguayan airplane, but nothing had been confirmed. They immediately jumped on a bus to Mendoza and arrived the next morning. With the help of the airport authorities, who were just as stunned as they were, they were able to hop aboard a cargo plane transporting frozen meat that had made a scheduled stop before continuing on to Santiago.

---

* Juan Carlos Canessa relayed this story on December 27, 2008, six months before his death.

Chapter 30

The day before, I had been barely able to walk, but today at least I could move around. I'd regained some of my strength and restored some of my body's electrolytes after drinking plenty of fluids and eating the bean stew and other food.

At around three in the morning, we had finally headed off to bed in one of the mountain farmers' huts, sleeping on cots with stretched-over leather instead of mattresses and covered in animal pelts for warmth. I lay awake thinking how, for the first time in days, we weren't sleeping on the rocky ground or suspended at the edge of a cliff.

I awakened before dawn just as I had every day on the mountain. When I opened my eyes, I did not remember where I was. I'd been waking up to a wide-open sky for ten days, but this morning, I was under a bower of branches twined together and vines of rose hips damp with morning dew. There were no frozen sneakers, no patchwork sleeping bag, no shredded remains of my friends stuffed into a rugby sock.

Still exhausted, I managed to get to my feet. Nando opened his eyes. Outside, I noticed Catalan, who waved hello. The carabineros were bundled inside sleeping bags. Two of them rose and began to stretch. I counted three of them . . . one was missing. I looked up and saw him making his way to the cabin through the fog. It was Sergeant Menares walking up from the valley below.

"Good morning," he said, winded. "The fog is too thick. I don't know how they're going to get the helicopters here."

We couldn't even see the river thirty yards away.

The carabineros lit a fire and warmed up some milk.

At around nine, we heard a commotion growing louder outside. I looked to Sergio Catalan to explain the ruckus, but he only shrugged as if he'd never heard anything like it before.

Out of the mist, on foot and on horseback, there emerged dozens of journalists with still and video cameras, microphones, recorders, and reams of notebooks.

The moment the plane had gone down on October 13, we had gone from being carefree young men to survivors fighting for our lives. And now, just as quickly, we had gone from forgotten shadows to unlikely heroes. For Nando and me, it all seemed like a hallucination. Catalan and the other two farmers slipped away and continued quietly with their work.

A short while later, despite the thick fog, we tried to head out on horseback, Nando and I riding with the carabineros. But a half hour into our journey, we were intercepted by the helicopters, which touched down in a nearby pasture. The two aircraft were commanded by Carlos Garcia Monasterio and Jorge Massa, the same two men who had been searching for the Fairchild FH-227D immediately after the crash and who had put together the C-47 mission. (Sadly, Monasterio would die in a plane crash five years later in Tierra del Fuego.) The two men looked at us in amazement, as the carabineros had.

When the commanding officer, Colonel Morel Donoso, saw me, he asked, "Are you Canessa's boy? Your father had been searching for you until yesterday."

"So that *was* him!" I said, more to myself than to him. "He was the one giving me strength." I had been right about my dad. He had never stopped looking for me, because he knew if he were the one who was lost, I wouldn't rest until I found him.

The pilots unfurled on the ground another, more complete map than the one Menares had shown us. And once again we pointed to the same spot we'd shown the sergeant the night before.

Massa's first reaction was disbelief, saying it was impossible because that was near the Argentine border, on the other side of the mountains, near Sosneado. But I insisted that the plane was on the other side of an enormous mountain peak, and that the situation was so dire that each minute could mean the difference between life and death.

It was impossible, they said. Respectfully, but unable to hide their astonishment, they added that maybe we just didn't know how to read a map or maybe we were still confused from the journey. They said that we should take a deep breath, calm down, and have another look.

Ironically, Nando and I were the ones who were the calmest—a remnant of our rhythms on the mountain.

"That's where they are," I repeated.

The helicopter commanders looked at each other. They could see we were sure.

Then Nando piped up. "If you won't believe us, they're as good as dead," he said. "For all we know, they're dead already."

They turned back to the map of the fathomless Andes, and we retraced our steps for them once again. They watched as we tallied the days on our fingers, recounting what happened on each day. They looked at each other and decided that if they were going to try it, they couldn't go out there blindly. They'd need one of us—because there was room for only one more on the helicopters—to go with them to point the way. Plus, it would mean one less survivor they'd have to bring back.

"It's a risky mission," Massa said. Later he repeated the warning to his crew and the rescue team, but no one begged off the mission.

I was exhausted, and Nando wanted to be the one to go. And so it was: Nando embarking on yet another perilous journey. That day, because of bad weather, only six of our friends returned to the land of the living; the other eight would be rescued the following day.

When I watch the grainy black-and-white film from that day, I'm always struck by the look in Nando's and my eyes. There was no joy or pride in them, only vestiges of our trek across the ages. The shepherd Sergio Catalan, who was sitting a few feet behind us in the pasture, had the same look, because he understood the painful secrets of the mountain.

When the first of the survivors returned that afternoon, I felt the rush of an emotion I had not felt in a long time: pride. I watched them alight from the helicopters, and it made me puff out my scrawny chest, because, at that moment, I realized we had not failed them. They had been right to put their faith in us. No one had to say a word to me; it was something I felt deep inside.

Before I got on the helicopter to go to San Fernando, I went over to shake hands with each of the shepherds and Sergio Catalan. When I thanked them, they looked at me with utter surprise, as if there was nothing to thank them for. These men, the guardians of paradise: Blessed are the humble, for they shall inherit the earth.

The helicopter rose into the sky toward San Fernando, and I looked out the window and wordlessly said goodbye to our society of snow and ice.

––––––––––

I walked into the hospital on my own two feet, wheelchairs, for all the doctors' supplications, be damned. They put me up in a room that seemed immense.

The first ones to come in to see me were Lauri and my mother. My father was still stranded in Buenos Aires, awaiting a flight to

Santiago. Then came my three siblings, Adriana, Conqui, and Juan Francisco, their faces radiant.

"You look like a little old man," my mother said, so calmly and peacefully that it seemed there was nothing else she could ever want in the world.

My siblings said that when my mother took the call in the middle of the night, she simply yelled from the other side of the bedroom door, "He's here!"

"We had to eat the ones who died, Mama," I confessed to her in a whisper.

Her next words absolved me of any doubt or tribulation, just as she always had my entire life. "That doesn't matter. I knew you'd never give up," she said.

The fact that we'd had to eat our dead to stay alive was irrelevant to my mother. What mattered was that we had never stopped trying to stay alive and had found a way home. "You were too young to die. You still have too much life ahead of you," she told me.

"I knew you were alive," she added later, "because I would have been dead and buried before I'd let them tell me you were dead."

I have several clear memories of being in that historic colonial hospital, San Juan de Dios. When the doctors ordered I be left alone to rest, I looked down at myself in the dim light from the corridor. I could move my arms and my legs in this bed that was much too large for me without any fear of falling off the side of a mountain. The ground, I saw, was not so far away.

My father arrived that night exhausted, emotionally drained, and overcome. He seemed like a soldier finally returning home from battle. I'll never forget the way he looked. He was overjoyed, I could see that. But in his eyes, as he rested his head in his hands, I could see his consternation over how society was going to react to us, to me, his boy, his son he was sworn to protect.

He asked me if I felt OK. The doctor in him wanted to make sure that the staff was being attentive to me, whether they had run all the appropriate tests; he wanted to know how the most important patient he would ever have was feeling. I told him I was fine, that the staff had been exemplary. But I conceded that I wasn't as well as I'd been the night I'd slept in the shepherds' hut in Los Maitenes on the day of our rescue. There, I'd slept under a canopy of twigs and straw, under the care of two Mapuches and Sergio Catalan.

"They cared for us better than any doctor," I told him.

Chapter 31

Laura Surraco Canessa

After the constant anxiety I'd lived with since October 13, I woke up feeling inexplicably heartened for the first time on December 19, 1972. It had been sixty-eight days since I'd lost Roberto in the accident. I missed everything about him more with each passing day. I missed the sound of his voice, which I couldn't remember and would make an effort to re-create in my mind. There had been moments of false hope: a cross in the snow, distortions in the mountain landscape, magnetic waves, visions—they were all fool's gold. They hadn't discovered anything new on this day, but I felt a quiet peace wash over me. The only explanation I've come up with over the years is that this was the day Roberto picked up the piece of limestone and asked me to wait for him.

Two days later, on December 21, my mother came into my room with a stunned look on her face and told me, "They say they've found two survivors."

My mind started racing. Until that point, I had lived in a world with open-ended possibilities. But now, hope ran up against reality. In my fantasies, anything could be real. But in light of two actual survivors, the mirage disappeared and I was left with one unshakable, tangible question: Could he be one of them? How did they survive seventy days in the Andes? Up till then, I had ignored my father's rational thinking. When he'd show me pictures of the mountain range, asking me to see how impossible it was to hope that they might be alive—because nothing could survive there for that long—I'd take refuge in Roberto's mother's house. She was resolute in her conviction that Roberto was alive. I couldn't stand the thought, the pain, of going on without Roberto, so I took comfort in his mother's hope. But now we would know without question who was right. We had only those words—"They say they've found two survivors"—to obsess over.

My father suggested I take a sleeping pill because it could be a long wait until we finally knew the truth. He didn't say so, but he thought it: The outcome could be devastating. The tension grew with each passing hour. It could be the best or worst night of my life.

At three in the morning, I woke up sitting in bed, with someone who was trembling, hugging me. It was my father.

"You were right. He's alive. And we're going to go get him in the morning."

Because of the sleeping pill, I'd slept through the phone ringing a few minutes earlier. Raquel, Gustavo Nicolich's mother, had called my mother to say the words she would always remember: "Canessa is one of them!"

My father was as elated as he was ravaged. He'd gone on so many flights to try to help find Roberto. In fact, shortly after returning from the first one, even though he had had only a few gray hairs at the time, he soon went entirely gray.

By morning, we were already at the airport. My father and me. Roberto's mother and his siblings. And a host of other passengers' family members desperate to know whether their loved ones were dead or alive. Soon we were on a flight to Santiago. (We were the only ones who knew for sure our loved one was alive, because even Nando's family didn't know about Nando's mother and sister.) From there, we drove to San Juan de Dios Hospital in San Fernando, where the survivors were convalescing before flying to a Santiago hospital.

Whenever I had thought he might be dead, I would think, *Please, let him be alive. Even if we don't end up together, even if he marries another woman, because I know he'll be a part of my life until my dying day.* Even if I got to see him for only a single minute for the rest of my life, I'd be happy. It was all I asked for . . .

That part of my dream had come true. Nineteen, as I was, I pictured him as my prince charming, who'd traveled across distant lands to find his way back to me. But I knew there was a chance he had moved on, that I had become part of a past he could not return to, another scar along his long and unimaginable journey. And yet, from what I'd been able to find out about his ordeal, it was typical Roberto: He'd managed to make his way, against all odds. I could only shake my head, not sure whether to laugh or cry.

I arrived at the hospital in a fog, as if entering another world. There was a deafening clamor of people I didn't know. I turned down a stark white corridor without knowing where I was going until I was stopped by three doctors, Dr. Fernando Baquedano, Dr. Jose Manuel Ausin, and Dr. Miguel Melej, who were attending to the survivors. Dr. Melej wanted to tell me what to expect when I saw Roberto; I can still remember the look on the doctor's face. But I couldn't concentrate on what he was saying. All I could think about, as he held me by the shoulders and tried to talk to me, was that Roberto was alive. I remember snippets of what he said: "We're still trying to find a way for the families to help these young men deal with what they've lived through . . . nothing like this has ever happened. . . ." He was resolute that I could stay only a short while because all the emotion might be too much for Roberto. He could pass out or worse.

Just then, a door to my left opened, and out of the corner of my eye, I recognized Roberto's feet.

"You have to go in slowly," Dr. Melej added, as I shook free of his grip and headed for that door.

I entered the room slowly. When I saw him lying in bed wearing a hospital gown, his beard long and scraggly, his face gaunt, I barely recognized him. Roberto gestured to me to come closer. I wanted to rush into his arms the way a nineteen-year-old girlfriend reunited with her prince charming should. But in my embrace, instead of a broad-shouldered prince, I found an emaciated skeleton of a young man, his beard so wildly overgrown, his lips so chapped I couldn't even kiss them.

Outside the room, there was confusion, euphoria, worry, nervousness, eager journalists, people crying and laughing at the same time. But inside, Roberto was the total opposite. He radiated a serene spirituality, as if his soul had occupied the space his shrunken body had left behind.

His movements were deliberate. There was a profound silence in the room.

He stretched out his arm and took a small package from the nightstand, holding it as if it were the world's most precious item.

"I forgot the rock I found for you. But I brought you this," he whispered. "Open it," he added, when he saw me hesitate.

I couldn't contain my surprise when, wrapped inside the red sweater I'd knitted for him, I found a small wedge of the cheese the shepherds had given him in Los Maitenes, yellowish and covered in sweater lint. I sat there unsure of whether he wanted me to eat it or what he wanted me to do with it.

"I saved it. For you," he stammered.

I began to understand something I wouldn't fully comprehend until much later. Despite the insatiable hunger that returned to him when he reached Los Maitenes—when he returned to the world of the living—he had deprived himself of this piece so that he could give it to me. It was no souvenir. He had brought me food so I wouldn't starve to death. As he'd done in the Andes with the others, he shared even his most priceless possession: the nourishment that would allow him to live another day. He had brought me a piece of cheese so that I might have the strength to continue fighting in the perilous journey of life.

"I was in the valley where the world's most beautiful flowers bloom," he added. "When we have a family, I want to take us all back."

I started to cry and couldn't stop.

He mentioned again how sorry he was that he had left the stone he'd brought me from deep within the mountains in the jacket the shepherd had given him. I tried to tell him I didn't care about the stone or the cheese or anything else; what I cared about was that he was back. But he seemed to misunderstand what I was saying. He couldn't comprehend how it wasn't important that he had lost the proof of his journey, the stone, and the vital sustenance, the cheese, that was going to keep us alive.

"I walked for you, Lauri," he mumbled.

And that's when I understood that we were speaking to each other from two completely different worlds. He was talking about the basic building blocks of life—a stone as proof, a wedge of cheese as nourishment—and I was speaking the language of another era, another time.

I threw myself into his arms again, but then I realized that this startled him. When I got too close, it was as if he was overwhelmed by the color and the feel of my hair, my perfume, the warmth of my touch. It had taken a superhuman effort for him to rip himself free of that world of snow and ice, but a piece of him, I sensed, would always be up in the mountains, where I was only a dream.

Meanwhile, it was hard for me to accept my role in his survival, that he had done all of that with me in mind. I didn't feel worthy of everything he had done; it was all too much.

I continued to cry as I took his long and bony fingers in mine, and he, too, began to sob. But it was a wailing unlike any I'd ever heard in my life. These were not the tears of a baby or a boy or even a man. It was the weeping of utter physical and mental exhaustion.

He cried both tenderly and intensely, an outpouring that seemed to emerge from the depths of his soul.

Just then, a nurse who was eight months pregnant came into the room, and behind her, while no one else was looking, so did a reporter. The first question he asked Roberto was whether he thought his survival was a miracle. And without missing a beat, Roberto gestured toward the nurse's belly. "There's going to be a new life in a few days. There's the real miracle," he said.

Then Dr. Melej came in, kicked out the reporter, and immediately led me out of the room by the arm. My father poked his head in long enough to say to Roberto, "What you two did, that's a man's job!" It was a running joke the two of them had, saying Roberto was just a boy and only my father was the real man, like Tarzan.

Later, my father took my arm and we paced the halls. He wondered aloud, "Poor kids. I wonder what will become of them." But what he was thinking was, *What am I going to do with this lovesick girl and this traumatized boy, who had to eat human corpses?* Little did he know that Roberto had already told me what he had had to do and that I had thought it a sensible and intelligent solution.

Of course, I hadn't fully comprehended everything that had happened. I didn't understand about the cheese or the rock, much less about the miracle in the nurse's womb. I hadn't understood about the valley where the world's most beautiful flowers bloom (which we would, indeed, see years later with our three children). Honestly, I think it was only recently that I truly understood—after our firstborn son, Hilario, fathered our first grandchild, Benicio, on October 9, 2012.

I've seen a lot of children come into the world, including our three. But I never made such a direct connection between a birth and something that had happened more than forty years ago in a San Fernando hospital. Just like Benicio, Roberto had been born that day—or reborn, rather. Benicio can understand so little yet, but we grown-ups ask a lot of him. The rest of us have many expectations for him, but he can meet those expectations only a little at a time. When they cut Benicio's umbilical cord from his mother's placenta, he was technically finished being born, but he would still be connected in other ways to his mother. In just the same way, Roberto would long be connected to the mountain—to the Andes, the fuselage, the hike, the shepherds, the cheese, and the stone. Forty years later, I finally realized what I could not on December 22, 1972: While children are born of water, Roberto was born of the eternal snow.

Part Two

Part Two

Chapter 32

When I returned from the mountain, I tried to pick up my life where I'd left off. It wasn't easy. Fortunately, Lauri was by my side.

We had both changed a lot, but we seemed to have grown in the same direction during our time apart. She had matured greatly in a very short time, and I lived in a sort of dichotomy. Lauri said my soul had grown exponentially but my body had withered. Early on, I was so thin that my skin was wrinkled and my voice was a whisper, like that of an old man or a child. It took us a while to begin acting our age again, a tender nineteen.

When Lauri and her family had seen me for the first time in the San Fernando hospital on December 22, 1972, they were shocked at my appearance. It didn't look as if I had spent seventy days on the mountain, but an immeasurable amount of time. As for me, I could barely make sense of reality. It was impossible to find myself awake in a dream that had become reality.

I think all the survivors and their families went through something similar. Lauri says that the survivors in the hospital looked like some kind of spiritual commune, a colony of bees buzzing at a frequency only they themselves could hear. We were overwhelmed by a deep, loving connection with one another and with God.

No one knew what to expect from us. Many said that the time

we'd spent away—which couldn't be measured by the hands of a clock—had devastated our bodies and minds. They predicted that we had aged way too much to ever live normal lives—that the event had left a scar that would never fully heal.

Some believed that we would never come off the high of our so-called feat. Others thought that the pain we had suffered was so great that we would never sleep again, never find peace again, never do the things that normal people do . . . never smile again.

I fought against society's expectations of me. I rebelled against the destiny it imposed. I hated the word "incurable." The world irresponsibly, unilaterally, tried to decree that I was either a hero or a monster—a cannibal.

One of the things that was destroyed when we crashed into the mountain was our connection to society. But our ties to one another grew stronger every day. What we did was stabilize the injury and stitch together new ties made of metal and glass, of strength and sensitivity, of intelligence and emotion, to protect us as a group and not as isolated individuals. We survived together, like separate organs working together to save the body as a whole. The ties between us were unconditional and as visible as sleeping together in one another's arms for warmth. It was a bond that would never be broken. A bond between the living and the dead. We call it resilience, but it was more than that, because we offered our very selves up to one another.

That's why I still carry their memory close to me, and why they comfort me during uncertain times. Not just because they gave me their bodies for nourishment, but because I am still one of them; I am a part of them and they are a part of me. Some of us crossed over; some of us carried on. Arturo Nogueira, Daniel Maspons, Gustavo Nicolich, Liliana Methol, Nando Parrado's mother, Eugenia, and his sister Susana, Numa Turcatti, Vasco Echavarren, Marcelo Perez del Castillo, Enrique Platero, and Flaco Vazquez were among the twenty-nine who crossed over. Nando, Coche, Fito, Moncho, Gus,

Carlitos, Tintin, Pedro, Alvaro, Javier, Roy, Daniel, Eduardo, Pancho, Bobby François, and I carried on.

Lauri says that she can see the different ways in which I'm actually trying to keep the society of snow and ice alive. The survivors get together every December 22nd. Each year, we play a rugby match in Chile in honor of the one that was canceled. And I make regular visits to see Sergio Catalan, which always renews my commitment to life.

Many people have told me that I never left my Andean experience in the past. It's something I can never leave behind; I carry it inside me.

On the mountain, dying was not seen as a failure. Life and death were not antagonistic states. We coexisted with the deceased, and it wasn't macabre, because they were simply the precursors of our own death. We weren't at someone else's wake, but at our own. They had simply been one step beyond us in our journey. They had arrived earlier, while we were still in transit. The twenty-nine who died were not gone and forgotten. Rather, they lived on inside us, as Gustavo Nicolich wrote in a letter to his girlfriend: "If I can save someone else with my body, I do it happily." And I know that at that moment of truth—a moment stripped of deceit and hypocrisy—I felt exactly the same way.

On the morning I'd awakened in the shepherd's cabin in Los Maitenes and a crowd of people emerged from the patchy fog, I asked the first man I encountered, a portly fellow, what he was doing way out there in the middle of nowhere. He told me he was a BBC journalist out of London and wanted to talk to me first, before any of the others did. "What do you want to talk about?" I asked. He answered, "Well, you were dead, and now you've come back to life. The whole world wants to know your story. It's an incredible feat." I was utterly confused.

After I returned to Montevideo, these two worlds would continue to clash—our struggle in the Andes and this supposedly incredible feat. It wasn't until arriving in Montevideo on December 28 that I realized how many people the tragedy had affected—the hundreds of friends and family of the forty-five people aboard the Fairchild whose lives had been on hold since our plane disappeared. For twenty-nine families, our reappearance was a double tragedy, because they had lost their loved ones first on the day of the accident and again two months later when it turned out they were not among the miraculously discovered survivors. Only sixteen families were spared this second death. And still others, such as Nando, who lost his mother and sister, and Javier, who lost his wife—the mother of his four children—faced the duality of joy and despair.

After I finally got home safely, I began to go door-to-door to the homes of my friends who never made it off the mountain and tell their families what we had lived through, how desperate it had all been, and why we'd had to do what we did to survive. I wanted to hand each family a keepsake from their loved one that Gustavo Zerbino had collected before we left. I didn't fool myself into thinking they might understand, because they hadn't lived through what we had. But I wanted them to hear from someone who had been there, and not from some third party—or worse, from the press— how horrible it had all been up in the Andes.

But the news arrived before I did. Some of the rescuers who were on the helicopters took pictures of the crash site and gave them to the press, exploiting our helplessness and exposing our wretched circumstances to the world. One of the pictures showed a rescuer standing away from the ignominious fuselage, his sidearm visible, as if he were standing guard against its ignoble inhabitants—my friends. On the other hand, others of the rescuers, such as Sergio Diaz, spent the night inside the fuselage caring for the survivors. It was Pancho Delgado who first told the world the story of how we'd had to feed ourselves. He did so on December 28, 1972, at a press conference inside the gym at Stella Maris–Christian Brothers, where most of our group was from.

I visited Flaco Vazquez's sister and Arturo Nogueira's parents, who begged to hear stories of their son, who, in death, had shown me I could not give up on life.

I also visited the four little Nicola brothers, whose parents had been killed in the accident. These sons of the rugby team doctor, Francisco Nicola, and his wife, Esther, were now orphans. Along with my grief, I was haunted by a deep uncertainty: What would become of these children? It's hard enough growing up when you have everything, but these children were left with nothing. Juan Pedro was eight, and his siblings were nine, ten, and eleven years old.

In the coming years, we did what we could for the children—but it was an uphill battle for them. The second oldest, Pepe, came down with lupus. However, he was saved thanks to a kidney transplant from an aunt on his mother's side. I gave the doctor's watch, a talisman from the mountain, to Francisco, the eldest son, who became a doctor for a nonprofit and eventually had two children of his own. Marcelo, the second youngest brother, eventually became one of the best rugby players the Uruguayan national team ever had. When he turned forty-eight, Juan Pedro came with us on a trip to the mountain with his own son, where he kneeled, kissed his parents' gravestone, and told his boy, "These are your grandparents, and these are the people who survived thanks to their sacrifice. I'm proud every day of the way my parents lived their lives." How many times must their sons have dreamed that their parents were not buried there but had come home to hug them the same way they had on the morning of October 12, 1972, when they had crept into their rooms before dawn to say goodbye for what would be the last time?

When I visited Gustavo and Raquel Nicolich, whose son died in the avalanche, I saw how they reached up from the depths of their despair to help us, the survivors, try to heal our wounds. How could we ever forget their dying son's letter to his girlfriend back home, explaining the sacrifices that had been made on the mountain? "I concluded that the bodies were there because God willed it that way. And since the soul is the only thing that matters, after all, I have no reservations about offering up my body, should that day arrive, so that I might help someone else live."

We had to live our lives in a way that would make his sacrifice count, in a way worthy of the price the deceased had had to pay. And not just us, but our children and our children's children. They had transferred their legacy, their progeny, onto us. That's why, when I returned to the mountain with my daughter, Lala, in 2006, I told them at the memorial site, "Just as I promised you, I made the most I possibly could out of my life. And I wanted you to meet the fruits of your sacrifice."

———

Even after returning to Montevideo, my mind was still back on the mountain. After spending months living inside a fuselage or out in the frozen open during our trek, I found I was most comfortable when sleeping outside in a tent on the hard ground, camping in Laguna Garzon in Rocha, Uruguay. Back home they thought I'd want a comfortable bed with clean linens, when in fact I felt at home only when I was living the way I had on the mountain, aside from the dangers.

I didn't walk very much during the first few days, fifty or sixty yards at most, because my heart would pound so hard from the effort that it made me nauseated. I slept a lot, as if I hadn't slept in months or years. And I ate a lot—too much. I would eat only hot food, while sitting near the stove or campfire. But what I loved most was breathing deeply, luxuriating in all the abundant oxygen that we had lacked up in the Andes.

My waistline expanded—I was gaining almost two pounds a day. I got the strength back in my voice. And one day, while walking out in the country with Lauri, I suddenly felt compelled to yell at the top of my lungs. The roar reverberated through the woods and frightened away all the birds in the trees. "I think I'm getting better," I told her.

I started riding a bike. It was actually hard at first, because I had to recover my sense of balance. One day, I decided to pedal to the next town over, and then the next. . . . After twenty days, I rode to Pocitos, more than ten miles from Carrasco, to visit the Strauch cousins. And when I returned after more than a two-hour ride, I was surprised to find I had energy to spare.

In February, I returned to medical school.

I soon had a first crucial test. In my anatomy class, I had to dissect a human cadaver like the ones I'd lived with on the mountain, and I could feel everyone in the room looking at me out of the corner of their eye, wondering what was going through my head. I don't know how I managed to keep it together.

In March, when I felt stronger, I started playing rugby again. I played harder with each game, with the same bull-rush intensity I had been known for. When my friends started calling me by my old nickname, "Muscles," I knew I was finally all the way back.

By April, I returned to what felt like a normal routine. In the mornings I studied medicine, and in the early afternoons I gave interviews about our time in the Andes. People had an insatiable appetite to know the details of what had happened, and we took the money from those various outlets not just for ourselves, but to give to the families of the deceased, whose lives had been torn apart emotionally and economically. In the evenings, I practiced rugby with the Old Christians club. It was a crucible of emotions playing alongside not only other survivors—the brothers of the deceased, other teammates who hadn't made the trip—but also with the ghosts of the teammates who remained in the mountains.

Chapter 33

When the book *Alive* was published in 1974, Nando and I were offered a chance to go on a book tour to promote it. Just a short while earlier, we had been among the most pitiful creatures on the earth, and now we were being painted as valiant heroes. Twenty-year-old masters of the universe.

Nevertheless, on my first transcontinental flight, I was terrified. Nando set a glass of water on his tray table. If turbulence made it slosh around, he would nudge me and say, "Should we get ready, just in case?"

First we toured the United States and then Europe. Everything should have been dazzling, since the journalists and celebrities we met were amazed at us and tried in turn to make sure everything was amazing for us. But all this amazement felt fake to me: They were only awed at the *idea* of us. They couldn't believe they were face-to-face with these two hikers who had come out of nowhere to reenter society with the shadow of death still in their eyes. Besides, we were so young, so normal, that we didn't seem real to them. And in fact, this image of us was not real.

In the course of the book tour, we met all kinds of celebrities. But the only ones I remember at all were the ones who felt truly genuine. The glitz and glamour of all the parties and dinners and the lavish attention never appealed to me. All of the praise for our "exploits" felt empty. What I truly appreciated was looking into someone's eyes and, instead of finding awe or horror, witnessing compassion.

We traveled nearly ten thousand miles crisscrossing the United States, and another six thousand in Europe. With each new consecration of earthly glory, with each celebrity I met or party that was thrown in our name, the now twenty-year-old Roberto was getting further away from the nineteen-year-old Roberto of the mountain, further from Sergio Catalan and the shepherds Armando Serda and Enrique Gonzalez.

One night, I called Lauri back in Montevideo. I was just starting to realize that being rescued was only the penultimate obstacle. The final challenge, it turned out, was finding a way to return to a simple, honest life. I began by telling her, "It's such a paradox, Lauri. I'm here, but it doesn't really feel like me. I was this unlucky creature, and my only real talent was my will to live." By the end of our conversation, I had taken the final step of my long journey: I asked her to spend the rest of her life with me.

I don't think I've ever been able to express so clearly and poignantly what love means as when I collected those two keepsakes for Lauri: a stone and a wedge of fresh shepherd's cheese. Although the stone was lost during the trek home, I had wanted to bring her a memento as a reminder of the terrible struggle I endured to make my way back to her. The piece of hard volcanic rock was from a place in the Andes where no person had ever been, something that had never before been touched by human hands. It was a reminder that sometimes our path is tough, as hard as a shard of mountain stone.

With that piece of cheese, I'd wanted to show her the other extreme. No food in my nineteen years of life had ever tasted or smelled as delicious as that shepherd's cheese. It had been made with care, by human hands, from the milk of cows that grazed on the most pristine, verdant pastures on earth. I wanted to show Lauri that life could also be this tender, as serene and caressing as a lullaby.

And given the chance, we should make the most out of the life we'd been given.

No sooner had I returned from the *Alive* book tour than I used the money from the sale of the book to buy a dirt bike and start racing with Nando. People wondered, *Why would these boys, who just barely escaped such a tragedy, tempt fate again by risking their lives with such a dangerous sport?*

Truthfully, I raced because I needed the adrenaline—some vestige of the rush we'd felt trying to out-will the mountain. People reproached my dad for not stopping me, but he told them, what could he do? I had been stubbornly independent since I was a boy, and after I had turned twenty on January 17, 1973, there was no stopping me.

Meanwhile, my mother cheered me on at every race.

I figured if I had survived the Andes, I could survive motorcycle racing. What was the worst that could happen, that I'd fly through the air and land on the packed dirt? At least there was no threat of falling off a cliff into an abyss below. Sure enough, I did crash: I hit a rock with my front wheel, flew in the air, and landed with a thud, dislocating my clavicle. No matter. As soon as it was healed, I was back on the bike.

On June 6, 1975, in preparation for my marriage to Lauri, I asked her grandfather, who had a spacious house in Carrasco, whether we could move into his third-floor attic. He allowed me to create a small kitchen and a bathroom there.

On June 18, 1976, we were married and moved in with the "abuelos."

We would live there very simply for years. I studied medicine and worked with Lauri at Hospital Italiano, where she was involved in coordinating patients in the Cardiology Department headed by my father, and he and I performed cardiac catheterizations on adults and children.

I was testing out a new bike on a course near Portones de Carrasco on December 20, 1976, when I noticed my mother-in-law drive up and park her car near the end of the track. After I finished my run, I stopped the bike near her car and pulled off my helmet.

"Lauri's test came back positive," she told me. "You're going to have a baby, Roberto."

And just like that, my need for speed was gone. I channeled all that energy and adrenaline toward the life force inside Lauri's belly, which had already started to grow. I sold the brand-new racing bike and bought a family car, a Citroën Ami 8, and went in with Jorge Zerbino, Gustavo's brother, on a touring bike that we shared. I soon discovered that having a family and a modest little sedan was all the adrenaline I needed.

When I had entered medical school in 1971, I'd asked myself what I wanted to do with my life. I was fascinated by surgery, because I saw the job as repairing broken parts or anomalies, and I'd always considered myself a Mr. Fix-It. But I couldn't imagine myself working as part of a team in an operating room, where everyone has to be totally in sync and remain in their roles. So I decided that I would align myself with the most knowledgeable people, our talents would complement one another, and I would discover my destiny.

Before I got my degree, I interned at Hospital de Mercedes in rural Uruguay as an on-call doctor. I was a surgical assistant and got to work on all kinds of procedures, as well as the routine appendectomies, hernias, and fistulas. Practicing that kind of rural medicine made me think fast on my feet, because a country doctor doesn't always have specialists at his disposal and must learn to improvise in emergencies. Funny, that's how my friends and colleagues at Harvard University refer to me, as a "country doctor," but sometimes also as a "wise doctor," not because of what I know but because of how I approach medicine. "The things you've seen, you don't find in a book or on the internet," they tell me. I had only ever aspired to be a doctor worthy of my country. But because of what I'd experienced in the Andes at age nineteen, in just my second year of medical school, some of the best doctors in the world opened the doors of pediatric cardiology to me. They told me I'd gone through what few other doctors had ever had to, and I'd lived to tell the tale. That kind of experience matters in medicine.

I returned to Hospital Italiano after my internship and began working in cardiology, developing angiocardiography films at the cardiac catheterization laboratory.

In time, I discovered what area of cardiology most interested me, or rather, as on the mountain, in which area I was most useful. I wanted to get to the very root of the matter, and that's how I came to fetal cardiology—and to Dr. Jack Rychik of the Children's Hospital of Philadelphia, who helped me with a patient in Uruguay, Agustin Vazquez Chaquiriand. Fetal cardiology is a field that's as tiny as it is enormous, as finite as it is infinite, because congenital heart conditions, unlike those illnesses that come from our environment or our bad habits, are the kind that appear suddenly and without warning.

One day in 1978, I heard that Pepe Nicola, one of the four orphaned Nicola children, had been diagnosed with lupus. His doctors weren't sure how best to treat him. So the sixteen survivors and everyone associated with the Old Christians rugby club decided we needed to do everything we could to help him. We raised enough money to fly him to the world's leader in treating lupus, the Stanford University hospital in California.

While Pepe was convalescing in Stanford, I started visiting the university's lab, and there I struck up a friendship with Dr. Norman Shumway, the father of heart-transplant surgery. He was a kind-faced man who wore a very old lab coat. And he introduced me to Dr. Richard Popp, one of the world's leading experts on a new kind of heart exam, the echocardiogram. I called him and asked what the requirements were to study under him. "To be able to speak English and have average intelligence," he said matter-of-factly.

When I returned to Uruguay, I switched to the other side of the operating table: Instead of assisting with heart catheterizations, I was doing them myself. I became so proficient at it, I could perform ten of them a day. One day, I began my shift at 8:00 a.m. by treating a month-old baby and finished at 10:00 p.m. by inserting a pace-maker into a ninety-year-old man.

With the help of Dr. Pedro Duhagon, one of my teachers who specialized in pediatric cardiology, we introduced the Rashkind method into Uruguayan medicine. Now it became possible to use a balloon catheter to treat infants born with a condition called trans-position of the great arteries. With it, we could breach the walls between the auricles and allow oxygenated blood to reach the right ventricle: The baby's purple skin would flush a healthy pink before our very eyes.

Later, my father and I began doing angioplasties and inserting stents. In 1983, I received a scholarship to study echocardiograms in Spain, where I worked under Dr. Manuel Quero Jimenez at Ma-drid's Ramon y Cajal hospital. "If you want to understand the living heart, you have to analyze the anatomy of many dead hearts first," Dr. Jimenez told me at our first meeting. And that's what I did. I spent countless hours studying still-fresh hearts, in my hands, at the Museo di Anatomia Patologica (Museum of Pathological Anatomy) with Dr. Manuel Arteaga.

The following year, I was making a house call to see a very sick child. He was suffering from aortic valve stenosis and endocarditis, and he was already showing embolisms in his hands. His parents had consulted several different doctors, and all of them had given dif-ferent diagnoses. After studying his case, I told his father he should have immediate surgery at the University of Alabama Birmingham Hospital with Dr. Albert Pacifico.

Since the boy's father was well-off and could afford the treatment, he had it done right away. They inserted an artificial aortic valve and the boy, Luis Pedro, was saved. His father was so overjoyed that when he returned, he told me I could ask him for anything—anything in the world. Other doctors had told him his son was fine, that he would grow out of his condition, but I had told him in no uncertain terms that his son would die without this operation. So I replied to him, "If you want to give me something, donate a 'blind' Doppler machine, which they only make in Sweden, to the hospital, so that we can diagnose other children like your son more quickly and effectively."

A month later, the boy's father showed up at the hospital with Uruguay's first Vingmed Doppler machine. Thanks to that machine, we were able to diagnose countless children less invasively than with a catheter.

This is how my path in pediatric cardiology was forged. But it started merely as a seed of an idea and needed many hands and hearts to germinate. I needed a committed and hardworking team to back me. Would we succeed? Would we overcome the odds? These questions plagued me but also always managed to strengthen me.

At first, I worked with the tools that were available at the time, back in the nineteen seventies. A stethoscope to discover a heart murmur. A chest x-ray, an electrocardiogram, my hands to feel for a pulse and to palpate the position of the liver inside the abdomen. Then came cardiac catheterization, which I learned from my father and Dr. Pedro Duhagon. By injecting contrast and a small tube up a vein and into the heart, we could watch as the dye revealed what manner of heart disease the patient had.

In my calling to fix babies' hearts, I found myself constantly returning to the lessons I'd learned on the mountain. I would again be in that gray area, standing at death's door, trying to keep others from passing through its gates. Beating inside me was the pact I'd made with my friends who would never get off that mountain in 1972: to live, and to continue bringing life, so that their loss would not have been in vain.

Chapter 34

If my life of nineteen years was put to the test during those seventy days on the mountain, my time there has been put to the test in the years since. Because my life did not end there, it only began.

Each of those days was a lesson, a rung on a ladder. But after being forced to grow up so fast, I had to return to the past to understand how I might be able to take my next step. On the first day, I had learned that to do something difficult takes incredible effort, and to do the impossible takes just a little more. And on that last day, when we reached the resplendent valley of Los Maitenes and I understood we finally were saved, I realized that our lives float on the air and that the difference between success and tragedy could depend on a mere breath of wind.

I had learned the soul of medicine on the slopes of the mountain and proved my knowledge in the university of the plains below. And while education is as vital as good parenting, a formal education only teaches you to respect standards and protocols, not necessarily how to challenge or overcome them.

In Chile, thirty-four planes had crashed into the Andes; there had never been survivors. In Uruguay, never before had a child been born with hypoplasia of the left ventricle and survived. "Never before." I had learned on the mountain that "never before" was a relative term. So relative, in fact, that we doctors would do anything in our power to disprove it, pulling that baby toward life, the way humble and merciful people like the shepherd Sergio Catalan did when he found us on the other side of that mountain range.

No sight can match the harmonious beating of the auricles and ventricles in a child's heart. A perfectly beating heart means life. I witness this life by way of a liquid crystal display, like the icy crystals on the mountain. There is no inherent beauty in this contraption made of plastic and metal. The beauty depends on something I see with my mind's eye, like that boy trapped on top of a mountain, reaching the summit, and looking down past the fog to see the valley of Los Maitenes below.

When I scan a heart with an ultrasound, I see souls hanging in the balance, teetering on a mountaintop, and on the other side, at a ten days' walk, a tiny kerosene beacon flickering inside the huts of the people who live below. People who are alive, who will offer us beans and bread and meat—everything they have—to help bring us back to life.

I look back in time and see my own mother, in tears, because her son has been hopelessly lost. I could almost hear her supplications from the other side, and I'd whisper for her not to lose hope, to have faith. I know that's why she waited for me, why she didn't lose her mind, because she knew I would make my way back to her.

Those tiny, unfinished hearts are simply waiting for someone to fix them. Those hearts that can beat only inside their mothers' wombs say the same thing to their own mothers: *Do not lose hope, I will make my way to you.* They only need a helping hand, the way a boy of nineteen once did. First they need someone to decide— yes or no. Then they need a concerted effort. All those wills must converge—as they did for us on the mountain—to bring forth the special radiance of these messengers. I can't help it: I identify with any living being who has to overcome impossible odds. To these mothers I say that what they've received is a diagnosis from doctors who have only experienced being alive, but I can give them the opinion of someone who also has experienced being dead.

A heartbeat is what signifies life. On the mountain, I would listen closely to people's hearts. The beating marked a very clear distinction: that they were still alive and that we would do everything in our power to keep them that way. To me, a person's heart became the expression of his very essence. Our objective high in the Andes was to keep our hearts beating, and to those who allowed mine to continue, my promise was that my own heart would beat for them.

The Old Christians rugby club had two penalty kickers: Arturo Nogueira, who died in our arms on the mountain, and me. I had spent countless hours practicing during after-school detention and well into the sunset. Months before the accident, in November 1971, the final game of the season depended on an overtime penalty kick at midfield, near the sideline. There was no time to put the ball in play; the only option was to attempt a forty-four-yard kick through the uprights. Since we'd never imagined such a scenario, we hadn't designated which one of us would take the kick. I studied it, and it looked like a difficult, almost impossible kick, at least for me. Maybe Arturo thought differently?

Just then, he came up and said, "I think you should be the one to kick it, Muscles."

The captain gave me the thumbs-up. I adjusted the ball, concentrated on the trajectory, took a running start, and punted it as hard as I could. The ball fired like a shot, spinning end-over-end through the sky, hypnotizing the fans as it took flight, and just as it was about to pass over the goalposts and the fans were already beginning to cheer, the referee blew the whistle. He said I had started my kick before he had given me the OK. I fetched the ball—you never argue with the ref in rugby—to try again as the fans and my teammates were still steaming. I placed the ball on the turf again, turned it until it seemed positioned just between the goalposts—waited for the signal, this time—took another running start, and gave it a mighty boot. The ball spun through the sky, high above. I watched it, open-mouthed, as I judged the wind, confident that I had hit it just as I'd hoped, but having no idea whether it would pass between those far-off uprights yet again. And when it did, the Old Christians' home field exploded in celebration.

The match ended, and as we headed back to the locker room, I asked Arturo why he had let me take the kick. "Because I knew if I missed it, I would never have forgiven myself. But if you missed, I knew it wouldn't bother you." That was the Arturo I remembered when he wrote that letter to his parents and girlfriend, as he lay nearly motionless with two shattered legs, death all around him. "Be strong," he wrote. "Life may be difficult, but it is always worth living, even through suffering. Be courageous."

Arturo had been right about me. If I'd missed that shot, I wouldn't have felt as if I had let down the team and fans. I wouldn't have felt responsible for the loss. And that helped me on the mountain. I didn't know how the injuries I'd treated or the fractures I'd set would turn out, but I jumped in to try without hesitation and did the best I could. Some turned out better than others. But I neither regretted the failures nor celebrated the successes. I just did what had to be done. I approached all the decisions I made later in life the same way; that had been my personality before the accident, but it was solidified in the Andes.

I take the same approach when dealing with my young patients. I visualize the trajectory before the kick. I imagine the ball flying through the air, spinning wildly through gusty winds that bend the cypress trees beyond the pitch, until it crosses between the goalposts. Only then do I attempt the kick. In much the same way, I visualize my sickest patients—the ones born with half a heart, their skin mottled purple, the ones struggling to breathe—running carefree in the fresh air, under a warming sun, enjoying their lives to the fullest. They are chrysalises, as we were, who either remain doomed to a larval state or eventually have the chance to come into full being as butterflies. That is my one and only goal—and my true reward. Let others be the ones to hesitate. I have no time for it.

If I had hesitated at any point in the Andes, I would not be here today. I'm sure of it. "Be strong. Life may be difficult, but it is always worth living, even through suffering. Be courageous." All my life, I've tried to follow Arturo's command.

I took advantage of every time I was invited to speak about the Andes to advance my other passion, medicine. I've always thought medicine was the best corollary to my time on the mountain. One prepared me for the other. Without the first, I would have seen medicine in a completely different way. The Andes were the unchangeable tribulation in my past, but medicine was a malleable future.

My next goal—applying the rules we'd set in the Andes—was to ensure that even the poorest Uruguayan child could have access to the same kind of medical care as the richest child in the world. I felt that a child from humble Mercedes, Uruguay, where I interned, should have the same level of diagnostic care as a child visiting the most advanced medical center in the world. As on the mountain, it was only a matter of distance—the distance between my level of knowledge with my echo in Montevideo and that of Drs. Jack Rychik and Meryl Cohen at Children's Hospital of Philadelphia. In any case, it was a much shorter distance than the hike from the Valley of Tears to Los Maitenes, which had become my standard of measurement—my own personal metric system—since 1972.

While I could try to stand in for the expert doctors—at least with the help of some of the best doctors in the world on the other end of a telephone—I still needed the appropriate equipment. That was the beginning of a long journey to acquire the same equipment used at the world's best medical centers for my own office.

The idea that a Uruguayan child—or any child anywhere in

the world, for that matter—should have access to the same level of diagnostic medicine started making its way around the world. It fell on the ears of Dr. Itzhak Kronzon, a transesophageal echocardiography pioneer in the United States who came soon after to visit me in Uruguay. When he saw that we had to lug a portable echo up sixteen flights of stairs because the elevators were broken that day at Hospital de Clinicas, he gave us an older color Doppler that New York Hospital wasn't using anymore. Now instead of having to undergo three catheterizations, my patients had access to one of the most advanced diagnostic tools anywhere in the world.

I traveled all over the world learning about the newest techniques at some of the world's most advanced medical centers while relaying my story. Not only was I learning the intricate details of many different heart conditions, but I also came to know where to send my patients when they had a particular disorder.

But it wasn't until the advent of the echocardiogram, or cardiac echo, that I found what I wanted to do with my life. What a marvel! Not just the machine and what it meant for the practice of medicine, but for what it meant to me. Every day we broke new ground with this machine, which so clearly showed the heart beating on the other side of the screen.

In 1989 I heard about a team of doctors, Bob Freedom and Jeff Smallhorn from the children's hospital in Toronto, who were using a new kind of scope to study the heart. Technology was advancing at a dizzying rate, and the images were getting better and more precise. I accepted the doctors' invitation to visit the Hospital for Sick Children in Toronto, and I stayed at the home of a literature professor who used the book *Alive* in his course. During the day I studied medicine, and at night I lectured about the Andes in my host's home.

It had been Dr. Itzhak Kronzon who first showed me how to use a color Doppler, which showed me blood circulating on the screen in swirls of red and blue. I was wide-eyed in amazement. It triggered a memory I could never shake off. Observing the depths of the human body through its LCD monitor, I recalled how long ago we had stared through the windows of our wrecked plane, shivering with fear, veering on starvation, huddling together for warmth, and witnessed the serenity with which the moon travels across the sky and sets imperceptibly, eternally. Inside, it was all suffering and chattering teeth; outside, the cosmos was showing us all was not yet lost. If I turned my eyes away, I was immediately racked with the stench and the pain and the sadness. But if I focused my gaze and directed my vision toward the moon floating by on the other side of the windows, I shuddered with the possibilities.

Through this echocardiogram machine, I had found a magical device that somehow allowed me both to visit and escape the mountains. It enabled me to keep asking the all-important questions: Can we continue? And if we continue, at what cost? Is it worth it?

Later, when a pregnant mother named Azucena confronted the same questions about her unborn daughter, Maria del Rosario, I was able to share with her what those questions have meant to me and whatever answers I have been able to find.

After we had been rescued, the psychiatrists that worked with us predicted that we would be traumatized, scarred for life, never again able to live a normal existence. The body might survive, but not the mind, they prophesied; we would never overcome our experience. They had studied similar horrors—shell-shocked soldiers, accident survivors—and applied their results to us. In many of those cases, people suffered depression, a meaninglessness in their lives, and lost their will to live. These doctors' mistake was to assume the worst for us.

If those same scientists analyzed babies who are born with congenital heart disorders—who have to undergo open-heart surgery the moment they are born, whose tiny chests are opened and doused with icy water to paralyze their metabolisms, who are kept alive by machines and must have a series of surgeries as they grow—they might conclude those children would have worse outlooks than healthy children. Personally, I believe that their lives are neither better nor worse, only different.

We, on the mountain, and these children with their surgeries, are sort of "abnormal," a kind of "mutant," because we both challenged our destiny and wrote a new ending. It's why I identify with them. When I'm with them, my life has meaning, and my heart grows. They are messengers of life, these children with voices made hoarse by the intubation that will often affect their vocal cords. In their raspy voices, they whisper to me that I was right to continue trudging over that mountain, to find that beautiful moon, and, if for nothing else, to spend my life searching for something that beautiful again.

Chapter 35

Azucena, Maria del Rosario's Mother

When I had first set out to make an appointment with Dr. Canessa at the end of March 2004, it seemed impossible. Then a friend who knew him suggested I call his office at Hospital Italiano and ask if he was in-country, and if so, I should sit in the waiting room until he would see me.

That's exactly what I did, staying until his office was about to close. What I discovered there was a scene unlike any I'd seen at other doctors' offices. It was like a nursery in which all the children were sick. Then I saw a man with white hair combed straight back and strong hands, like a farmer's or a mechanic's, rushing around from one room to the next. He would occasionally pop into the full waiting room to speak with mothers and children whom I later learned he had known for years.

When the doctor was finished with all his patients, he came back to the waiting room to find me still there. He conducted the ultrasound, then ushered me into a room next to his office to discuss the results. I later called it the "Glass Room," because it was the only one in that wing of the hospital from which you could see the sky.

I knew that something terrible lay ahead after that ultrasound, which had seemed to last an eternity. I sat across from the doctor. My hands were sweating, and my heart was pounding like a loco-motive. But he seemed at ease. His disposition might have calmed me in any other situation but not in this one. During the ultra-sound I could see the worry on his face. Or maybe it was just my imagination.

The doctor started by asking me what I did for a living, what my husband did, and what neighborhood we lived in. Suddenly, he paused. He looked past me, at some point over my head, out the sec-ond-story window, with a look I've come to know over the years, one in which he's still with you but is also somewhere else, wandering off into some unknown world. Over time, we'd learn that whenever Dr. Canessa got that faraway look, we would soon be up against a serious challenge—but he would already be searching for a solution. At first it made us nervous, because we thought he was distracted. But on the contrary: He was steeling himself.

"Your unborn daughter is missing half of her heart," he told me. "We can take heroic measures to save her. But if we go down this path, you have to understand there's no turning back. Your life as you know it will change forever. It'll be as if you had been in a plane crash. The procedures alone are going to cost a fortune. You and your family could be financially ruined. This is the decision you have to make. But know this: Whatever you decide, I'll be by your side to support you."

On a windowsill in the Glass Room there was an old faded teddy bear. When I asked Dr. Canessa what it was doing there, he told me a patient, a little boy, had placed him there, "looking out" at his new home.

"That little boy. Did he survive?"

"No," he said flatly.

I have remained captivated by that moment. There, in that room, where a teddy bear belonging to a boy who had died looked out the window, Maria del Rosario's life began in earnest.

Those next few days would be the most desperate times in my life and that of my husband, Juan. We have two other children, Juan Francisco and Jose Maria. We didn't have any problems with our first two children, and I considered myself an experienced mother. Our decision was complex and horrifying. Would a decision to save the baby drag the rest of our family down a path of destruction? Would we know how to live constantly on the edge? Was it all worth it?

The name we chose for our unborn daughter has a special meaning for us. After my first day in the Glass Room, searching for answers, I took up my rosary, and since that day, I've prayed. That's why we named her Maria del Rosario, a name given to her before she was born, when the world was still harmonious and predictable.

I had a feeling that when we visited Dr. Canessa at Hospital Italiano to tell him our decision, he already knew our answer. He'd told us that after they had gotten off the mountain, when they had told the world what they had lived through—because the world demanded to know—they had somehow put a price on emotion, on suffering. Disney had bought the rights to make the film *Alive*, and he had felt as if they had sold their pain, as if tears were legal tender. We then understood that our pain would also have a price: How much was Maria del Rosario's life worth? The first surgery would cost one hundred twenty thousand dollars. But Dr. Canessa's challenge involved us stepping out and walking on the ledge. It was no longer a matter of something physical, but something spiritual. Of course, it would eventually become something quantifiable.

Dr. Canessa has a saying: "Without joy, there is no success." If he believes that the struggle to save the life of a child who ends up dying will inflict an unbearable amount of pain—on the child's mother, father, siblings—then the fight is not worth the pain. But if he believes that the adversity will not overwhelm you, then you charge on, betting everything on success.

Before that fateful decision near the end of March, we had had to make a previous huge decision earlier in the month, before we had even seen Dr. Canessa. Uruguayan law forbids ending a pregnancy. But these cases fall into a gray area that depends on the parents' wishes. There is no hard-and-fast law, no judge. There is only a child and the child's parents. And in between them, doctors like Roberto Canessa. When we'd learned about the pregnancy and that there would be complications—though we didn't yet know the details of what was wrong—Juan and I decided to take a little time to think it over, freely and honestly. A few days later, when we went out to celebrate our wedding anniversary on March 2, each of us finally shared how we felt, and we had both come to the same conclusion: We were no one to say who should live and who should die. These were God's decisions, and we did not want to end the pregnancy. But it was one thing to let the pregnancy continue. It was quite another to make the decision we faced later in March.

———————

Roberto was waiting for us in his office, sipping what looked like a *cafe con leche*. When we came in, he didn't ask us if we had reached a decision. He calmly sipped his drink, making small talk. We had a lump in our throats.

He began testing our boundaries to see how far we were willing to go. I remember he started by saying that these kinds of operations were done only overseas, primarily in Boston. I responded with one word: *viajo*—"I'll travel." He paused. He implied that I would have to travel well before the birth, and before he got into the details, I interrupted him: "I'll fly there fifteen days before." He paused again. He asked me what I planned to do with my other two children, and I told him Juan would stay behind and fly in for the operation. This time he sat silently, waiting for me to come to my own conclusion.

"We are going to *do* this," I said.

182

When he realized I was willing to do whatever it took to save my daughter's life, he calmly set down his mug and told me, "Take this pen and paper and write down these email addresses." He gave me the contact information for three of his colleagues in the United States. He told me what I would have to write in my emails to them, and I remember I had to ask him to spell the medical terms in English, because some of the names didn't exist in Spanish.

Roberto was probing to see if we were up to the challenges that lay ahead: months of battling against the odds, with the likelihood of success slim. There were other complications, beyond the medical, which further reduced her odds of survival. But we learned to believe in success despite the harrowing odds.

We understood the magnitude of what it would take for Maria del Rosario to survive—and that a bad outcome would mean she'd be kept alive with a feeding tube until she inevitably died a slow death.

That's why our second decision was so much more complicated. And it was one of the fundamental reasons we finally resolved to embark on this strange, unprecedented, and unpredictable journey. Roberto's final words to us when we left his office that day were: "If you decide she should live, know that I will be there with you every step of the way." We would be explorers through undiscovered country, never knowing what tomorrow might bring.

From the moment we agreed to take on this quest together, the initial nightmare ceded to another until we were faced with a seemingly endless stream of challenges. A series of fragile links in a chain that could easily snap as we groped along in the dark. A passage that was as common as it was singular: the journey into existence.

Maria del Rosario was born on Tuesday, August 17, 2004, in Boston. They performed surgery on her two days later. (Her godmother calls to wish her a happy birthday every August 19, because she says Maria del Rosario was truly born that day.) By Saturday, August 21, she was out of imminent danger. I was still in the hospital following the birth, and only then did we call our children who had stayed behind in Montevideo to tell them that their sister had been born.

The chances of Maria del Rosario surviving that first operation and all the subsequent surgeries were low. She hung by a thread during every operation. "Hanging on." I got too used to that phrase. Twice when we arrived in Boston she was hanging on to her last breath. They had to rush her from the airplane to the hospital in an ambulance. Dr. Jane Newburger, a cardiologist and Roberto's counterpart at Boston Children's Hospital, asked us to say our goodbyes before every surgery, just in case.

We learned to exist in that in-between state, always saying goodbye. All the doctors' appointments, scheduling the surgeries, figuring out our finances, traveling with oxygen tanks, the endless bureaucracies—it pushed us to the limit. Before long, it didn't matter whether we were optimists or pessimists. We just *were*. On Maria del Rosario's first flight to Boston for her second operation (technically, she made her first trip inside my womb), we had to make a stop in Buenos Aires, but there was no protocol for someone remaining on the plane while they cleaned and refueled. I told the agents I wouldn't get off the plane because we couldn't move the oxygen tanks. True desperation is trying to explain—without breaking down into tears—to some bureaucrat, who won't deviate from rules and regulations, that if your child arrives in Boston even one second too late, it could mean the difference between life and death. We weren't traveling for business or pleasure. Ours was another kind of voyage altogether: a matter of life or death.

Before another surgery, she arrived cyanotic, with a blood oxygen level of 58 percent. While she was in the operating room, I waited for her in the lobby. Time seemed suspended because Dr. Canessa had also warned me that I should be ready to let her go.

When Maria del Rosario was born, there was not a single other child in all of Uruguay who had survived her kind of heart disorder. She is now the oldest person with her condition in Uruguay. Today, there are several cases of children in Uruguay who were born with hypoplasia of the left ventricle and who have lived. But back then, there were none.

Maria del Rosario's condition was supposed to require three surgeries: the first, upon being born; the second, after six months; and the third, at age three. That was the best-case scenario. Instead, three weeks after she was born and we'd returned to Montevideo, we had to put her on oxygen, and she needed surgery again after two months, not six, to fix an issue with her shunt. We flew back to Boston, where her recovery from the surgery took not one week, as we had been told, but forty days. And in between, she needed another procedure to fix a problem with her intestines. We flew home to Montevideo, but less than a month later, her condition worsened and we had to fly back to Boston to put in a new shunt. Two months after that, we were back in Boston after yet another complication. Her situation was far worse than we had expected. By the age of ten months, Maria del Rosario had needed four surgeries when we'd hoped she might need only one or two. None of the models applied to us anymore. When we asked the doctors in Boston what to expect next, they told us to consult with Dr. Canessa.

Fortunately, we had a great copilot—as Roberto liked to call my mom. She's tough, determined, and always ready to jump in and help. She accompanied me on every flight to Boston and shone a ray of light during my darkest hours, when I could barely breathe. She always managed to see the bright side. Even when the doctors gave us grim odds over a procedure, she always managed to focus on the best possible outcome.

I was just on autopilot; there was so much to do. My friends say I go into "Boston mode" when a problem with Maria del Rosario arises and that I do whatever it takes to find a solution. I didn't cry for eighteen months, yet today, I'll break down during a sentimental movie.

Before Maria was born, Roberto told us about a conversation he had had with his father. "My father says I shouldn't be giving you all such high hopes, because that little girl is going to be born, she's going to die, and you're going to lay all the blame at my feet." He stayed quiet for just a moment, then added, "Then again, when my father went to search for me in the Andes, he assumed I was dead."

I remember one morning when Maria was struggling to get enough oxygen, and Roberto came to spend the day with us in her room, so he could observe her and decide what the next step should be. As Juan and I were discussing what to do next, Roberto got that faraway look in his eyes and, very calmly, started telling us the story of the conversation he'd had with two of his friends when they were getting ready to make the final, dangerous leg of their journey through the mountains. "We did the right thing in pacing ourselves. That's how we reached our destination," he said.

Maria is a living case study today. She was born with half a heart, and the oldest survivors of this condition are thirty years old. Will she die at thirty-one? At forty? We just don't know. We've done all we can for her. The best we can for her. What if there's a complication? She might need a heart transplant and also a liver or lung transplant because her hepatic portal vein was rerouted to the inferior vena cava. Will I ever be able to say that she's finally healthy? What if I say she's healthy and then she needs a transplant? My friends and family ask, "How can you live like this?"

At the start of all this, I didn't know how I'd live this way either. But now I don't know any other way to live. She's alive thanks to medical advances and because we all had the will for her to live. No one knows what the future holds: It's only a saying, yes, but it's also the embodiment of joy, of gratefulness for being alive. If I allow myself to worry about tomorrow or the next week, I'll get depressed, and worse, I'll miss out on the joy of appreciating today. There's no point in worrying about the unknown because there's no way to eliminate those risks.

After everything we've lived through with my daughter, I realize that every day is a gift. Maria del Rosario is living proof. We are not the family we were years ago. *This* is our life. And it's our greatest gift.

Chapter 36

I have come to observe human life by way of the screen of an ultrasound machine. And when I witness it failing, when I watch a tiny human heart beat ever more slowly, I must do all I can to save it. One day, as I was preparing to treat a serious heart defect in a baby who was still in utero, Lauri asked me, "Who are you to change God's destiny?"

"I don't know. But I have to try," I told her, because that was the philosophy that saw me through the Andes.

Night fell quickly on our first day of hiking after sixty-one days on the mountain, and we found ourselves without shelter as we reached a frigid 15,000 feet above sea level. Darkness enveloped us, and the wind howled harder with each passing moment. I experienced the fear of knowing that we could die in an instant. The end was near. Each step took a Herculean effort as I watched my legs disappear into the snow. The air was so thin, the mountain so steep, and ours was nearly a vertical climb. The summit wasn't where we expected, and the mountain was much taller than we had imagined. Nothing we had experienced to that point could have prepared us for the magnitude of what we were facing. A blizzard devoured us and the snow whipped us like a lash.

As desperate tears froze on my cheeks, there came a sight: a rock jutting out from the cliff wall, an alcove the wind had whipped clear of snow. It was as if it had been waiting for us since its formation millions of years ago when the earth was still cooling. This horizontal sliver of a rock, barely big enough for us to lie beneath in our improvised sleeping bag, was all that kept us from freezing into blocks of ice—there, at 15,000 feet, in 30-below cold, not even able to offer our frozen corpses to our friends. We huddled and dared to dream we might live just a little longer.

The stone outcropping held firm against the blistering wind and snow. It was just wide enough for us and our sleeping bag, as if it had been made for exactly that purpose and exactly that night. One wrong move and we knew we would tumble down the precipice, hopelessly ensconced in our bag. When we huddled inside it, exhausted, it was clear that the temperature was just warm enough to keep us alive. Yes, it was cold—freezing, in fact—but our body heat kept us warm. Everything outside our bag froze, but inside, our bodies remained alive. Our bizarre sleeping bag, made from leftover scraps, withstood the Andean cold!

I lay down near the edge, closest to the abyss. We could make only small adjustments. And if we dared to sleep, it had to be with vigilance, knowing we could easily fall. I watched as the moon eventually rose over the snowy peaks that night, high above us, and I took it as a sign that we still had a chance: We were allowed to continue living. Just a few minutes ago, I was as good as dead. Now I was alive, and the moon had come back once again to tell me so. I wanted to throw my arms around its pale moonlight—light that illuminated the valley, just after we'd been about to give in.

Sometimes, my patients' hearts are the same way, on the verge of quitting. On some occasions, they ask for a brief respite, a moment to catch their breath before continuing on. Life has taught me that this moment can be so narrow as to keep life from slipping through or wide enough to invite me to stay forever. The brink, the edge, is the place where I exist, my home on the side of the mountain.

What surprises me most is that my loved ones, Lauri and my three children, keep me company here in this place that others find so foreign.

Chapter 37

Hilario Canessa, Roberto's Son

The first time I set foot on the crash site—standing there in 1994 amid the towering Andes mountains with my parents and my siblings—I was overcome with emotion. We'd had to cross over from the Argentine side because reaching it from Chile was impossible. We had traveled a long way to be there. When we rounded the last mountain, our guide stopped his horse and spread his arms out toward a valley encircled by jagged peaks: the Valley of Tears. *This is where my family is really from,* I thought to myself. That treacherous tale I'd been hearing for nearly twenty years originated in this desolate and majestic place.

My name even comes from the ridge that blocks the western pass: Sierra San Hilario.

We had come during one of the few times of the year when this place was accessible on horseback, even though it remained a rough, snow-covered journey. At that moment, staring at that absurd, impossible scene, I realized why I had always valued effort as the greatest of virtues, the results be damned. The one thing that always stood out to me about my father's epic journey was the night he, Nando, and Tintin reached the top of Sierra San Hilario and decided to fight on instead of giving in. They would reach their destination or die trying. It moves me every time I think about it, because my father had shown me over the course of my life that effort in the face of adversity is what makes you a stronger person. That decision transforms you, forever and for the better. I realized he learned that lesson way up here. It was one thing to hear him tell it in the comfort of our home. It was quite another to see it, to live it, to experience it there at the top of the world.

My mother has told me that when she first saw him after the trek he did not look like a normal man. And it wasn't because of his appearance or his whisper of a voice or the fact that he sobbed uncontrollably. It was because he looked like a being who had no age. One moment, he looked like a boy. The next, like a wise old man who radiated a spirituality that engulfed everything, a state of grace. He was, in my mother's words, a man who was soon to die, on the threshold of transition to another state. Someone who had made an extraordinary physical journey and was now ready to make a supernatural one.

I realize that in everything I do, I tend to favor someone who tries his best, who never gives up despite the outcome, over someone who has better luck and achieves his goal with less effort. If my father and Nando had fallen on the ninth day, their effort would not have been in vain, even if no one had ever known about it. Because *they* would have known. That's what makes you a better person. Because it doesn't matter what anyone else thinks, but what you think deep inside.

When I was an architecture student, I started designing three-dimensional computer models of homes. I loved it because I had to combine the logic of mathematics with the freedom of design. When science and creativity intersect, that's when great innovation happens. That's how I always describe my dad: as an innovator and a pragmatist. Was that a virtue born in the Andes? I can't say for sure, but if it was just a spark before the accident, it grew into an inferno up there. The moment he decided not to quit, the pragmatist and the innovator became one.

As kids, he taught us to respect precedent but to reject dogma. It was up in the Andes that he witnessed the two sides of life: reality and imagination, beauty and pain. He fused them together into a new force he used to keep moving forward. And that became a part of his personality.

In my career, I build computer programs so that homeowners can see their houses in 3D. And although my dad isn't an architect, he's been doing the same thing all my life, building little lean-tos and sheds and simple country homes. They're rudimentary structures, so he never uses plans but just innovates as he goes—the way he did on his escape from the Andes. But there's always one common theme with the little houses: They're always built around a fireplace, whether it's made of stone or brick or metal. If he builds an outdoor patio, he might build it around a fire pit. Out on the ranch, he builds the bonfires. Wherever he builds something, it's always a place where people can gather around for heat. And one day, it hit me: He's not building houses at all. He's building shelters where people can come for warmth.

When I picture my dad, he's either wearing simple work clothes and putting up drywall or installing a corrugated metal roof or fixing an old motor, or he's in his lab coat, coming home from the hospital in the wee hours of the night, exhausted. In my mind, he's always working, always struggling.

Everything I know about my father I learned from watching him. He has such a quiet, humble demeanor and an attitude I've rarely seen in clergy or missionaries or politicians. He respects everyone as equals. The other thing that stands out about him is that he never gives up. Whether he's working on a car engine or a water pump, he can't conceive of something being broken beyond repair. He feels the same way about people. The sicker a person is, the more intent he is on helping them. I've never met anyone else who lives his life that way. Sometimes, he'll hire a recovering drug addict and put that person to work right alongside him, or he might hire a man who just got out of jail—all without anyone knowing about it. That brings him immeasurable joy. I've never seen anyone have quite that reaction. Pride or compassion, sure. But joy? Is that something he got from the Andes? I wonder. In large and small ways, the Andes always seem to be there. And I'll never forget that what drives him today was born up on the Sierra San Hilario.

In a few days, October of 2012, my wife, Macarena, will give birth to our first child. This will be my parents' first grandchild. I wonder what my child will mean to my father. I think he'll see that life goes on, that he no longer has to struggle and strive and push the way he has been since the age of nineteen. I think when he sees my child take his first steps, my father will finally be able to rest. Perhaps it will be the end of that arduous journey and the beginning of a more serene one. He will finally have arrived at his destination, from the arid peaks of the Andes to the verdant pastures of Los Maitenes.

Chapter 38

Isabelle, Agustin's Mother

My husband, Diego, and I had our first son, Juan Diego, in 2005, two years after being married. Agustin came two years later.

While both of our families had been well-off, we worked hard as a young couple to make a life for ourselves. I got my accounting degree at twenty-five and started on my master's at twenty-six. I began in March and two months in, at some point in the rat race between work and school, I learned I was pregnant with Juan Diego. I had the tenderest bond with Juan Diego you could possibly imagine. Even the birth was amazing. It was sheer joy that radiated from my pores and was utterly contagious to everything and everyone around me. He was born at one thirty in the morning and by six, I was so overjoyed, I was ready to have another one. *This must be what heaven is like,* I thought.

Shortly after finishing my master's degree, I got pregnant again, but had a miscarriage during a work trip to San Pablo. It was the most devastating thing that had ever happened to me, to lose the pregnancy while I was so far away from home, all alone. But the sadness didn't last long. Three months later, I got the news: I was pregnant again, this time with Agustin. I was nearly nine weeks along when I got my first ultrasound.

Everything was magical again, as it had been with Juan Diego—until the fifth month when I went in for a second ultrasound. The memory of that moment is so strong that I can recall every sight, every smell. I was in the waiting room when I said to Diego, "I don't know why I'm so nervous." They started with the routine five-month ultrasound scan, the technician pointing out every organ, and then he stopped at the heart for a long time before moving on to the rest. He came back to the heart and stayed there until I asked, "What's wrong?" He remained silent, still studying the tiny heart inside my womb until he finally said, "I can't see the four chambers very well. But relax, I'm going to order a fetal echocardiogram, a special ultrasound of the heart."

We were left up in the air, suspended in time. "It can't be that bad," we told ourselves. Because bad things only ever happened to other people, or so we thought. I went to my obstetrician and dropped off a copy of the exam, as the ultrasound tech had instructed. A few hours later, I got a call. My doctor suggested I see our neonatologist, whom we knew well because he was our older son's primary doctor. There, he told us, "Isabelle, I know how you are, so I'm not going to sugarcoat this, and I'm not going to lie to you. This could be nothing, a hole between the ventricles that will close by itself in the next few weeks of pregnancy. Or, it could be as bad as what we call hypoplastic left heart syndrome—that your son Agustin only has half a heart. You need to make an ultrasound appointment as soon as possible with Dr. Canessa so you can make a decision."

We had to wait three weeks until I was twenty-three weeks pregnant, when the baby's heart would be large enough to be diagnosed. Those were excruciating days, having to keep up a smiling facade when people said, "How's it coming along?" "How's the baby doing?" and "Oh, it looks like a boy!" Since that day, I rarely ask inane questions to make small talk, nor am I ever surprised by an answer that doesn't jibe with society's expectations. Those who did know what was going on asked us questions we couldn't yet answer or offered words of encouragement that gave us no solace. During those weeks, I just wanted to crawl into a deep, dark hole and never come out.

I met Roberto Canessa on November 27, 2007, the day of my appointment. I was supine on a hospital bed when he came into the room, said hello, and got right to the exam. After a few minutes of scanning the heart, despite how nervous we were, he started to ask us questions about our lives, wanting to know who we were, where we were from, where we lived. I wanted to scream, "Stop the stupid questions and just tell me what's wrong with my son!" I realized later he was probing to find out whether we had the economic where-withal as well as the emotional stamina to withstand what lay ahead.

Then, as he watched the ultrasound monitor, he stopped asking questions and a quiet descended on us.

"This is a complicated case," he said finally.

I choked on my tears and couldn't speak. I tried to hold still while he continued scanning my womb, but I shook from the uncontrollable sobbing.

"He has hypoplastic left heart . . . a part of his heart hasn't been fully formed," he said.

He spoke calmly and confidently. He told us exactly what he was seeing and didn't try to downplay it.

We eventually moved into the other office, and the first thing I asked was what kind of life our son could expect to have.

"He has a very serious condition, and he has some tough years ahead," he said. "But if everything goes as it should, he may never be an athlete, but he will be able to have a normal life."

"Normal?" I asked.

"Happy," he answered.

We ended up making the same choice for Agustin as Azucena had made for her daughter, Maria del Rosario. Her decision had been in the second month of pregnancy. Ours was in the sixth month. At first, we thought everything would be easier for us because we managed to get loans to pay for the procedures. We didn't realize that money would be only a small part of the ordeal. It all happened in exactly one month, twenty days less than we had imagined.

On the day we were set to leave, during our last visit to see Dr. Canessa, I broke down into inconsolable tears. Roberto hugged me and I told him, "You know what's wrong? Deep down, I thought if we didn't need to make this trip, then Agustin really wasn't that sick. But the fact that we're leaving means it's really serious." He held me and said, "Don't worry, these children have a good prognosis through age twenty. After that, who knows? Twenty years from now they might have artificial hearts."

In the days leading up to the trip, we spent a lot of time talking with Azucena and her husband, Juan. Our children would be among the first cases to be treated for hypoplastic left heart in all of Uruguay. Until now, the few who'd had the condition were stillborn or died shortly after birth or surgery. Azucena walked us through it. "You'll most likely have a cesarean section. They'll hand you your son for a few minutes, you'll kiss him, and then a nurse will come in and put him in an incubator. Your husband, Diego, will accompany him as he's wheeled across a tunnel to the children's hospital side while you go into recovery in a separate area." And that's exactly how it happened. But nothing else was quite that orderly. We continued to walk along a high wire, without any rest until the end.

Agustin needed to be delivered in Boston Children's Hospital, which is affiliated with Harvard Medical School and specializes in these kinds of surgery. But I would not be able to travel after my thirty-fifth week of pregnancy. It was March 4 when we left Montevideo, and I was in week thirty-four.

We flew to Boston at night on a Tuesday, Diego at my side and Agustin in my womb. I'll never forget the look on my son Juan Diego's face—he was two at the time—when we said goodbye in Montevideo. We arrived in Boston on Wednesday at 11:20 a.m. We

Stella Maris de Carrasco Church, June 18, 1976: Our
wedding, in the church where Lauri would go to pray for us
when we were lost. (Courtesy of the Canessa family)

Uruguay, 1975: The first time Nando and I
invited Sergio Catalan to visit us in Uruguay. We
were at Lauri's family's house. When she heard
Catalan say that we had fallen in Sierra San
Hilario, she realized that would be the name of
our first son, to make good on her promise when I
was lost. (Courtesy of the Canessa family)

September 12, 1977: With Lauri
and our elder son, Hilario, as a
newborn. (Roberto Canessa)

1980: Departing for South
Africa, where I was part of the
first selection for the South
American rugby team, the 1980
South American Jaguars rugby
union, to play a championship
to denounce and fight against
apartheid. (Roberto Canessa)

Los Maitenes, 1988: When I was reunited with Lauri at the hospital in San Fernando, I promised her that when we had a family of our own, I would take her to the valley where the richest flowers grow: Los Maitenes, where the farmers had made their homes. I made good on that promise sixteen years later. You can see Sierra San Hilario in the background. (Courtesy of the Canessa family)

Aerial view of the Valley of Tears (Valle de las Lagrimas), 2015: The valley is distinguishable by the yellowish color of the earth. This photo was taken in April, when the snow on the mountains had already thawed. While we, the survivors, were there, the whole mountain was covered in snow. (Diego Errazuriz)

The Valley of Tears (Valle de las Lagrimas), February 2001: With my sons, Hilario and Tino. I returned six times to the site of the crash, during the few days of the year when you can gain access to the valley, after two days on horseback, because the rest of the year it remains covered in snow. (Courtesy of the Canessa family)

The Valley of Tears (Valle de las Lagrimas), March 2006: With my daughter, Lala, in the Andes at the site of the accident; at that time I wanted to present her to my friends who remained on the mountain, because now they were all the same age. (Courtesy of the Canessa family)

The Valley of Tears (Valle de las Lagrimas), February 2001: At my friends' grave. (Courtesy of the Canessa family)

Grave site at the Valley of Tears (Valle de las Lagrimas): On a rocky hill 2,625 feet away from the fuselage, a grave was created in January 1973 for those who died on the mountain. Years later, on an iron plaque, the survivors and I left this message: "In memory of our visit, the 16 to our 29 brothers as always united." (Roberto Canessa)

Santiago, October 2002: Lauri says that I have a tendency to remember and repeat the scarce good moments of our 1972 tragedy, like when we met Sergio Catalan. Among those rituals, year after year we keep playing the same match that we couldn't compete in, in 1972, the so-called Friendship Cup ("Copa de la Amistad"), awarded by the International Rugby Board. In 2002, thirty years after the accident, we returned to, symbolically, play the match. As part of the remembrance, a helicopter brought Sergio Catalan to the center of the field, and then I led him to his horse. (Alfredo Alvarez)

December 22, 2008: Since the accident, the survivors reunite each year on December 22 to remember the day we were saved. Here I am with Nando and his daughter Cecilia, my goddaughter, and my son Hilario, his godson. (Courtesy of the Canessa family)

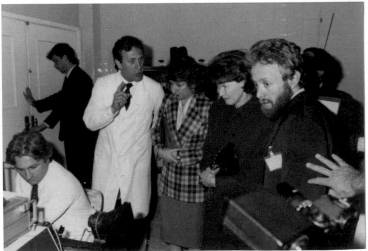

Hospital Italiano, 1986: The First Lady of Uruguay, Marta Canessa de Sanguinetti (*left*), and the First Lady of France, Danielle Mitterrand (*right*), visited the Institute for Infant Cardiology at Hospital Italiano, where I worked on an echocardiography machine of the time. Beside them is Dr Pedro Duhagon (*far left*). (Courtesy of the Canessa family)

Chile, 1999: At Lake Villarrica, with my friend Dr Itzhak Kronzon, Director of the Cardiac Imaging Department of Cardiovascular Medicine at the Lenox Hill Heart and Vascular Institute in New York. (Courtesy of the Canessa family)

Uruguay, March 2015: At the Pereira Rossell Children's Hospital, undertaking an echocardiograph on a newborn in an incubator. (Natalia Dadalt)

1995: Jojo Buere Beraza in her kindergarten uniform. (With the kind permission of the Buere Beraza family)

2014: Jojo Buere Beraza in her nurse's uniform. (With the kind permission of the Buere Beraza family)

November 18, 2002: Tiago in his father Jacinto's arms on his first birthday. I brought the candle closer to his lips so that he could blow it out. (With the kind permission of Martha Mesa and Jacinto Desouza's family)

October 21, 2010: Tomas the Great, the bravest boy I ever met, with his mother, Adriana. (With the kind permission of Adriana Mazza de Klimas and Bernardo Klimas's family)

Cambridge, November 2010: Agustin Vazquez Chaquiriand with his parents, Diego and Isabelle, at John F. Kennedy Park, after his last surgery in Boston. (With the kind permission of the Vazquez Chaquiriand family)

Boston, June 16, 2015: Agustin and his brother, Juan Diego, with Dr. Jane Newburger, Commonwealth Professor of Pediatrics at Harvard Medical School, and me. (With the kind permission of the Vazquez Chaquiriand family)

Boston, June 14, 2015: Dr. Neil J. Weissman, president of the American Society of Echocardiography (ASE), presenting me with a plaque that named me an honorary fellow of the ASE. (Courtesy of the ASE)

Boston, June 14, 2015: Speaking at a conference in which I thanked the ASE for the honorary fellowship they granted me. (Courtesy of the ASE)

2013: With my *chambergo* tilted, dancing a tango with my wife, Lauri, in our home. (Courtesy of the Canessa family)

2014: With Lauri in the winter garden of our home. (Courtesy of the Canessa family)

checked into the hotel and I told Diego, "My stomach hurts a little. I shouldn't have had that soda on the airplane."

"You're probably hungry. Let's get something to eat," he told me. We had a hospital appointment at 3:00 p.m. for a fetal echocardiogram.

We crossed the street to get a bite to eat, but I felt worse and worse. At the crosswalk on the way back, I could barely stand. I staggered into our room. When I went to the bathroom, I felt my first contraction. We grabbed my passport and a nightgown and raced toward the hospital in a taxi. The only address we knew in all of Boston was the Children's Hospital, where we had the appointment.

In my broken English and with strengthening contractions, I tried to explain to the nurse that I was in labor, but she misunderstood and said that according to the computer I was early for my 3:00 p.m. appointment. "Please, call a doctor or a nurse at the women's hospital. The baby's coming!" I tried to say. She finally realized what was happening, and they put me in a wheelchair and rushed me through the tunnel Azucena had told me about to the women's hospital. By the time we arrived, I was dilated six centimeters. Then I had to wait another fifteen minutes because the nurse had trouble spelling my Armenian last name and heaven forbid I give birth without that crucial hospital tag on my wrist. I yelled in pain, but the nurse just said, "Don't push yet, hold on!"

When it was finally time to push, I didn't know where I would find the strength. I hadn't slept on the plane, and I was eight months pregnant, in a foreign country, in a strange city. It was unreal.

Back in Montevideo, Roberto had told me, "Don't trust technology too much. The machines, the sophistication, what have you. At the end of the day, it all depends on you. Boston has a great team that has more experience than the one in Uruguay. They've done this several times before, and that's the only difference." And that's exactly what happened. I was at Harvard's medical center, apparently in the best situation possible for my son. But I was tired and hungry and desperate, and I barely had the strength to push. My son was coming early and they couldn't so much as figure out my last name. And I didn't even speak the language. All of it, because Agustin had decided it was time.

From that point on, it all happened just as Azucena had told me. They asked Diego to leave the room, and I was left alone with a nurse, on my hospital bed, shaking from nervousness. I spoke on the phone with the surgeon, Frank Pigula. My son hadn't even been born yet, and I blathered on and on about his impending operation. When I stopped to catch my breath, the surgeon simply said, "You read too much." He was right. I was constantly sharing books and articles I'd read with Roberto because I needed to know. I'd learned that the crucial number was 5 pounds, 8 ounces. If Agustin managed to weigh at least that much, his chances were good. Less than that meant that everything would become much more complicated.

The second he was born, I whipped my head around to look at the scale. I blinked and squinted, my eyes blurry. It read . . . 4 pounds, 13.6 ounces. That was it. "God, don't do this to me!" I yelled. "You can't give me so much. You can't keep kicking me when I'm down!"

That night, Diego pushed me in a wheelchair down the hall to see Agustin, all 4 pounds, 13.6 ounces of him, and we ran into Jane Newburger, the renowned Harvard cardiologist. From Montevideo, we'd been in touch with her and the famous Harvard surgeon Pedro del Nido (who is Chilean born), who had operated on Maria del Rosario. This was the original team for children like ours: Roberto in Montevideo, Jane and Pedro in Boston. The first time I met Jane, she talked about her close relationship with Dr. Canessa, and that helped put me at ease.

Jane is a petite, caring woman who gives off a maternal warmth. I think that's why she hit it off with Roberto and why she's our pillar in Boston. But even Jane's demeanor couldn't stave off the bad news. "Agustin was born prematurely, and the surgeon we'd planned on,

Pedro del Nido, is in a conference in Madrid. We have two options. Either we wait for Pedro to arrive next week and increase the risk for Agustin, or we go with another surgeon who also has had excellent results with these types of cases." I asked Jane what she would do if it were her son, and she said, "I think we should speak to Roberto." We called Roberto from my cell phone. I told him Agustin had been born. Silence. He finally asked me how much he weighed. "Four pounds, thirteen point six ounces," I said. Silence, again. After another long pause he finally said, "He's right on the edge." I knew he was small. He asked me, "What does Pedro think?" "Pedro's not here." Another long, arduous pause. "They've had great results over-all, not just with Pedro," he finally said. Since Agustin was stable, we decided to do the operation with the staff that was available. We spoke with Jane, and she agreed.

The surgery was scheduled for early the next morning.

We kept vigil that night, and at 6:00 a.m., we crossed over from the main hospital to the children's hospital, where surgeon Frank Pigula was waiting to do the operation. He asked me again if I understood precisely what was wrong with my son, even though we had spoken about it the previous day when I'd been in the throes of labor. Roberto had already explained it to me in detail and so I recited it from memory.

Since the left side of his heart hadn't developed and the aorta was also affected, they would perform surgery so that the right side of the heart would do the job of the left. They would connect the pulmonary artery to the aorta to help it do its job, and they would widen the upper section of the aorta. They would insert a tempo-rary artificial pulmonary artery in the meantime until subsequent surgeries. They would connect the two venae cavae—which bring the oxygen-depleted blood into the heart—directly to the lungs. The oxygen-depleted blood would travel to the lungs not through a heartbeat but by a change of blood pressure. And this way, Agustin could survive with only half a heart.

Dr. Pigula was surprised at my detailed explanation. "Yes, that's exactly what we're going to do," he said. He asked if we had any other questions, but all I could think of to ask was whether he'd had a good night's sleep—whether he was calm and well-rested. He just smiled. He told us that the operation would last at least six hours.

He said we should go back to my hospital room. They would keep us updated on their progress by phone. Every hour, they would call us to let us know what they had found and what lay ahead. They would lower Agustin's body temperature to 64 degrees, stop his heart, and connect him to life support that would breathe and pump his blood for him. Then they would complete the open-heart surgery, raise his body temperature, and restart his heart. If all went well, they would close up his tiny chest. Otherwise it would remain open for the next few days. I had read that if they kept him on machines for longer than five hours, he risked neurological damage.

After the surgery, we were told the surgeon would meet us in intensive care at 1:30 p.m. to talk to us. We were already waiting when Dr. Pigula arrived. He told us that everything had gone well and that the recovery would take four to six weeks. The next few hours would be critical, but the surgery had been a success.

An hour later, I returned to the ICU to see Agustin. When I arrived, I was told to wait a minute, that a nurse would be out to speak with me. That unnerved me, but I figured it was just standard procedure. The nurse arrived and told me there had been a problem. The doctor was on his way to speak to me. I fired a text to Diego (who had gone to rent me a breast pump) to hurry back; there had been a complication.

Jane and another doctor who spoke Spanish arrived to tell me there had been post-op complications, and Dr. Pigula was deciding what to do next. Jane said, "He developed blood clots and suffered a few small heart attacks. The entire team is with him now and they're working on the heart. We can't really say anything else right now because we don't know; it could go either way. They're giving him anticoagulants and deciding whether to put him into a medically induced coma or take him back into surgery. He had a heart attack, recovered, but then he had another."

Jane left and I drifted off into limbo. Diego arrived a few minutes later, just as Dr. Pigula came to tell us that they had taken him back into surgery. Things had taken a turn for the worse. It was 8:00 p.m. and it had been fourteen hours since Agustin had first gone into surgery. My baby weighed just 4 pounds, 13.6 ounces, and he was lying in a room with his chest open. Our minds couldn't take any more. Everything was up in the air now, frozen in space and time. We trudged down to the cafeteria to wait, and there, calmly eating a sandwich and reading the newspaper, was the surgeon. I will never be able to erase that image from my mind. *He was reading the newspaper while my son was fighting for his life!* Diego noticed my stunned look. "This is a good thing," Diego told me. "He's been at the hospital for nearly twenty-four hours now, working on that tiny heart. Let him take a break and distract himself with the newspaper. We want his mind to be clear."

At one in the morning, after we had been waiting in limbo for more than five hours, Dr. Pigula returned from the operating room. He had been working on Agustin's heart for nineteen hours. He told us Agustin had survived the second surgery and we were back to square one, where we had been this morning: wait and see. In half an hour we could go in to see him.

A half hour passed. Then another. Two hours went by and still we had no word. Then Jane and Dr. Pigula emerged to tell us that while the second surgery had gone well, Agustin went into momentary cardiac arrest as they wheeled him to the ICU, and they immediately hooked him up to an external breathing machine called an ECMO (extracorporeal membrane oxygenation). There were two possibilities. The first was that his tiny half a heart had been too badly damaged during surgery and would never recover; the more hopeful option was that two consecutive surgeries had been too much on top of his low birth weight, and his heart only needed to rest. "We have to wait and see how he responds," they said. He was just 4 pounds, 13.6 ounces, and only two days old, and he'd already withstood two surgeries. They'd run a battery of tests to determine whether his nervous system had been affected, but all signs were good—although we wouldn't know for sure for days, or even years, as he grew and matured.

At 3:00 a.m., we finally got to see Agustin. I didn't have strength left in me to even cry. It had been twenty-one hours since his first surgery, thirty-nine hours since he had been born. This was all too much to be real. I had figured this would be difficult, but I had never imagined how much we would all suffer.

We spent four days tumbling in limbo without knowing whether Agustin would live or die. On his fifth morning, his tiny heart started to give signs of responding. It hadn't been so far gone, after all, but had needed only a little time to regain its strength.

That evening, the doctors told us that although he'd been sedated with morphine, Agustin had opened his eyes, looked around the room at each doctor, and then closed them again. On one hand, they were shocked that the baby was strong enough to do that—they increased the sedative so he wouldn't exhaust himself after that—but they were delighted to see him respond.

The next day, they began weaning him off the artificial heart pump and slowly allowed his heart to take over the work, to see how it responded. Then they unhooked him completely and let his heart work on its own for half an hour before putting him back on the machines. It was the longest thirty minutes of my life. Six doctors were watching over him. The next day, they took him off the ECMO for good, and we were back where we'd been after his first surgery: waiting in purgatory.

We stayed in Boston for a month, experiencing the duality of being in a place with the world's best medical technology while suffering through physical and mental exhaustion. Life and death were juxtaposed.

They fed Agustin my milk through a feeding tube because they feared he might have lost the ability to suckle. Eventually, we started him on a bottle as the cardiologist and nurses looked on. The goal was clear: When he could drain an entire bottle, we could leave the hospital. The day he finally did, I broke into tears.

A week later, we had a follow-up appointment to decide whether we could fly home to Montevideo. Agustin checked out perfectly, and I cried again. How many times had my baby been reborn during those four weeks? I had lost count.

After a long flight with a cyanotic baby of less than five pounds, while carrying an oxygen tank with a lead connected to his nose and going through tedious U.S. security with bottles of liquid medicine, we finally returned to Uruguay on April 6, 2008.

I'll never forget the moment in the airport when Agustin first met his brother, Juan Diego. The two looked each other over, amazed. I stared at my baby and thought, *Life hasn't been easy for you so far, my love.*

Chapter 39

Lala Canessa, Roberto's Daughter

On the eastern side of the San Hilario Sierra on March 14, 2006—
my second trip to the crash site—Dad told me about the night he
slept standing up over the abyss.

We set up a tent in the Valley of Tears, the accident site, but Dad
wanted to sleep separately in a smaller tent. I could see he was emotional. So I decided to spend the night in the small tent with him. It
was very cold that night, and we could hear avalanches breaking loose
in the distance while we struggled to breathe in the thin Andean air.

"The night we slept standing up," he told me, "I asked God to
make it hard for us, very hard, as much as we could stand, but please
don't make it impossible. I prayed he would let me sleep lightly
enough so that I wouldn't let my foot slip off the pole. I promised if
he let me survive this, I would come through."

"Coming through" meant not only surviving. It meant coming
through for his mother, who could not have lived with the reality
of a dead son. Coming through meant finding help for his friends
in the airplane.

An avalanche rumbling in the distance startled me. Dad paused.
I couldn't seem to get comfortable in the cramped space only dimly
lit by a lantern.

I'd rarely seen my dad this troubled. He'd asked me to accompany him on this journey to the Valley of Tears, which took two days on horseback through the mountains, so that he could introduce me to his deceased friends.

"This is my daughter, Lala, who is the same age as you now," he said.

He confided that on all the previous occasions when he had returned to the mountain, being there was like a nightmare because he could still hear the cries of his friends in pain. But on that day, they only whispered in his ear.

"I'm white-haired and old now, while they remain forever young and healthy, like the pastures of Suspiro," he said. Suspiro is our family's forty-acre country home in the sierras of Lavalleja in northeastern Uruguay. With his eyes glistening with tears, he told me the story of Flaco Vazquez.

Flaco Vazquez was studying medicine with my dad, and he was one of the best, brightest, and most sensitive people Dad had ever met. Dad encouraged him to come with him to Chile. Flaco hadn't been really excited about it, but Dad was insistent. And so Flaco went, and sat across the aisle from Dad. After the crash, when the plane finally came to a stop, Dad noticed that Flaco's legs were badly injured. Still in shock from the accident, Dad asked him if he was OK, and Flaco answered, "Yeah, go help the others." When Dad came back to do his "rounds" two hours later, Flaco had bled out. A propeller blade that had shorn through the fuselage had all but amputated his leg.

"His attitude became my guiding light: 'I'm fine, help the others.'" It was the mantra that would guide my father.

Lying inside the tent, my father closed his eyes and listened to the distant rumble of avalanches in the Andean night.

To me, there are three Roberto Canessas. There's the Roberto Canessa of myth and legend, the one people want to hug and commiserate with, whose shoulder they want to cry on. Then there's Dr.

Canessa, who dresses in white while making the rounds into the night at hospitals all over Montevideo. The third one is the Roberto who lives in my home, who merges the myth and the medical practitioner. That's my real dad.

I tell him, "Dad, you always tell people to enjoy life, but you're the one who least enjoys his life." He's always concerned with other people and whether they're OK, so he often neglects himself. He forgets that he needs to feel emotion, too.

I feel as if my dad is still guided by the mission of his mountain trek: If you fall, get back up and keep going. This belief is supported by what he's seen and done. If someone tells you, "Your child is going to make it despite the odds," you might answer, "Who are you to say such a thing?" But if you know my father's story, if you know what it took to survive that long in the snowy mountains and to hike across peaks and spend the night sleeping practically standing up on a pole above a chasm, you realize he has the credentials to make those kinds of statements.

Of everything that happened in the Andes, the thing that stood out the most to me was his trek. How did two emaciated young men, ages nineteen and twenty-two, who knew absolutely nothing about climbing and had already been stranded for such a long time, make that journey? After spending two months living in a broken fuselage in the snow, thinking they were going to die, knowing that the rescue had been called off and that their friends were dying around them, and after hiking and failing so many times? After all that, they still had the wherewithal to say, "If they won't help us, we'll help ourselves—and we'll do it for our friends, too"?

A friend of mine came to me one day and said, "I have to talk to your father. It's an emergency."

"Why, what's the matter?" I asked.

"I failed a big test and I need your dad to help me."

Everyone comes to my dad for help. But to whom does he go for help?

The same thing happens with his patients. A desperate mother needs someone to give her strength, and Dad is the kind of person who gives people hope. He forgets about himself and focuses on helping the other person, as if life were eternal and he will eventually have time for himself.

At the same time, he wants to live life to the fullest. If it's a beautiful Sunday morning, he'll come and wake me up at 7:00 a.m. because he says I can't waste a beautiful sunny day. But even if it's dark and rainy, he'll say I'm wasting a beautiful rainy day. Sometimes I feel that because of his crash in the Andes, I'm obligated to enjoy every day, whether it's sunny or stormy, happy or sad. I have to be grateful for a cup of coffee or a glass of tap water, because that's what I was taught at home. And if I'm not, I'm being terribly ungrateful to those who died on the mountain and their families.

My house wasn't a normal home. We always had people who weren't family members staying over, people coming and going at all hours of the day. Last year, my mother put up a Christmas tree in a room whose roof is made entirely of glass, so you can see the sky and sun. One day, I found a bird had made its nest in the tree. When I got close to it, wondering whether it was real, it hopped up on a branch, among ornaments and Christmas lights, while its chicks popped up their heads begging for food. It hit me all of a sudden: We were the kind of people who had a family of birds living in our Christmas tree in the middle of summer.

However daunting the Andes might have been, my father's trek to escape it was even more impressive. When your entire life has been an intense journey—and my father continues to live his life this way—you become a beacon in the storm for others. That's why people come up and tell him they have so much they want to say to him but end up hugging him and crying in his arms. In truth, the things they have to say are to themselves. Dad is just the catalyst. He's the pilot in the storm, a glint from a lighthouse amid a troubled sea, preventing others from crashing against the rocks.

What most impresses me about him isn't so much what he gives of himself to help others, it's that he truly delights in doing it. That's why his career in medicine fits him like a glove. And why his experience in the Andes only amplified that gift. He made a commitment at nineteen that he continues to honor today.

When I look back on things, I always reach the same conclusion: The reason Dad made that trek was so that his mother wouldn't have to live her life without him. He had to survive for his mother's sake—although she says she always felt he was alive. And that's why he exists in that special place, not one of life and death but of rebirth, like the helpless children he treats. Children who cannot live without intervention. And desperate mothers who need support, the way his own mother did. His mother needed to know that she was right, and the only way for that to be proven was for Dad to make his way back to her. To bring that message to her in person. That's exactly what he does today in his career: He is the messenger of hope between desperate mothers and their children.

One weekend, I could see Dad was worried and anxious as he awaited a pregnant mother whose baby had a serious heart problem. By the time she left, completely at peace an hour later, I thought, *That mom's mind is at ease but she must have left my poor dad emotionally drained.* But when I went in to see him, he was glowing, full of energy.

"What happened?" I asked him.

"She decided her baby was going to live," he said.

The prospect of a new life is what fuels him. It is not only his endless source of hope, but also of purpose: to help another mother continue to believe.

Chapter 40

Mercedes, Jojo's Mother

My youngest daughter, Maria Jose, whom we all call Jojo, is now twenty-one, but her tumultuous journey began when she was too young to remember it.

Jojo celebrated her second birthday in an intensive care unit. And today, just days after her twenty-first birthday, she finds herself in a hospital bed again, following another ICU visit. But in a few days she may be able to leave this place, never to return to an intensive care unit again.

Jojo had her first operation when she was two and a half, her second at age five, her third at nine, and her final one in August of 2011, all of them in Uruguay.

A month before Jojo turned two, in December 1991, her doctors discovered a congenital heart defect: a mitral valve stenosis and an aortic stenosis. A month later, we met Dr. Canessa. After a month of intensive treatment in Salto, we came to Montevideo for an appointment at Hospital Italiano. She was set for a Doppler echocardiogram to determine exactly what was wrong with her heart. That afternoon, when Dr. Canessa gave us her diagnosis, I burst into tears and felt as if I would never stop crying—that I would cry for the rest of my life. He put his hand on my shoulder and very soberly told me to stop sobbing for a moment because he had something very important to tell me: "You can't cry, because it's time to get to work."

After Jojo's second surgery, I was going down an escalator with Dr. Canessa and a reporter from *Life* magazine who had come to write a story on him. I was clinging to Roberto, sobbing uncontrollably like that first time, and the reporter asked him what was wrong with me. "Those are tears of joy from a mother whose daughter has successfully come out of surgery," he told her.

Ours has been a race against time to add years to Jojo's life. Going into the first surgery, I admit we didn't have high expectations, because there just wasn't experience with these types of cases here in Uruguay. Over the past twenty years, they kept going back in to do corrective surgeries on her heart valves, buying time until we reached this critical surgery just six days ago. They replaced two of her heart valves in an eleven-hour surgery.

It was a race against time because Jojo was constantly at risk of sudden death, something we had understood since she was first diagnosed. We lived each day with our hearts in our throats, permanently in a state of watchfulness, because every cold was another possible complication, every flu a trip to the emergency room; every sickness could bring on tragedy. She also suffered from endocarditis. She had a limited life: She couldn't overexert herself, couldn't run, couldn't eat anything that wasn't part of her low-sodium diet.

Dr. Canessa will often sit with Jojo and just talk. Sometimes I tiptoe close enough to hear them talking, often about very intimate things. Sometimes they talk about death, and so simply and straightforwardly that it breaks my heart. I can see that occasionally she argues with him, and I'll think she's right on the verge of rebelling, but then she's always at peace, serene, after their conversations.

When Dr. Canessa first got it in his mind that we had to save Jojo, he spared no effort to find a solution. He had a surprising effect on us. Even when things were grim, Dr. Canessa would give his opinion and we would breathe a sigh of relief, because he gave us hope that things would get better. And when things were really dire, he found a way to make them seem a little less so. I've told him before that he's not just healing hearts; he's mending souls.

We live in Salto, more than 150 miles from Montevideo. I remember one time, before the third surgery in 1998, when Jojo was seven and close to death. Roberto was just as desperate as we were, searching everywhere for an answer, until he called us one day, moved and uplifted, to tell us he had found a solution. Not an option or an alternative or an experimental procedure, but an actual surgery that would resolve Jojo's condition. You could hear in his voice that he, too, had found peace. By coincidence, a renowned New Zealand surgeon named Roger Mee, who practiced at the Cleveland Clinic and was a friend of Roberto's, was going to be at a conference in Montevideo that very day. He was one of the world's only surgeons who performed a particular type of procedure called the Ross. It was unbelievable luck: He was going to be at a nearby conference, and Jojo had precisely the condition that this doctor was an expert at treating. Jojo was dying and there was no time to waste. Dr. Canessa picked the doctor up at the airport and took him to his home, instead of his hotel, to ask him to please do the surgery to save Jojo's life. Dr. Mee hadn't arrived expecting to jump right into an operating room. But at 11:30 p.m. that very night, he emerged from the operating room after performing surgery on Jojo.

"I did everything I could, and it appears that everything turned out fine, but I have to apologize for not having my whole team with me," he told us.

He usually performed this kind of surgery with a specific team of doctors, and he told us he might have been able to do even more if they had been in the room with him. As it was, he ran out of time to do further repairs to her heart, he said, because they couldn't safely administer any more anesthesia to Jojo. But that operation—in which he removed the excess tissue from two valves that had been blocking the blood flow to the aortic valve—was enough to keep Jojo alive until her surgery just six days ago. I'll never forget that moment: A doctor who had traveled across the world from New Zealand, walking out of an operating room near midnight, asking my forgiveness because although he had done absolutely everything he could for my daughter, he could have done a little more with his team. I was clinging to Lauri, Dr. Canessa's wife—who worked at the hospital and had been with Roberto during Jojo's ten-hour surgery—and began crying again.

Dr. Canessa repeatedly asked me to learn to live with Jojo's heart condition instead of seeing it as a tragedy. And I think I was able to. Because I've seen so many terrible things over the past twenty years in hospitals and ICUs, I'm thankful Jojo's condition was treatable and that we've been able to continue forging ahead day after day. What we needed was someone by our side, that's all. All we ever wanted was a healthy daughter. But if we had to face a life-threatening illness, I'm glad it was this one. It was hard to learn to live with it. I went long stretches of my life not sleeping, not eating, and not caring about what happened to me. I had a daughter in the ICU and two other children at home to think about. They were my priority. I would think, *I'll sleep some other day. I'll eat some other time.* And when I finally learned to live with my daughter's illness, I finally was able to rest.

I remember the night we raced desperately from Salto to Montevideo with Jojo in critical condition in an ambulance. The skies had opened up and it was pouring rain. I had asked Dr. Canessa to meet us at the hospital. And when we arrived with the sirens blaring, I looked out the window through the torrential rain and saw him silhouetted against the night. I knew right then that we were going to be all right. He could have been waiting for us inside. Instead, he was outside as the wind and rain buffeted his umbrella so that his would be the first face Jojo would see when they opened the ambulance doors. That image of this man waiting for us in the stormy night told me that he would be there with us always, until the very end. "Look, Jojo!" I said to my daughter. "We're saved, my love. We're saved."

Chapter 41

There's a branch of medicine that focuses on extending an elderly person's life, but I worry about the roots, the beginning. Adults generally have more resources, and the elderly often have people to look after them. But there are few advocates for those who haven't yet been born. When a major problem arises in such cases, sometimes parents, other adults, family members, and doctors will say, "Let him go; you can have others." Or, as they told one mother shortly after her baby was born, "Resign yourself to the fact that there's not much else that can be done for your son."

Who's going to speak for those children, the ones who are told there's no way they can possibly survive? The decision isn't up to them, but to those outside the womb. Doctors tend to run from these cases, which are undoubtedly hazardous. But these children don't have a union or a voice or even a face to turn to. They're even worse off than we were in 1972. There's not even a photo of them, only a hazy ultrasound image.

When I came to be involved in politics circumstantially in 1994, I did it with one goal in mind: How could we rescue the 10 percent of children living in poverty, the forgotten ones, in the most egalitarian country in all of Latin America? How could we make it so that all those children had a chance to be rescued from their own personal mountaintops?

In 1994, I'd been involved in the cases of about 100,000 sick children. When I told my father my plan—to use the fame I'd garnered from my experience in the Andes for something beyond helping the patients that came to my practice at Hospital Italiano, multiplying those 100,000 patients to reach Uruguay's population of three million—he tried to dissuade me. My mother told me, straight-faced, she'd help me round up votes.

People tried to talk me out of it. They said it was a quixotic dream, that I had no party affiliation or support, that I lacked experience, that I lacked the necessary ambition for power—something considered crucial to win. Yes, I understood it seemed quixotic, and no, I didn't have a lust for power, but none of that had stopped me from helping rehabilitate drug users or saving children with hypoplastic left heart or trekking across the tops of the Andes mountains on foot. You didn't have to be power hungry, you just had to dedicate yourself to caring.

It was the first time in my life that I took a more systematic approach to solving the problems that stumbled into my life.

My country had history on its side. Uruguay has a very inclusive society, ever since the start of the twentieth century, when it established the world's first social democracy. It was called a "model country" and the "Switzerland of the Americas." When Albert Einstein visited Uruguay in 1925, three years after winning the Nobel Prize for physics, he wrote: "I found a genuine warmth in Uruguay like few others I've ever felt in my life. They have a love of country without delusions of grandeur. Uruguay is a small, happy country."

I had always felt that my "small, happy country" with none of those "delusions of grandeur" had laid the foundation for me personally, as well as for our group in the mountains, to be saved in 1972.

Of course, the first reaction when I announced I wanted to enter politics—forming the Blue Party and staying in long enough to en-sure it would continue after I left—was total disbelief (as it usually is whenever I've taken an unexpected path in my life).

Soon I realized that this would be a career for the long haul, and it would preclude me from helping in all the other ways I liked. I couldn't just jump in for a few years and jump out. It would be a life sentence. And it turned out that you did, in fact, have to have a lust for power—something I definitely didn't have.

I'm not sure what would have happened if I'd stuck with it, whether, like any politician, I would have celebrated a few successes after a long line of failures. Who knows if I would have had what it took to become president, something I'd wanted back then only out of a desire to help others on a wider scale? But I know this much: The heads of almost every political party in Uruguay asked me to join theirs—to come inside instead of trying to make it on my own, instead of sleeping outside in an improvised sleeping bag, so to speak. I declined all their invitations. It turned out I could be more useful in other arenas.

Measured by the total number of votes I received in 1994, my candidacy was an abject failure. But measured in other ways, it was a success, because, as the Brothers had tried to teach me in my youth, I finally learned something about my limits. The nineteen-year-old Roberto of the Andes had returned once again to teach me humility.

Chapter 42

Adriana, Tomas's Mother

We were married in the year 2000, with Lucia born in 2003 and Tomas in 2005. He lived for only five years, yet somehow he managed to become Tomas the Great. What did he do that was so great? He taught all of us, beginning with his parents, the true joy of life. It's not fair to say that he lived "only" five years. He lived five years, period.

He spent his first few months going from hospital to hospital, surgery to surgery. He barely rested. When he finally came home, he wasn't a normal boy with toys and diapers and a brightly colored nursery. Tomas was more like a wounded veteran. He had a breathing tube and an oxygen tank and was fed through a feeding tube. And yet, despite everything he was missing, the one thing he had in never-ending supply was sheer joy. Roberto Canessa always says that Tomas is a higher being. How else does one explain the way he radiated absolute vitality despite all the odds being against him? When Dr. Canessa speaks of Tomas, he uses the present tense.

Tomas was never afraid of the surgeries. And to him, Dr. Canessa wasn't just a doctor: He was his friend who looked at his heart—and was also his doctor. "Are we going to see my friend so he can look at my heart?" he would ask.

Tomas was born via C-section on August 16, 2005. He weighed 8 pounds, 14 ounces, and he was beautiful. His neonatologist Jorge Speyer delivered the baby and later listened to his heart. The three of us spent the night together in my recovery room. The next day, Dr. Speyer came by, listened to his heart again, and ordered an ultrasound of his heart. But the test didn't clearly show what was wrong with him. Dr. Speyer told me to take Tomas to Dr. Canessa at Hospital Italiano. I went with my mother-in-law, who had been taking care of me. We weren't really sure what was going on. When we met with Dr. Canessa, he had this look on his face, which I now understand meant that something serious was going on. He hadn't examined Tomas yet, but he was worried about what he had been told.

He carefully performed the ultrasound, but when we asked him what the matter was, he told us he'd better let our primary doctor speak to us first. Dr. Speyer had driven nearly one hundred miles from Colonia to Montevideo to be there. We went into the next room, that very special room in which Dr. Canessa has all of his private chats. Dr. Speyer told us that things didn't look good. Tomas had a heart condition called hypoplastic left heart. His aorta was constricted, and blood was flowing through something called the ductus, which could close at any moment, at which time the baby would die. "If you had gone home, the child would have died in a couple of days," he said. We had caught it in time, he said, but now there were a couple of serious possible outcomes. If we did nothing, Tomas would surely die. If we did operate, he could die during surgery—or he could live. They had been doing this surgery in Uruguay for only the last five years. It was so new, there were only two children alive who had survived the procedure. "Those are our only options," he told us. Had he been diagnosed before he'd been born, we would have had other options. As it was, our choices were limited.

It's hard to describe how I felt at that moment. The only thing that comes to mind is that it felt like a bomb had gone off inside me.

We could take him overseas, where they had more experience with this type of surgery, but it was riskier. At the time, I was a school receptionist (now I'm a nurse), and my husband was an accountant. We didn't have a lot of money or the resources to get it in such short order. The doctor told us, "Of course you would give your life for your child, but you have to keep in mind that you can't lose your home [which we didn't own yet] in the process. Where would you and Tomas live afterward?" Plus, Tomas had already been born, and a baby in his condition might not survive an airplane trip, which would have to be specially equipped. If he had been diagnosed while I was pregnant, I would have taken the risk. But there was no way to turn back time now. Plus, we knew Dr. Speyer and his team would do everything possible for him. So we decided to stay and do the surgery at the children's heart institute in Uruguay.

Thinking back on it is like an earthquake of emotions, dotted with flashes of memories that are etched into my mind. One of those moments was when Dr. Canessa came in after we'd made our decision. Dr. Canessa, my husband, Bernardo, and I stood over Tomas in his crib. I asked him, "What are his odds?" He stared at me. "I mean, what are the percentages?" I added. I wanted to hear someone tell us there was a chance, even if it was 10 percent, just to give us a concrete number to tie our hopes to. He looked into my eyes. "The hardest thing I ever had to do in my life was to hike across the Andes. And this condition, this is Tomas's Andes. It doesn't matter whether it's one percent or ninety percent. To Tomas, only one hundred percent matters." I never again spoke of life in percentages after that.

They got Tomas ready for surgery by giving him the drug prostaglandin and, on August 29, thirteen days after he'd been born, they operated.

The procedure lasted eight hours. They came out every now and then to tell us how the operation was progressing as they faced and overcame obstacles. After the operation, we saw Tomas as they took him into intensive care; he looked completely disfigured because of how babies bruise and swell during surgery. He soon stabilized; the surgery had been a success. What we kept hearing over and over throughout Tomas's surgeries was, "It's amazing how well he's coming along." Dr. Canessa told me, "He has a strong will to live."

In that first operation, they installed a tube to ensure that the blood from his heart reached his lungs.

After we went home, Tomas stopped eating—he wouldn't nurse—and we returned to the hospital. They performed another surgery to install a feeding tube that took nourishment directly to his stomach. Although the surgery was a success and he started gaining weight, soon he started having trouble with his breathing. He would choke and pass out. They brought him in for more tests and discovered that a nerve had been cut during his initial heart surgery that had paralyzed his vocal cords. They would have to do a tracheotomy. We had known this was one of the risks. It was hard to see our baby with that tube in his neck, but Dr. Canessa told us that now he'd have a deep, strong voice, like a wise older man. And, in effect, Tomas became a boy who was wise beyond his years.

Tomas came home on October 31, but he soon started having problems with the tube that took oxygen to his heart, and we had to return him to the hospital so that Dr. Canessa could help stabilize him. Then at just four months old, he had to have another surgery because the tube was obstructed. Plus, he was having trouble with the tracheotomy tube. We didn't return home until the end of December.

When a normal baby is discharged from the hospital, he just goes home. Tomas came home with an oxygen tank to make sure his blood oxygen level remained steady, a feeding pump and an NG tube, a tracheotomy, a pulse oximeter, and a nurse named Domingo that our insurance had paid for. Domingo told us a few days later that the doctors had felt Tomas should be able to be at home, and not in an ICU, if he were going to live only a few days more.

No sooner had we gotten home with all that equipment on December 31 at 10:00 a.m. than the nurse informed us that Tomas's pulse oxygen level was down to a frightful 55 percent. We had two options: race back to the hospital or give Tomas a chance to stabilize here, on his own.

And so, I decided to ask Tomas. I looked into his eyes and together . . . we decided to stay. That day, he earned the nickname "Tomas the Great." And I broke down into tears.

The second surgery in December had been a success, and it improved Tomas's quality of life. He was more stable and we no longer ran the risk of the tube blocking and having to rush him to the hospital. After a while, we even stopped keeping the oxygen tank in his room. It was a sign that there had been a change in our home. Tomas was transforming from a patient into a child. He grew and developed, and when he was just over a year old, he no longer needed a round-the-clock nurse. Instead, a nurse came when needed, as did Dr. Speyer, who had spent so much time in our home that I joked he now had privileges there.

On May 25, 2006, they took out the feeding tube and Tomas learned to eat. Later, they got him a phonation valve and he quickly learned to speak. Sometimes he would cover up the tracheotomy cannula as a joke. He was coming along so well . . .

You'd think that after a child had gone through everything Tomas had, he might be timid or rebellious. But the opposite was true: He was radiant and loving. We raised our children, Lucia and Tomas, to live life to the fullest. We weren't going to raise Tomas like a sick child. Sure, he had some "manufacturer's defects," as we liked to say, but we would raise him like a normal boy. And we did everything we could to make that the case.

We put Tomas in preschool at a year and eight months. People told us we were crazy to send him to school with a tracheotomy. Some of the other children would touch his tracheotomy tube out of curiosity. But we wanted Tomas to have a rich, normal life, because each day was a gift. He had already proven himself a survivor. We wanted Tomas to have the best life he could, not live trapped indoors watching the world outside go on without him. On October 6, after two years, the doctors removed the tracheotomy and he began breathing normally. The other children immediately asked him where his tube had gone, but it was quickly forgotten, and Tomas simply became another one of the kids.

The teachers were scared for Tomas. Sometimes they would call me frantically, saying, "Tomas's breathing sounds off!" When I rushed down to the school, he was always surprised to see me in the middle of the school day and would say, "Why did you come get me early, Mama? I was having fun with my friends." I would make up a reason for my visit, casually check him over, and send him back running to play with his friends. And he wouldn't stop running.

A few days after his tracheotomy tube was removed, we signed him up for hydrotherapy classes at Casa de Gardel, a rehabilitation center. And Tomas discovered what he loved most in the world was the water. He learned to swim in just a few days. I'd go to the pool and see this little boy, with his diminished lung capacity, dive to the bottom of the pool and wave at me, trying not to swallow water as he laughed under the surface. He was too delighted not to laugh.

He started school at three and quickly showed himself to be one of the smartest, hardest-working kids in his class. One day they asked him to sculpt an animal out of clay, and it was so marvelous, I still have it on my shelf in the most visible place in the house.

I feel as if the world lost out on a truly great person—or had him for much too short a time. I still speak to Tomas's last teacher, and she says she can't remember a time when she saw Tomas sad or down. He always managed to find the good in everything and everyone. Whenever an argument broke out between children in class, Tomas was always the one to smooth things over. He believed in a world where there was always a peaceable solution, where we could always find things to unite us instead of divide us.

A year before Tomas preceded us to heaven, we started the foundation *Corazoncitos*, Little Hearts (to which Dr. Canessa contributes his time), to help the families of children with congenital heart disease. We work on early detection so that each of these children can live as full a life as possible.

Tomas touched so many lives that in his final days, the hospital was overrun with people who stood watch over him, hoping against hope. The hospital administrators told us to ask people to stop coming because they couldn't handle the huge crowds. But how could we tell them not to come?

Nowadays, when I see someone stranded in the pouring rain when I drive by the bus stop, I offer them a ride. Sometimes one or two people. We figure out where they're headed and we make it happen. My husband says one day I might pick up the wrong stranger. But I don't think so. You can tell which people need help, on the inside or the outside.

We live in a small apartment, so every Saturday, we hop in our little green car and venture out for a picnic in the park as a family. When you'd ask Tomas what he wanted to be when he grew up, he would say, "I want to be like Papa and go on a picnic every Saturday in my little green car."

The greatest praise a child can give you is to say he wants to grow up to be just like you. Not because you want him to be like you, but because you know you did something that brought him joy. That's why I happily drive around in a little green car, like the one Tomas dreamed of, helping others reach their destinations.

Tomas's life was positive. He didn't suffer because he had to take several medications a day. Instead, his life was like a song—like a bird who perches itself on the highest branch on a sunny morning and will not stop chirping. Once I was pushing him along in the stroller at a fair, with his oxygen and his feeding tubes attached, and a woman stopped me and said, "Oh, poor baby." And I said, "No, quite the opposite. Look at his eyes. He's a happy baby, and not only is he living the richest life he can, he's enriching our lives as well."

His sister Lucia thought it completely normal for him to be hooked up to machines to help him breathe and eat. When anyone asked how her brother was doing, she would answer, "Oh, he's fine. He eats through his nose and breathes through his neck, but he's just fine." People were stunned. So were some doctors, who said I was the only mother they'd ever heard of who regularly took her son to the beach. But Dr. Speyer was happy about it, especially because he knew a fellow parent who had made a filter for Tomas's tracheotomy tube that kept out the sand.

The day Tomas died, I remember scores of people hugged me and whispered words of encouragement in my ear—but I don't remember a single word of what they said. Not a one. The ones I appreciated the most were the friends and family who sat outside the ICU that morning of December 7, 2010, and didn't say a word. My husband and I would emerge every so often from the room, shaken, and they simply hugged us and stayed with us in total silence before we went back in. I learned that silence can say something words can't in a situation like that: *We can't imagine what you're going through, but we can be here to hold your hand.*

Nowadays, after Tomas's passing, I look at the children around town differently, those whose age Tomas would be. I know it's not good for me to imagine what Tomas would be doing if he were in their place. I always remind myself that if Tomas could see me like this he would be very sad. And I'd hate that. I'd want him to know that Mama misses him so much, but that she keeps pushing ahead. He showed me better than anyone else that you can live a full, rich, jubilant life despite the tracheotomy, the feeding tube, the oxygen tank, the eight pills a day, and the pulse-oxygen meter that drove us half crazy. He showed us the simple truth: that he didn't die before his time; he lived five years longer than anyone ever expected him to.

Whenever I meet with Dr. Canessa or when we bump into

each other on the street, I always come home with the names and telephone numbers of people he thinks can help the foundation do its work. He has an entire network of people who are always at the ready. Whenever I see him, he says something like, "Adriana, I was thinking, and you know who you should talk to . . . ?" He gives me a name or a phone number or some kind of minuscule detail that later turns out to be important.

The last case he asked me to collaborate on was that of a baby girl named Clarita, who had been born with the two major blood vessels to her heart transposed and a ventricular septal defect. Roberto called me and said, "Adriana, Clarita passed away. Is there something you can do?" I tried calling the mom; no response. Called the dad, no response again. So I left a message saying I, too, was a mom whose child had had a heart condition and died at an early age, and that if there was anything I could do, I was at their service.

A week later, the dad called me. He said they'd heard my message and wanted to speak to someone who had gone through something similar—because they had no idea how they were supposed to go on living. So Bernardo and I went over to meet them. At first, we were all very formal, but it didn't take long for us to find common ground and begin sharing stories. And it was actually the moments of levity that brought us together. We thought back on the phrases we'd heard at our children's funerals, like, "Don't worry, you can have another one someday." As if we could just make another one like him. We couldn't help but laugh, because we knew people didn't mean any harm by it. They just couldn't understand what we were going through.

I sometimes tell Roberto, "What you need to do is somehow connect the fresh, green valleys of Los Maitenes with the cold wreckage of the fuselage fifty miles to the east in the Valley of Tears." That is, attempt to merge those two lives into one. He always listens without saying yes or no. He had to find a way to make his own peace, the way I needed to make mine. We each have our own way of uniting the two parts of our lives divided by tragedy. Whenever I tell Roberto about my meeting with other parents, how we commiserate and even laugh, he listens to me attentively, silently. But I can see the sparkle in his eyes: He has brought Los Maitenes to the Valley of Tears.

Once, I asked him why he does all this. "I have to give back for everything life has given me," he responded.

And so I, too, have become part of this goal, helping mothers bring in their babies for free heart screenings. I've dedicated myself to helping stitch together this quilted, nameless community so that we can grow stronger as we're tied to one another. One moment that I'll always remember was after one of Tomas's doctor's visits. Roberto had just performed an echo on Tomas and we were headed out through the waiting room when a mother came up to me and said, "I'm sorry to bother you, but is your name Adriana? And is that Tomas? I've heard so much about you, and I admire you both so much. I'm Isabelle, Agustin's mom."

Chapter 43

Tomas is the bravest person I've met in my sixty years of life. Usually, children are scared when doctors approach them to listen to their hearts; they drop their eyes or they flat-out cry. But Tomas would ask, "Are you going to check on my heart?" as if it were no big deal.

He had gone through so much in his short life that when he came for an appointment, I was the one who was intimidated, who felt small in front of this giant of a human being, a boy who radiated kindness and tenderness. Since he had a raspy voice, I told him he was a "man child"—a man in demeanor but with all the tenderness of a boy. "I'm like you," he would say. He was only three, four years old. But when he said, "I'm like you," I could see, then, that he was a child of the mountain. He was one of those beings who had known what it is to struggle to survive.

Chapter 44

Isabelle, Agustin's Mother

In December 2010, two and a half years after our surreal month in Boston at the time of Agustin's birth—and a month after his fourth surgery at the same hospital—we had an appointment at Hospital Italiano in Montevideo. I was a few weeks pregnant with my third child, my daughter, Valentina. Some people said, "Wow, you're brave!" But for us, having another child was just part of life. Life goes on. Agustin wasn't a baby anymore, but a playful toddler. The office was backed up because Dr. Canessa had had an emergency at the Centro Hospitalario Pereira Rossell (Children's Hospital). When I finally got in to see him, with Agustin at my side, I realized Roberto was in one of those moods where he was more interested in listening than talking. Agustin, all energetic two-and-a-half years of him, was all over his office, touching everything, running around, and Roberto was just as calm as could be. I was more worried he might break something than Roberto was.

"I want to show you something," Roberto said to me. He opened up his wallet and took out a handwritten note. He said, "You didn't keep your word to me, because Agustin isn't playing golf." I took the note in my hands and I was reminded of the deal we'd made.

Three years ago, in my twenty-third week of pregnancy, Roberto had confirmed my son's heart condition. After the shock and the tears, learning the minuscule odds of survival, he'd asked us if we wanted to go to a neonatal conference at the Sheraton Hotel in Montevideo to meet Dr. Jack Rychik of Children's Hospital of Philadelphia. One of the world's most renowned fetal cardiologists from one of the United States' most renowned hospitals in dealing with infant cardiology just happened to be in town. Rychik was hosting a session with Roberto. We didn't believe we could be so lucky to have such a knowledgeable doctor in Montevideo at that very moment, much less to be able to ask him to help our son.

When we arrived at the hotel and went up to the ballroom where the conference was taking place, we waited in a nearby sitting room with other parents who apparently had had the same idea. We weren't sure what was going on. The couples would go in one at a time until only we were left waiting. Then one of his assistants came out and told us Dr. Rychik could meet with us during his fifteen-minute break between sessions, and not in front of the entire panel, which is what the others had been doing, presenting their clinical cases as part of the conference. During the break, we were taken over to a side conference room, where a hospital bed and an ultrasound machine had been set up especially for us. From where we were, we could hear the murmur of the other doctors on break, drinking their coffee. They asked me to lie down on the hospital bed while Rychik and Roberto did the ultrasound, and I tried to understand with my basic English what the devil they were saying about my son. Rychik asked me about my life and my background with calm good-naturedness, as if he had known me my whole life. He watched the screen with such quiet confidence, as if it were something he saw every day, completely different from the awestruck expressions we had seen on other doctors' faces to that point.

Two men came over and told Roberto that the break was over and they should probably get back to the conference. But Dr. Canessa didn't pay much attention to them and remained with us for quite some time. After speaking to Dr. Rychik alone for a few minutes, Roberto told us it was just as he suspected. Agustin's condition was operable (I'll never forget his exact words) and he added, "Now the decision is up to you. You have a long and difficult path ahead, but it can be done." By the time we'd processed what he'd said, he had already gone back inside the conference. *Decision?*

It was only the second time we had met with Roberto, so I don't know why I did what I did. Maybe it was out of resentment toward all the doctors who had told us to really think about what we wanted to do, as if we should quit because there was no chance of saving Agustin. That's when I grabbed a notepad from the conference room and scribbled a note to Roberto. It read: "Thank you so much for giving us the chance to meet with Dr. Rychik. God has put a difficult test before us, yet I know we're in good hands. I want you to remember this name: Agustin Vazquez Chaquiriand, because he's going to be a famous golfer, one day." I still don't know why I wrote that. What did I know about golf? It's just that one of the doctors had told us that, at best, Agustin would never have an active life, would never be able to play sports because of his heart condition. But now I thought, *Why wouldn't he be able to grow up and have a full, active life and maybe even play a sport like golf?* I folded the note, found Roberto's wife, Lauri, and asked her to give it to him, because we hadn't had a chance to say goodbye.

And now three years later Roberto was handing me that note, which he had kept with him. After I finished reading it, my hands shook and my eyes filled with tears. He took the note and put it into Agustin's chart. So much had happened since that day. *Why in God's name had he held on to a note from a couple he'd just met? What goes through his mind when he deals with a case like ours?* And then, I thought about the Andes. To him, we were another plane crash, and he would do whatever it took to save the survivors.

Today, Agustin is the kind of boy who's bursting with joy and energy. He's small and skinny for his age, and he has a raspy voice after being on a respirator for so long. But he's so sure of himself that he has no idea how small he is. He's always ready to face the world. He's mischievous and inventive and extremely smart. He's the life of the party, a born negotiator, and he has no idea what it means not to get his way. He's even playing soccer, and he's good at it, not because he's the fastest or the strongest, but because he's agile and pays attention to details. He attends the same school that Roberto did, Stella Maris–Christian Brothers. The day the school's headmaster realized who Agustin was, he said, "He's a Canessa junior!"

Agustin and I traveled together so frequently, often just the two of us, to places like Boston for his surgeries and to regular doctor's visits, that we became close companions. Our trips to see Roberto every three months became more like a social visit and less like a doctor's appointment. Roberto is his friend, a friend he doesn't have to share with any of his siblings or the rest of his family. That's what makes it so special. That's his exclusive space, his universe. Maybe that's why it's the only place I'll let him use my cell phone to play games, so he can be entertained while they do his echo and I chat with the staff. That office has become his domain.

One day Agustin decided to draw a picture for Roberto's birthday. He drew us all: himself, his brother and sister, and his father and me, next to Roberto, who is wearing a cowboy hat, boots, and a wide leather belt and is next to his grandson Benicio, who had recently been born. Above the picture he wrote, "Our Family."

Thanks to those long talks with Roberto and watching how he leads his life, I learned a lot of things. I learned that being a hero means more than persevering through one huge, life-changing situation. Rather, it is being a hero in the day-to-day details. I learned that helping others and being passionate about what you do are not the exclusive domain of a person who survives a plane crash or a parent who endures a child's long illness. They are not reserved for a select few who are all of a sudden superior to you because they survived some enormous tragedy. What makes each one of us different are the blows we've suffered and overcome in life. The Roberto that became part of our family, as Agustin so aptly put it, the one we came to love and respect, did so because he is a noble, humble, and grateful spirit, and not because of his fame from the mountains. He's a person who inspires those who know him to be better people. And that's a miracle in itself.

Agustin never knew of Roberto's episode on the mountain. None of us ever mentioned it to him. In 2012, on the fortieth anniversary of the tragedy, the school paid tribute to the incident and told the students about the accident in the Andes. That night during dinner—the time we tell one another about our day—Agustin, who could hardly contain his news since coming home from school, let me know what he'd been saving up all day to tell me. "Mama, Mama! Did you know that forty years ago, some of the kids from our school were on an airplane that crashed into the mountain? And I bet you'll never guess who was inside . . ."

Chapter 45

Tino Canessa, Roberto's Son

To this day, I can see the mark my father's trek left on him. I spend a lot of time watching him, not just because he's my father, but because I've worked with him for eight years since I became part of the medical staff. First, I can see the effects the Andes had on him. Dad suffered so much in the fuselage and on his journey that he turned into a "life addict."

I'm always surprised that his commitment never wavers. He watches a heartbeat inside a mother's womb, and it's the doctor's job to counsel her on the best course of action. Despite all the complications, he always aims to save the baby. Even in the most complex cases, when most doctors would rather wash their hands of it.

When a child is born with a single ventricle, it's a tumultuous event that will affect the child and his family for at least the first twenty years of his life. But my dad never gives up. Even in the worst cases, I have never heard my dad doubt or hesitate, never heard him say, "Just let the child go." I have never heard him say, "There's not much else we can do," or "Maybe you should reconsider."

He always bets on life, against all odds, as he did on his trek. He came so close to death so many times that he truly values life much more than most people do.

It's no coincidence that he became a cardiologist, and moreover, a pediatric cardiologist, because he knows a child has much more life to live than an elderly person. When the parents of a child say, "Here comes Dr. Canessa," they know it means *Here comes hope.* Because my father is addicted to life.

Dad doesn't worry about society's conventions and he often forgets his patients' names. He knows who the patient is, all the details of their lives . . . not to mention that he can recall a clinical history down to the slightest detail, but he can never manage to remember someone's name. I always die of embarrassment, but neither he nor the patient seems to care. They're both on a different wavelength, where something like a name is irrelevant. They're focused on what's important.

Nothing about my father's life is conventional. The second floor of Hospital Italiano, where his office is, sometimes looks like a birthday party. There's always a commotion—laughing, crying, yelling. The only difference is that the room is full of children in wheelchairs. What surprises most people is what sounds like a barking dog. Soon people realize it's not a dog, but my dad, trying to distract a child to whom he's giving an ultrasound. He does a good job, too, throwing his voice without moving his lips, like a ventriloquist. The child is so surprised that a dog is in a doctor's office that he stops kicking and screaming. Dad turns back to the ultrasound, and when the child starts squirming again, back comes the barking dog. Dad points to the child's heart on the screen, pointing out how his heart sounds like a woof. The child is mesmerized. When the child starts to squirm again, the dog whimpers again to grab his attention. Dad tells him the dog's name is Bow Tie, because he has a white patch on his chest that looks like a tie. The next time the boy comes to the office, the first thing he does is ask Dad where Bow Tie is. "Right in there," he says, pointing at the room with the ultrasound.

The second floor of Hospital Italiano is like an entire universe itself, complete with planets and stars and moons. And from that cosmos comes the other mark the trek left on my dad: In the face of adversity, he always marches forward. My dad set out on that journey knowing he might die. But he always said he would rather die trying. In the face of fear, he doubles down on courage. And he doesn't worry about anything else. It's like a formula for life that he learned at nineteen.

The other imprint the mountain left on him was his desire for harmony. He existed amid chaos for so long that he needed order in his life. The same thing happens to me: I have this compulsion for trying to make sure everything is in its place. If I think about it, it's what my dad does all the time. I do it physically, but he does it figuratively, with his patients.

He knows how to create a calming environment for his patients. He can be rough in a lot of ways, but when it comes to weaving together a peaceful atmosphere, he does it with the skill of a surgeon.

On the balance of it, his journey has served him positively. After suffering in the Andes, some people would have been perpetually worried about all the unexpected horrors life could have in store. But for my dad, it was the opposite. I don't know how he did it, but he convinced himself that the positive always outweighs the negative. He's the rarest example of the worst-case scenario. But he uses that in his favor, to expand the circle of virtue to encompass others. He abhors resignation. He won't tempt fate, but he doesn't fear it either.

He suffered so much. I wonder, *Why didn't he perish? What was the reason for him having to suffer the way he did?* And I think he has answered that question: He invites you to take a chance with him. He invites you to believe, to forget the odds, to imagine a world filled with people who should not have survived—and, of course, he's the prime example.

Chapter 46

Marta, Tiago's Mother

We are a very humble family. On November 18, 2001, our son Tiago was born. He left the hospital doing just fine, but five days later, we had to admit him because there was a problem with his heart. Later they discovered he was born with just one kidney. With each passing day, he got worse. No one communicated anything to me, but I could tell he was getting worse. They were paying attention to his kidney instead of his heart, which didn't make sense to me, even though I don't know anything about medicine, because it was his heart that was making Tiago regress. Then, on December 4 at 6:00 p.m., the doctors called his father and me into a conference room and told us, "You should resign yourself to the fact that there's nothing more that can be done for your son. It's hopeless." It was the worst day of my life. It was rock bottom. I asked my husband to give me a few minutes alone. Meanwhile, I could hardly be with my son, who was in the ICU. Just a few minutes every three hours or so. I headed for the chapel to pray, and I asked God to help my son. Because it felt as if there was no help for me in the realm of medicine.

I didn't leave the chapel until 11:50 that night, completely heartbroken. I staggered into the small waiting room set aside for parents whose children were in the ICU. I was all alone. And then I heard footsteps and the ICU page Dr. Roberto Canessa. I can still hear it, and it makes me as emotional as I got that day.

My heart felt as if it was going to pound out of my chest because I realized in a flash that this was going to be my son's salvation—the help I'd just asked God for in the chapel. I wondered, *Would he even have time for me?* I now know that he is one of the most approachable and caring men I've ever met. But back then, Roberto Canessa seemed unreachable: the legend of the Andes. Plus, my husband, Jacinto, who works as a baggage handler at the airport, said he had seen Dr. Canessa often and he always seemed in a rush, like a man on a mission, with important things to do. But none of that stopped me that night of December 4.

I stood in the hallway, blocking the exit. Twenty-seven minutes later, Dr. Canessa emerged with two other doctors who were talking with him. With my heart in my throat, I kept pace with him so I wouldn't delay him.

"Doctor, could you give me a minute of your valuable time?" I said, just barely containing my emotions. The phrase seemed to strike a nerve in him. He couldn't believe that I would beg him for only a minute of his "valuable" time.

"Of course, I can give you a minute. I can give you all the time you need," he responded.

"Can you save my son?" I asked.

"Is your son Tiago?"

"Yes. Is there anything you can do to save him?"

"Of course there is. Why wouldn't there be?" he responded, surprised.

"Because the other doctors told me it's hopeless, that there's nothing more to be done for him, that my son is going to die . . ."

"Hold on a minute," he said without hesitation.

He turned around and went back into the ICU. Through the glass, I could see him looking at Tiago's chart. He made a phone call—and then several more phone calls—and he was talking on the phone for a long time with different people. He came back out and took my hands, which were holding a pair of small medals of Saint Pio of Pietrelcina, to whom I had also been praying.

"I want you to try to relax. You should have some news tomorrow. If you don't hear anything, I want you to come find me at the Institute for Infant Cardiology at Hospital Italiano. I'll be there." Touching one of the medals, he added, "And never lose faith."

The next day, I got a call from the hospital. Three doctors—a nephrologist, a cardiologist, and a pediatric specialist—called to tell me that they were planning to operate on Tiago that afternoon. I asked where the operation was going to take place, and they said at some other hospital. I said, "No, I want him to have the surgery at the Institute for Infant Cardiology, where Dr. Canessa's team is." When one of the doctors asked why, I responded, "It's a matter of faith," because I knew that God and Saint Pio had interceded to put Dr. Canessa in my path when no one else in the world was there to help my dying son.

That day, on December 5 at 8:00 p.m., Tiago underwent surgery at the Institute for Infant Cardiology. And thank God, he is here with us today. All of his kidney tests have come back normal. He's now twelve years old and weighs 110 pounds.

Tiago never again had to step into a hospital, aside from the routine tests he undergoes with Dr. Canessa.

"You know, you were right about what was wrong with your son," he once told me. "You didn't use the medical terms, but you knew it."

Tiago had a persistent ductus, which is how a baby gets oxygenated blood from his mother in the womb. It usually closes by the time the child is born, but when it doesn't, as in Tiago's case, the baby has pulmonary edema. Tiago had received too many diuretics to try to compensate, and instead he had become dehydrated. What he'd needed was surgery to close the ductus. When he was born, he didn't nurse, because he didn't have the strength to suckle. He'd sip a little bit and fall asleep and he had to be fed through a tube.

One day, Tiago was at Hospital Italiano for an echo. "Before going to sleep every night, I pray," I told Dr. Canessa. "I pray and I thank God for putting you in my path on that night in December, at that last possible moment. Every day, I pray for God to bless your family—and to bless you."

When Tiago turned two, Dr. Canessa and his wife came to his birthday party at our house.

"Laura, what a pleasure it is to have you here for Tiago's birthday in our humble home. Honestly, I didn't think you two would come," I said.

Laura seemed surprised. "Why wouldn't we?"

"Well, it's such a long way, down a nameless dirt road . . ."

"Did you forget it was a shepherd who has a much more humble home than yours who saved Roberto's life? Where do you think he feels most at home?"

I didn't say this to them, but it was nonetheless true: I had cooked with him in mind, because I had a feeling he would come.

Years passed. In 2010, my niece had a baby girl, but when she was less than a year old, they rushed her to the hospital in critical condition. I ran to her bedside with my Saint Pio medals. "I brought Saint Pio so you could ask him to protect her," I told my niece.

But the baby only got worse. I had gone home at night and was preparing a *mate* to try to relax when I got a desperate call from my niece. "Oh, Marta, the doctors say it's hopeless for Delfina. . . . But you know who I'm looking at, at this very moment? Dr. Canessa!" It was happening all over again. It was a different hospital, a different illness, but the same situation.

"Wait, where exactly is Dr. Canessa?" I asked.

"He's right here, walking right by me."

"Go after him! Walk with him so you don't slow him down and hand him the phone!"

She did just that, chasing after him and handing him the phone with me on the other end.

"Dr. Canessa, it's Marta, Tiago's mom," I said.

"Oh, and how is Tiago?" he asked calmly.

"Oh, he's fine, fine. But I'm also Delfina's aunt, and they say her case is hopeless. Is there anything you can do for her? My niece who just handed you the phone is the baby's mother."

"Let me speak to her. We'll talk later," he said.

He saw the baby, called me back, and said, "I want you to relax. There's nothing wrong with her heart. They consulted me because she was retaining too much fluid, but the problem is with her lungs. It's serious, but it's not hopeless. Call me in two days; I'm going back to look after her." I called back two days later and he told me Delfina was about to go home from the hospital. She walked at a year old and, today, at age three, talks like a parrot.

I think Dr. Canessa is the way he is because of all he lived through, that horrible life lesson. But that doesn't explain how his wife and children, Hilario, Lala, and Tino are just the same, caring and humble. I think he was like that to begin with, but the Andes only intensified his personality.

I consider him a good friend. I call him for his birthday on January 17, on Christmas Eve, and on New Year's Eve. I call him on the anniversary of his father's death, July 19, and his mother's on August 14, and on national cardiologists' day.

This year, when I called to congratulate him on his anniversary, he was on the roof. I heard loud banging. "What's going on over there? Are you OK?" "I'm hammering some shingles in place on a leaky roof," he said.

Dr. Canessa's spirit is always in my home, because when I look at my son, I can never forget what he did for us. One of the pictures I have prominently displayed in my home is of Tiago's first birthday. He was still too little to reach over and blow out his candle. So Dr. Canessa pulled it out of the cake and brought it close to Tiago's lips. The picture captures that moment and signifies what he's meant to our family: Dr. Canessa is reaching out his arm and bringing light to our son.

Chapter 47

In May of 2007, the Royal College of Surgeons in England organized an event titled "Risky Business" and invited accident experts and people with dangerous jobs to talk about their experiences. There was a man who worked on the rescue of the submarine *Kursk*. A mountain climber who rescued two people on Everest. A firefighter who saved several people from a burning building. A rescuer who saved a group of oil well drillers on a rig in the Pacific Ocean. A neurosurgeon who attends to Formula One drivers. A renowned emergency room doctor. The pediatric cardiologist Allan Goldman (one of the organizers). An astronaut. And me.

When I heard the astronaut speak, I felt as if we had had kindred experiences. He said that when he left earth's atmosphere and looked back on the planet as a blue marble in the vast black vacuum of space, he found it almost impossible to return to a conventional life back on the ground. Mostly, he was baffled by the provincial battle lines arbitrarily drawn between different countries and cultures—in much the same way that I couldn't understand why children separated by geography were denied the same level of medical care.

We spent a long time talking before and after the event. He spoke like a man who had traveled far—too far—out in the expanse of space, while I acted like a man who had plumbed far too deeply the depths of human suffering. He had seen the world from on high, and I from far below.

Our travels outside our known worlds had left a mark that ran deep within us.

Brain damage, particularly to the substantia nigra, causes a specific kind of memory loss. A person can look at an object, recognize it as something familiar, but have no idea what it is for. Damage to the soul, however, causes a completely different kind of psychological injury.

The psychologists and psychiatrists who cared for us after the accident admitted we were something entirely new to them. They'd never had a single patient with our particular kind of trauma. They didn't even know how to classify us.

I feel such empathy when I cross paths with someone who has survived an unusual trauma, because I know what they're dealing with. It's not physical or even psychological damage. It's an injury to the soul. And worse, usually there's no one to blame, no one who cocked a gun and pulled a trigger.

There were moments on the mountain that left indelible marks, memories that left an imprint, fingerprint swirls on my psyche. There's the loneliness, the feeling of abandonment. That desperate feeling of isolation—and the desire to escape it—is something that's deeply imprinted on me.

In the Valley of Tears, there was nothing but rocks and snow, and our fuselage buried within it. I spent too many desperate days searching for any signs of life: lichens on rocks, forgotten food in our luggage, flies, mountain birds, traces of airplanes coming to our rescue, even life in the form of electrical wires we might use to repair the radio and communicate with life beyond the mountain. Our hike off the mountain was the ultimate form of that search.

But the mountain also imprinted me with compassion. Why had we been left alone for so long? Now, I think, *What can I do to make sure those victims of tragedies I meet along the way are not left alone, abandoned, on their own paths?*

I also have this deep desire to know the person beyond the "character." I'm aware now that each person wears a mask, and his true self is hiding behind that mask, crouching, waiting. In my time on that mountain, I found there were different people behind my friends' masks, and that I, too, wore a mask. Our true selves were revealed. Sometimes that true self is buried deep within the psyche, and I feel it's my job to find it. In each one of us on the mountain, those who perished and those of us who survived, was the glowing light of goodness. A generous, honest, compassionate, and just being. A courageous soul.

Another vestige of my struggle was a heightened instinct to fight until the end. I am convinced that we were saved in the nick of time, that we would not have lasted another day. Similarly, in the crash, we were saved by a hairbreadth because the plane slid down the mountain. Just as my surviving the avalanche was by a matter of seconds. And the day we began our trek, December 12, we found the stone outcropping for the night at the last moment; and nine days later, Nando still had a sliver of energy left, but I could not take another step.

I now recognize in myself a deep desire to build a personal space, to make a home. On the mountain, in that endless time, our home was fashioned out of a crumpled fuselage, and later, in an improvised sleeping bag to protect us against the life-threatening elements. That lack of a home left a deep and lasting mark, as did that oasis of a mountain ranch in Los Maitenes, which will always feel like paradise to me. That feeling of home, of safety, resonates inside of me. And when I see people who are homeless, I instantly feel their anxiety—and my desire to help them reach a sanctuary of their own immediately kicks in.

An accident is just that. Something unforeseeable. I never set out looking to get into people's business, it's just that when I come across someone with a problem, I feel compelled to help. No, I haven't started a foundation to help drug addicts or starving children. I would never compare myself to the great philanthropists; I'm just an ordinary man.

I've realized this about myself, though: I just can't simply ignore it when a problem falls into my path. I've come across children, homeless people, and others with all kinds of problems, and I've always tried to help—albeit with mixed results. Similarly, when a person has come to me asking for help, that person stumbles into the unforeseeable, too. What I see is not an elderly homeless person, or an invalid, or a drug addict, or a baby with hypoplastic left heart. Instead, that person desperate for help . . . is me. It's me at nineteen, standing at the edge of the abyss on the day I couldn't survive even one more night in the cold, imploring someone to help me reach Los Maitenes—to reach salvation. If I turn my back—if I don't offer a plate of food, or a coat, whatever—I'm denying myself the bread that Sergio Catalan flung over the San Jose River when we were at the breaking point, or the bowl of beans that the shepherds Armando Serda and Enrique Gonzalez offered me from their own table. It's not that I'm betraying someone else, it's that I'm betraying myself.

When a mother comes to my office with the tired expression of anguish in her eyes begging me to help her child, I cannot turn her down. When someone comes to me for help, as an elderly woman did in 2010 and told me that I was the only hope to help her drug-addicted grandson, I'm not just another resource: I'm the shepherd from the mountains. We are inexorably committed to one other from that moment on.

And since you may wonder, I can confess that, yes, it sometimes causes collateral damage to my family. In a way, my loved ones are unintended hostages to my trauma in the Andes. Because they have food on the table and a roof over their heads, they are saved, and so I feel as if I must turn my attention to that lonely wanderer who has waved to me from the other side of the San Jose River.

Back on the mountain, when one of us was ready to give up and lose hope, it was the others' job to do everything possible to keep them moving forward. We would leave no one behind. We would try to heal their bodies and their minds, sate their hunger and pain in any way possible, and above all, give them hope.

I've put up all kinds of people, for all kinds of reasons, in my own home. I can't turn away anyone who stumbles upon me and needs help. I have known all too well what it means to have nothing—no food, no clothes, no shelter, not even a proper place to die.

Why do I open my home or my family's forty-acre ranch in the Pan de Azucar foothills in Lavalleja (a ranch I call El Suspiro or "The Sigh") to strangers who need my help? It's not out of charity or generosity or even kindness. It's out of compassion, out of the empathy of being able to put myself in their shoes. It's knowing that one can go from joy to tragedy in the blink of an eye.

When we were freezing to death on the mountain, oh, how we fantasized about being rescued. Oh, how we dreamed of a hot meal in place of frozen human flesh. . . . How can I not help people? Now that I'm not surrounded by snow and cadavers and thin mountain air but rather a comfortable home and a wide-open pasture with fruit trees and a tin-roof house, which is usually vacant?

Sometimes I dream I'm back in the Andes. I dream someone throws me a rope I can use to climb out of that quagmire. Now I'm on the other side of the cliff, and I can be the one to give that nineteen-year-old kid a helping hand. That kid in need has many names: Alvaro, Tomas, Agustin, Santiago, Maria del Rosario, Jojo, Tiago. . . . I find I can relate closely to some aspect of all their tales.

Alvaro has been living and working out of my home for ten years now. When he stumbled onto my path, he was jobless, and I, in turn, had a lot of work to give him. He is pure energy. Tireless. He's so bright, he can fix anything. The second I met him I thought, *God, could we have used someone like him in the Andes!* Maybe he would have fixed the radio when we found it in the tail section. I can't imagine someone who could have been handier in the Andes for improvising hammocks, partitions, crutches, and sleds, and fixing a broken radio to connect with the outside world.

The one thing I know is that when he makes some forgotten, broken-down machine whir to life again, Alvaro and I share a look of pride that we've brought something back from the grave. From broken pieces, he has made something useful again. What was once forgotten metal becomes, say, a machine, an automobile that can be used to change someone's life—the way a group of doomed people on a mountaintop were saved by helicopters.

Every now and then on weekends, Alvaro will invite some city children from a poor neighborhood on an unusual trip. Together, they visit El Suspiro in the countryside, where several people with dependency issues are recovering at my ranch under my guidance. I usually join them. It's a sight, those ten or twelve children who have never seen the country or farm animals, sitting side by side with adults. Alvaro is their host, and the patients cook the meals and entertain the kids—applying a skill that becomes a life lesson: giving without expecting anything in return. I like to slip away from the group and watch them from a distance, sitting under the shady canopy of an Ombu tree.

Sometimes they whisper; sometimes they laugh out loud. It's a motley group and an unexpected scene, each person carrying his own heavy burden: poverty-stricken children from humble homes and addicts trying to find the road to redemption. When I watch them, I can't help but feel that this diverse group, each of them looking for a second chance, is playing out life in the fuselage, the place that sowed the seeds of my second life.

Chapter 48

Laura, Santiago and Nicolas's Mother

When I was six weeks pregnant, I was told I was having twins. I was going to be a mother for the first time at age thirty-two, and it was going to be two boys. At my five-month ultrasound, they said there was some issue with one of the twins, but they couldn't say exactly what it was. At thirty-one weeks, on February 26, 2013, a day before I was supposed to have an ultrasound that would tell us more about the anomaly, my water broke. I had to have a C-section. They performed the ultrasound while the boys—whom we named Santiago and Nicolas—were still in the incubator. They told my husband and me that Santiago had such a complex heart disorder that there had never been anything like it. They explained to us that all heart conditions were named for the person who discovered it, diagnosed it, or tried to treat or cure it. But Santiago's heart condition was so incomprehensible that it didn't have a name, because it had never been seen before. What was worse, no doctor could even imagine it was possible for someone with Santiago's condition to live. They were stunned that he was alive at all, although they assured us he would not live very long. I was shocked. I asked them whether they meant days or weeks or months. "Hours," they said. "Maybe minutes." As complicated as his case was, it was made all the more difficult by the fact that he had been born prematurely. My husband and I should prepare ourselves for the end, they told us. That was in February. As I write, it's September, and Santiago is still with us. He refuses to give up: He apparently doesn't want to leave me, because he keeps breathing and growing.

The night they told us Santiago would not live until the next morning, my husband and I wept all our tears—tears of joy, of doubt, of a sense of cosmic injustice. But we made a pact that night: We would never cry in front of the baby because we were ashamed at the thought of us crying while he was fighting for his life. If the end came, there would be plenty of time to cry later.

When Santiago didn't die, the doctors adjusted their diagnosis but still stressed that he had the most complicated heart condition that had ever been seen. The risk of death was still imminent, though now, instead of minutes and hours to live, they gave him days.

The one constant with all the doctors who came to see Santiago—that is, until I met Dr. Canessa—was their utter bewilderment. They'd come into the room, and no matter how hard they tried, they couldn't mask their surprise at the fact that he was still alive. The most amazing thing, they said, was that he was alive without any kind of life support. They had no idea what to do to treat this new condition.

Seeing my tribulation as I paced the halls of the ICU where my son was a patient, a mother told me I should go see Dr. Roberto Canessa. "This is a case for him," she said without any hesitation. When we saw Roberto, he analyzed the information carefully. "It's definitely a complicated heart condition, but it's not something that doesn't have a name or that we've never seen before," he said finally. "In fact, it has three doctors' names. It's such an intricate case, because we're seeing anomalies that are usually present in three different kinds of heart conditions. But here, we have all three in one little body." First of all, the veins that bring oxygenated blood from the lungs were connected to the heart in the wrong place, the right atrium. Plus, instead of having two valves leading into the heart, Santiago had only one. And he had two exit valves from the right ventricle. Finally, the passage between the ventricles was too small, as was the pulmonary artery, slowing the flow of blood from the heart to the lungs. But the interesting part, as Dr. Canessa explained (I noted he didn't say "amazing" or "terrifying," but just simply "interesting") was that this confluence of three conditions made it so the blood reached the brain, the liver, and all the other organs without any of them experiencing a great lack of oxygen or lowered blood pressure. From the outside, it wasn't evident that such babies had a complex heart disease. "All heart conditions are different, and this is just another one of them," he told us. "There are surgeries available to us. You don't have to lose hope."

The first thing that struck us about Roberto was his simplicity. It's the same trait that all of his doctor friends who are helping us with Santiago's case exhibit. Roberto organized a council of doctors to look at Santiago's case at Pereira Rossell Hospital in Montevideo, and he later took his case to an international cardiology conference in Minneapolis in June of 2013.

Meeting Roberto made my heart open up, and I like to think that the same thing happened to Santiago. I had never met a person who cared so much and showed so much dedication toward children. I see how he treats the other children, and yet when he's with us, he treats Santiago as if he's his only patient. I'm sure the families he sees before and after us feel the same way.

The future is a mystery to us. But right now, we're just waiting for Santiago to gain weight so he's big enough for surgery. Because he definitely will have to have surgery. The bigger he gets, the better his chances will be to come through that first surgery.

In such a short time, from February to September, I've learned more than I have in my entire life. I've learned that each child has a special strength and a particular light inside, as Roberto likes to say, that makes him different from every other child—and even different from his parents. And while a lot depends on Santiago, on his will to live, I know that a lot depends on those of us who are here to help him. I can feel it in the way he hugs my arms when I pick him up, as if he never wants me to let him go.

Meanwhile, Santiago has something other babies with heart conditions don't often have: a twin. Nicolas is a mirror for Santiago. Santiago spends hours staring at his brother, trying to talk to him, watching his every movement as if he wants to copy it. And you can tell that it brings him so much joy, because they go on and on in their shared baby language, laughing.

I've learned something about myself, too. That I am a desperate mother who cannot act on her desperation. At first, I couldn't understand why life would give us these two little souls just to rob us of one. But when I watch the way Santiago reacts to Nicolas, I think I understand why life has placed me at this crossroads: Santiago couldn't have done it alone, but he may just survive with his brother's help.

Since I've been coming to see Roberto at his office in Hospital Italiano, I've learned to hope. My husband says it's been a light in the darkness. I see things I never saw before, have feelings I didn't know existed. And my bond with my son grows stronger every minute. Sometimes, I completely forget about his heart condition.

Roberto says he carried that same uncertainty and hope as he crossed the Andes. When he came to the end of his trek, there were twin peaks awaiting him on the horizon.

Just as he did during his odyssey, we have to take it one step at a time with Santiago. I can't allow myself to think of the incredible distance. I can't think five years into the future. Or one year. Instead, I have to take it one month at a time, one week at a time, one day at a time, because children have a way of surprising you by developing in ways you never expect. Every child blazes his own trail.

I remember asking Roberto once what he thought about the prospects for our situation. Without hesitating, he told us that we were walking along a dangerous gorge, tiptoeing along a narrow ledge. But if we managed not to look down and to keep moving forward, not to lose our balance and to concentrate on the road ahead, we might just make it through. We have to take it slowly, step by step. And it feels just that way, as if the five of us, Santiago, Nicolas, my husband, my mother, and I, are tiptoeing along the edge of a canyon. (I had to leave my job to care for Santiago, and my husband, who has been with me every step of the way, has to work twice as hard.) The path is so narrow that we can only walk single file, one at a time. And yet, we are all in this together.

Some children with heart conditions will not have a good outcome. But others remain on track. Santiago may never be fully healed, but as long as we have room to keep moving forward, we will walk bravely, hopefully.

And I know it's important for me, too, to keep on track, to keep moving forward, because I don't have just one life depending on me; I have two. If Santiago were to leave us, I cannot stop to rest. I have to keep going. I don't have the luxury of quitting. Roberto told me that although it was just the two of them hiking across the mountains, they were making the trek for the entire group—both the living and the dead. If Santiago doesn't make it, I have to go on for Nicolas's sake. And he will carry on for both of them.

Chapter 49

Sometimes I feel as though our vicissitudes in the Andes mirrored those of early mankind. We seemed at times like the first humans on earth, with no one before us, no ancestors or history. So we had to improvise, to make our own way, to invent.

Unmoored from any link, subject to the elements, humans seek to organize and to protect one another in order to survive. After overcoming our anxiety, it was time to get to work. We had to find a way around all the dangers surrounding us in that wilderness—the freezing cold, the lack of food, the snowstorms and avalanches—while looking after our young and healing the wounded. Then, once all hope seemed lost, it was time to move on to new lands, like nomads. We became explorers, learning, bit by bit, what other dangers the landscape had in store for us—because there were always dangers, and we always tried to vanquish them. We could never give up—or it would mean the extinction of our species.

I think of my life in the same way. My patients are different now. They're not named Maria del Rosario, Jojo, Tiago, Tomas, or Agustin. Now they have names like Pily, Santiago, and Angeles, the next generation whose cases keep me up at night and whose ultrasounds I use to consult with doctors all over the world, because I believe that all children should have access to the best medical care possible.

In 1998, I collaborated with the team, headed by professor Jose Nozar and Dr. Beatriz Ceruti, that performed the first heart transplant in a newborn at Hospital Italiano in Montevideo, with the help, via Canada, of Dr. Lori Smallhorn, the wife of one of the pioneers of echocardiology, Dr. Jeff Smallhorn. Then came the second transplant, and the third, and so on, until the procedure became routine.

Organ transplants, to me, are intimately connected to our experience on the mountain, to the point that the survivors created the *Fundacion Viven* (The Alive Foundation), whose goal is to raise awareness of the benefits of organ donation. The very first transplants were taking place around the time I was in the Andes. Anytime I can, even if it's serving in a minor role, I try to help out with transplants. Regardless of the time of day or night, when I hear there's been an accident and there's a potential donor, I hop in the car with my portable echo and head to the hospital where the donor is to scan the heart and see if it can continue beating within a new body. In a way, I'm continuing to do what I learned in the Andes: trying to ensure that a heart that has stopped beating can continue on in some form. It will never be the same; you can't just exchange one life for another. But as we used to say on the mountain, it would be a generous death.

It's a recurring theme. A few years ago, Dr. Jeffrey Jacobs, a renowned infant cardiac surgeon from All Children's Hospital in St. Petersburg, Florida, invited me to the third joint conference of the U.S. Congenital Heart Surgeons Association and the European Congenital Heart Surgeons Association at the Drake Hotel in Chicago. Two other physicians were set to speak along with me. One was Dr. Antonella Rastelli, whose father, Giancarlo Rastelli, classified the atrioventricular canal defect, which is one of the most common heart conditions in children with Down syndrome. The other was Dr. Leonard Bailey, who was the first to successfully transplant a monkey's heart into a newborn human baby. I spoke about the medicine I practiced in the mountains.

Sometimes I think I understand children with heart conditions because I know how they feel. Half of all heart diseases are cyanotic, which means that they aren't getting enough oxygen in their blood. The other half have too much blood in their lungs, which makes it hard for them to breathe. We on the mountain had both problems: pulmonary edemas and low levels of oxygen in our blood.

I made that same argument at an Orlando, Florida, symposium hosted by the Children's Hospital of Philadelphia, to which Drs. Gil Wernovsky and Meryl Cohen had invited me. To track the progress of patients who have received a heart transplant, you have to measure the force with which the heart contracts and how that strength varies over time. You can't compare hearts in the same body in which they were born to those that have been transplanted into other bodies. Nature will always show there's a difference. You can't compare isolated pictures, but rather still frames of the same film.

When it comes to health, it doesn't matter where you've come from or where you're headed, but rather where you are at the moment. Just as in the Andes, I set short-term goals and meet them. I don't think about the end. When you come across a child with a heart condition, when nothing more can be done, people will say his prospects are very bad compared to a healthy or "normal" child. The mother might ask me, "What do I do?" And I tell her, "Take him to the pool and let him swim around and enjoy life, because he will know his limits; this *is* normal to him." You can always grow and develop; the rest is just a mirage. You shouldn't compare yourself to anyone else. You have to evaluate the transplant patient based on where he is at the moment, not compared to where he *might* have been had he never needed a transplant. Rather, set short-term goals and achieve them. Some people think these members of society are somehow diminished when, in fact, they are the ones who truly show us how to live. They may have only half a heart, but they have twice the vitality and zeal for life.

Chapter 50

Maria del Rosario's Parents

Azucena, Her Mother

In a few days, Maria del Rosario will turn nine. She's in her second year at her new school, and she's getting good grades. She plays sports—field hockey, gymnastics, swimming, dance—and she wrestles, too: every time she disagrees with her two brothers.

Maria del Rosario lives a totally normal life, and that's exactly what we wanted for her. But we can't deny that our lives have been different since the day she was born. Maria del Rosario has a mental toughness that's hard to describe. She knows the difference between what's important and what's irrelevant better than most adults, which sometimes makes it hard for her to follow certain routine rules. Yet none of this makes her any less clever and mischievous a child.

Sometimes I catch myself thinking about the past. Recently, I put together all the photos and paperwork I had shoved into a box in a scrapbook detailing the six operations she had in the first eighteen months of her life. Looking back, it sparks all kinds of memories. What I was feeling during the hours-long surgeries. The sense that I, myself, was floating between life and death because my daughter, essentially, was standing at the threshold. It was a bizarre feeling. As if there was barely any distance between life and death, that the line between them was blurrier than I'd ever imagined.

There are two ways to look at her future. One is to be completely rational about it, looking at statistics to dictate what kind of life we can expect for her with this kind of heart condition, and that makes it almost impossible to imagine. Looking at the statistics alone, every surgery seemed doomed to failure. But there's another way to look at it, a purely emotional view not based on statistics or similar case studies. It's based entirely on observing my daughter approach her life. And when I do that, this strange sense of peace washes over me, an intense serenity, and I realize we've done our part for her. Maybe it's because she's so strong, so preternaturally wise. In her short but full life, she already has made a long journey. Her father, Juan, and I can do only so much. Parents won't be around forever, but we've given her the tools. I get this sense that she knows a lot more than she lets on.

There's an anecdote that explains just how I feel. I'm the kind of person who loves to control the variables, and that's what I do in my job as an economist. When we returned from Boston, I put together a checklist of the countless medications Maria del Rosario would have to take and when, and I made three copies, one for each of my sisters and my mother. "This is what you have to give Maria del Rosario in case something happens to me," I told them. It sounded absurd, because I was young and healthy, but I felt the information regarding Maria del Rosario's care was too important to rest with me alone. Now, nine years later, they all still have that checklist, but the one person who knows exactly what to do without looking at it is Maria del Rosario herself.

She's keenly aware of what's going on with her. She understands what was wrong with her, what she went through to fix it, and what she needs to do to stay healthy. And that makes me believe she's ready to take on her life. She's going to be a success. And she's going to be happy—because she already is.

Yesterday I asked her if she wanted to be part of this book about Roberto, and she answered, "How could I not be, especially after he saved my life . . . ? It was hard, but I survived."

Juan, Her Father

On one of the many days when Maria del Rosario faced yet another complication, I sought out Roberto Canessa with what felt like a void in my own heart. "Remember, Juan," he told me, "not too long ago, we were talking about a fetus inside of a womb. And now, we have Maria del Rosario."

As she grows and changes, so do the questions surrounding her future—questions we have to answer. That's why we take her to a psychologist to help her with these issues. Maria del Rosario says, "I like going because I can express my emotions in front of her."

When I think back on these last nine years, I think a lot about her brothers. Juan Francisco was only six and Jose Maria only four when we had to take her to Boston. They were so young to be away from their mother for six months. Meanwhile, doctors and ambulances and oxygen tanks and machines were always in and out of the house. There were people coming and going who wanted to help, who left everything from prayer cards to envelopes filled with cash. I often look at my children for traces of damage from all this, but I can't say that I've found any.

About two years ago, when Jose Maria was eleven, we were sitting on the couch and he had his biology notebook with him. He started asking me questions about the heart, which is what he was studying in school. So I said, "Do you want me to tell you exactly what happened with Maria del Rosario?" I brought out a more advanced biology book and explained all the details. He stared at the book without so much as blinking—and then he began to cry. It was a slow crying, like a release of anxiety. And that's the way it was in our house, combating fear with facts. Always the truth. Of course, some people, including some close to us, didn't understand our methods.

Shortly before the third procedure, we had an appointment with Roberto and he came to see us at home the next day. Juan Francisco guessed right away what Roberto's presence meant (that we would soon be leaving for Boston again). "Papa, if you leave again, I'll be the one who'll die this time," he told me.

From then on, I stayed in Montevideo with the boys.

Over time, I've realized a few things. Although I wish things could have been different, I feel that all of this has made us stronger as a family. It has taught us to appreciate the love we have, to be thankful for the people in our lives, and to appreciate all the things we might otherwise take for granted.

One of the things I learned, with Roberto's help and example, was never to give up, to find the strength to keep going, even on your hands and knees, when it seems you don't have the energy to take another step. Fight to the end and give every last ounce of what you've got.

For a long time, that uncertainty about Maria's future tied my stomach in knots. That is, until I went to Roberto Canessa's house one day. He told me, "Juan, stop worrying; that phase where your stomach is in knots, wondering whether she's going to need another surgery the next day is over. This is a success story. She's not going to have any problems for a long time." So I asked him, "So you mean I can relax for a few months?" "You can relax for a few *years*," he told me. We'd lived day-to-day for so long. That was as far into the future as we could see. There was a time we were weighing her every day, because if she didn't gain a pound, we had to rush her to surgery. But on that morning, Roberto was telling me, "Widen your horizon." From that point on, I could look into the future without anguish. Very simply, it felt as if the battle had been won, and each passing day was a victory.

Blows are softened over time. Memories become easier to bear.

Time files the rough edges off of our pain. Through it all, this little girl has been a hero to us, to her family, to anyone who has followed her journey. To the point that people cannot separate the girl from her odyssey. In this way, she's like Roberto and the mountain: People can't think of one without thinking about the other.

When she and I are together, I just let go and enjoy the day. I'm just happy to be with her. I don't think about tomorrow, only today, this very moment; that's what's real. We'll worry about tomorrow, tomorrow. *What will she be like in a few years? In ten years?* All those unknowns parents worry about, I never do.

Thanks to her, I feel like I've been given an insight into something deeper. As if death came for her and she somehow won. She *beat* death. Whatever happens later, I don't care. We've stolen from death time she might not otherwise have had.

Chapter 51

Jojo Buere Beraza, Nurse

The second floor of Hospital Italiano is a cherished place for me because it has been an intimate part of my life since I was two. Yes, my refuge is my family and my home in Salto, but this hospital is my second home. When I visit now, as an adult, every minute detail of this place brings back memories of my childhood and adolescence. I might see a poster that has been there for years and be flooded with old images. Usually, young people recall memories of being at a party or a friend's house. I find them in a hospital. In the machines used to examine my heart. In the people like Hilda, Roberto's assistant, who has been there as long as I can remember.

Every time after Roberto finishes doing my ultrasound, we go into the next room to talk. Roberto says his experiences in the Andes are a toolbox he reaches for when he needs them. Not like delicate laboratory tweezers or test tubes or graduated beakers. But the heavy-duty tools of a mechanic. Or a blacksmith. A pair of pliers and a hammer, a wrench and an anvil. There's no room for anything delicate on a mountain, he says, only for things that are strong and tough. And that's how he is.

Ever since I was a little girl, he talked to me about my heart condition, clearly and without calling it a problem. That gave me

275

a strange sense of security, because I always pictured him with his toolbox, ready to come to my rescue. He told me that my heart condition wasn't a disability but simply a series of life's hurdles to be overcome one at a time. And the latest hurdle was when he replaced two heart valves so that I could live a more normal life. After that, I should be able to live like any other young woman. But as Roberto says, I'm not like other young women, because I've had to climb precarious cliffs and brave snowy gorges, just as Roberto did when he was nineteen.

Once, he blurted out to me, "Well, it looks like your heart valves are all rotten; we'll have to go in and swap them," as simply as if he were talking about a broken pipe, which made me burst into laughter instead of tears.

Sometimes people ask me how I manage to stay upbeat despite my illness. But honestly, although I had several major surgeries before the age of twenty-one, I can't say that I have bad memories of them. I think that's because I have always had Roberto's support, because we have always focused on the positive and the facts. Knowing the truth, I've come to learn, is always a positive.

I may have had physical limitations, but I never had emotional or psychological barriers. Maybe that's why I never looked so harshly on my condition. I never saw it as a great tragedy. It was just part of who I was. If I'd loathed it as something scary or horrible, I'd only be loathing myself. Before this last operation, Roberto told me, "Life's greatest challenge isn't dying, it's living." Of course, I went into the surgery knowing the risks. I may not have been aware of the gravity of my situation at two or at seven, but today, as an adult, I understand.

As a nursing student in Salto, I fell in love with the profession because I love the human body and how it works. I'm a perfect example: I was broken and now I'm not. And, oh my, did the nurses help me! That's what fascinates me: No matter what is wrong with a person, you can always try to fix it. As a nurse, I can help fix all those "rotten" valves and help people feel well again.

When I study the human body, the mystery of the human heart, the perfection of this machine, I feel as if I understand life. The heart is more than just an organ that helps keep you functioning; it's what gives you warmth. I love the idea that there's a toolbox I can use to help people regain their warmth—that I can be a part of that.

I used to hate it when my parents saw me sad. I felt as if I had already given them enough pain and anguish and should not add to it. But when they told me about the final operation—besides being scared because it was going to be a long and complicated procedure—I felt nervous because everything I had lived up to that point was riding on this one surgery. Everything I'd gone through was leading up to this day! That's when I finally allowed my feelings and emotions to show. After the operation, I cried more than I could control. Dr. Canessa said he experienced a similar feeling when he finally saw the valley of Los Maitenes after leaving the mountain. Before, he had constantly been on alert. He hadn't even allowed his body to get sick. But when he saw those green pastures, every tension was released. (He even got violently sick with dysentery.) He could barely take the last few steps because he had finally let loose the emotions he had guarded so carefully.

I used to tell my family, "I can't allow myself to cry until August 8, 2011, after the final surgery to determine whether I'll live or die." It was a luxury I couldn't afford, because if I started crying, my mother, father, siblings, and grandparents—everyone—would break down in tears. *Who was supporting whom?* I had to be strong for all of us.

At the same time, I owe my siblings a huge debt because during those years, their wants always came second. When my sister wanted or needed something—a new dress, braces, money for a school trip—my parents always had to evaluate whether they could afford it, because "Jojo came first." And my siblings never once argued. Jojo always came first because my parents didn't know how long I would be around.

That's why every day, I ask my family, my parents and siblings, how I can possibly repay them for everything they've sacrificed for me. They always respond the same way: "You can thank us by being healthy." In my twenty-one years, I've tried to pay them back by studying and working as hard as any normal young woman who wants to better herself as a person would. But I know I'll never be able to pay them back for everything they have done for me.

Before that final surgery, I went to see Roberto. I was feeling depressed, and he asked me what was wrong. I told him that I didn't know but that I was feeling very emotional and was crying all the time. I told him I was afraid of dying during surgery because it was a long and risky operation. He just said to me, "You can't worry about this, Jojo. If you're going to die, you're going to die. It's nothing unnatural. Believe me. I lived it."

"It's not dying that I'm afraid of," I responded. "I'm worried about the people I'd leave behind. I'm not as worried about my heart as I am about the hearts of my mother and father. How can I possibly console them? How can I help them? That's what's worrying me . . ."

He thought about this and responded, "You have a point. But don't you worry about that part of it. I need you to worry about yourself. I'll worry about your parents."

It's been two years now since my last operation. I'm twenty-three, in my final year of nursing school, and I work in Salto's Regional Norte hospital.

I like working with people, especially with children. I could have chosen to work with adults or in maternity, but since I like challenges—I guess since my whole life has been a challenge—I chose the more difficult specialty. Because children are at the most delicate stage of their lives. They say kids are resilient, that they fall and bounce right back as if they're made of rubber, but I've learned that they are, in fact, quite fragile. If you're not careful, the slightest injury can leave a mark that could last a lifetime.

A nurse has a very intimate relationship with a patient. You're the one who holds their hand during a difficult time, something they often don't feel comfortable doing with a doctor. That, to me, is everything. No one is closer to a patient than a nurse.

My childhood was intense. When other people my age talk about childhood, it seems like something distant. They have sporadic memories, here and there, but not a solid sequence. Me, I remember being in this very hospital many times, particularly in the intensive care unit. My childhood is seared in my mind, a raw and real memory. It feels as if it were yesterday and not twenty, nineteen, ten, or even two years ago. I look at some of the child patients here and realize I was once their age.

Whenever I approach one of these children, I can look into their eyes and tell exactly what they're thinking and feeling, because I was that child. Their eyes say, *I don't want to see anyone else dressed in white.* No one else in scrubs with their names embroidered over their shirt pockets. No more doctors in lab coats. Because people in white mean injections, IVs, pressure cuffs, thermometers—pain, discomfort, and exhaustion. As a patient, I understood they were doing things to help me, but I needed them to understand how tired I was of all of it.

That's why I spend a lot of time talking with the children at the hospital, even if they can't understand everything. I tell them as often as I can—sometimes with just a look or by stroking their heads—that I understand they're uncomfortable, in pain, or tired.

So, we make a deal. Children really do understand everything, and I, who am not so far removed from my childhood, remember it just as it was. I liked it when the doctors would make a deal with me: "Look, we're going to have to poke and prod you a little bit now, but I promise we'll leave you alone after for a solid four hours." *Four hours to myself! Without anyone in white bothering me!*

I've learned things you don't learn in textbooks, because I lived them. I've learned a child understands gestures and facial expressions and the look in someone's eyes. I knew when someone was coming to bring me pain or comfort. So when I step into a hospital room, I find myself in two places at once: both coming into the room, and lying in that bed watching the nurse come in.

I don't think it's a coincidence that I, who was surrounded by nurses throughout my life, have gone into health care. You'd think after all I'd been through that I'd run from any field that brought me in contact with doctors and nurses and hospitals, but it's quite the opposite. Because I've found a real treasure in this field.

Sometimes I think I'm like Roberto's disciple. That's probably why I've always wanted to go into the medical field, just like him. When I was little and I'd get an injection, I'd secretly keep the syringe so that I could use it in my job in the future. Once, in 1998, after they removed some cables from the pacemaker in my chest, I squirreled them away in my keepsake box so I could use them when I was a doctor to help a girl who had my condition.

When I turned eighteen, I enrolled in medical school. But I soon realized that each one of us had to blaze our own trail. Just as my role model was strong, I realized so was I—strong enough to make my own choices.

I felt that a lot of doctors were too distant. They recognized their tiny patients not by their names and smiling faces, but by their room and bed numbers. These doctors seemed like very smart and dedicated people, but they generally interacted with their patients at arm's length—not up close, as Roberto had when I was a patient. So I asked myself, *Who was at my side when I was a patient? Roberto and the nurses.* But since Roberto was one of a kind, I decided I would be a nurse.

I started to think about each of the nurses I'd come in contact with over the course of my life. I remembered their dedication, their kindness, their tender loving words. *This* was my calling. *This* was my passion: to use the field of nursing to repay the people who had not only treated me, but cared about me. To them, I was never "Bed 6," never just a series of notes—the patient with the heart condition—on a chart. I was Jojo. And my mother wasn't "the patient's mother," but rather the sweet woman who slept on an uncomfortable pullout next to her daughter's bed for weeks without complaint. The people who saw that every day and appreciated it were the nurses. They were the ones who witnessed my mother coming to my aid when I so much as whimpered in the middle of the night, to comfort me, to hug me, to love me. When the night nurse would come in to help in any way she could, it was as if my mother's love was multiplied. By the time the doctor came back to do his rounds the next morning, an entire lifetime had passed between three people who had been in the room that night: me, my mother, and the nurse.

I know that in some ways, I'm trying to be like Dr. Canessa. My childhood is like his proverbial toolbox. He uses adversity to try to solve other people's problems and, humbly, I try to do the same thing in my own way. It's the only way I can make any use, any sense, out of the bad things that happened in my childhood. Bad things will always happen, but you can't let those things define your future.

I have to see Roberto every six months because of my heart issues, but now I take these visits in stride. The last time I had an appointment with him I told him, "I'm doing something I've never allowed myself to do before: make long-term plans." I even make long-term plans for the children who are in my care.

It's a curious feeling to know someone has kept watch over you, day and night, for as long as you can remember. To know that, no matter the hour, he'd always be there, just a phone call away. You feel protected. Because of that, I feel that I in turn can protect and care for all those other children at the hospital, and so we keep paying it forward.

Chapter 52

Sitting by my mother's deathbed on August 13, 2011, I leaned in close and whispered, "It's OK to let go, Mama. You've done enough."

My mother had been suffering from a progressive neurological disorder that had hindered her brain from communicating with her body since the age of seventy-two. And in the last few years, her memory had begun to fade as well.

That day, knowing she was in that in-between zone where the will to live and the will to let go are in constant opposition, I gathered myself—I knew what my opinion meant to her—and told her softly: "It's OK to let go, Mama. You've suffered long enough." *You've tasted real joy and real sorrow.*

We had talked it over. My brother Conqui and his wife, Virginia, who had cared for her for years. My sister Adriana and my youngest brother, Juan Francisco. We weighed her will to live and her will to move on, and we felt her slipping away. I'll never know if we made the right choice, but it's clear my mother took me at my word. She would not awaken to another sunrise.

It's OK to let go, Mama. You've done enough. I can't help but think at that moment of finality that I was referring to what she had meant to my own story, to the long and intense battle when she had held my hand from a distance and guided me through the abyss. *You did it, Mama. You did it forty years ago, and you kept doing it every day over the course of my life.*

When my mother heard me, I felt she had not only understood me, but had actually been waiting to hear those words. A harmonious aura settled over her, and she floated off to sleep. That night, as I left her room, I turned to look at her one last time, lying in her bed. The next morning, a Sunday, as I was driving toward the hospital, I got a call from Conqui with the news that she had died. I wept in silence. *You've arrived, Mama. Life is a journey to reach this place you now know.*

I'd lost my biggest supporter, my mother.

After the avalanche, I felt I'd come to know something about death. Whether suffocating beneath tons of snow as I nearly had. Or dying peacefully in bed, like Mama. Or, like my father in July of 2009, who tore out the tubes that were keeping him alive in an ICU so that he could let himself go.

Sometimes, the memory of his death sneaks up on me like a ghost.

My father was as strong as an ox at eighty-two years old. We were stunned to learn he had developed a tumor on one of his kidneys, seemingly overnight, that had spread close to his heart, overtaking the inferior vena cava. He underwent a complex operation, but by that night, I figured he would survive it. I went into the ICU and debated whether I should spend the night with him, watching over him the way he had stood vigil over me while I had been on the mountain. In the end, I decided against it. That night, while the intensive-care staff was distracted, he tore out every tube and wire connected to him. By the time they'd realized what he'd done, it was too late. When I arrived that morning, I found the staff giving him CPR, and he died.

I've spent countless hours wondering what happened that night. Deep down, I think my father crossed over that blurry area between wanting to survive and wanting to end. A hazy region I had known personally the night of the avalanche. Maybe he couldn't imagine living with a reduced quality of life and ripped out the life-support tubes. Or, who knows, maybe he ripped them out involuntarily, in a daze. And maybe if that had been the case, and I had been with him, I might have been able to stop him, to save him. It seemed as if there was still so much he wanted to do, like find that taxi driver he had met on the morning of December 22, 1972, and later searched for, a man who still appeared to him in his dreams.

Chapter 53

There's a common denominator to my happiest moments, even though those moments are completely distinct. Sometimes, my life might have been in danger. At other times, I'd arrived at an unexpected place in life. And during others still, it seemed like nothing obvious was going on.

What's at the essence of my happiest moments? First, that what happens is unexpected. Second, that it's something internal, not external. And third, that it involves another person.

I can't define it, exactly, but I can take stock of all the moments I have felt this blessing.

I felt it the moment the helicopter arrived with the first of the fourteen of my friends who were languishing in the fuselage.

I felt that blessing watching Tomas the Great run.

I felt it the moment I saw my mother come into my hospital room in San Fernando with a look in her eyes that said, *You're finally home.*

I felt that blessed when I met Sergio Catalan face-to-face, this man who was the first to believe in us, and I felt it later that night when the shepherds watched over us as we slept.

I felt it when I handed Lauri that wedge of cheese from Los Maitenes at the hospital. And I felt it a second later, when the pregnant nurse came into the room with a new life just days from emerging from her womb. She seemed to restore a balance, an order that we had lost up in the mountains.

I felt these blessings when my children were born, and when Hilario placed my grandson Benicio in my arms and said, "Thank you."

I feel it the moment a desperate mother regains hope, and her eyes fill with tears, and all she wants to do in the world is hug someone, because she has just realized that her child is going to live.

There's a fourth element involved, and it's that we're not limited to being a single person, but rather that we can stretch the boundaries of who we are and become much more.

The fifth is that adversity makes you a better person.

The sixth: Perfection is always unachievable, always seeming to move farther into the distance. And when I feel passion for what I do, the barrier between the possible and the impossible vanishes. I don't know if it exists, but I no longer perceive it.

I feel blessed in realizing that these children who are born with a heart ailment through no fault of their own are not survivors like me; instead, I am a survivor like them.

But the greatest miracle is that all these truths converged to reveal themselves to me at my personal nadir, the most difficult moment of my life: as I watched the moon rise over the Andes while I was on the brink of death. All my blessings crystallized at that moment, when I was just nineteen. My joy is not linked to anything tangible or something that can be won. Not even the prospect of staying alive. My happiness lies in that spiritual moment, when I was able to put my arms around that celestial light and feel its incandescent radiance. It's a light that never fades, that strengthens me and allows me to share it with those who seek my help. Who would have guessed? It's the light from the mountain that continues to illuminate my path, in life and in death. That was my ultimate discovery, the one that explains all the rest.

A Note from Pablo Vierci

I've known Roberto Canessa almost all my life. I was born in the Carrasco section of Montevideo, Uruguay; he was born two and a half years later, just seventy-five yards away. We went to the same school, where our parents took turns carpooling, and we grew up playing at the same playground, located exactly halfway between our houses. He was so intense and bright, his personality so unconventional, that even as a kid it surprised me. We became instant friends and have remained close all our lives.

When the airplane Roberto was on crashed into the Andes in 1972, I couldn't believe that he, along with so many other friends and classmates, had disappeared. That group of rugby players had exuded such an aura of youthful immortality. But only Roberto, Nando Parrado, and fourteen others were to return.

Over my journalism career, I've written many articles trying to elucidate exactly what happened on that mountaintop from October to December of 1972. In 2008, I published the book *La Sociedad de la Nieve* (The Society of the Snow), in which all sixteen survivors tell their stories, providing not just the facts of what happened (as in the book *Alive*) but a unique glimpse into their inner turmoil.

It was while I was in the process of interviewing Roberto for that book that he came to me with an idea: He wanted my help in delving into the larger picture of how his ordeal on the mountain had influenced the course of his life. I agreed to do the project. It was a huge challenge for me. My esteem for him had grown into profound admiration over the years, not just because of what had happened in 1972, but because of what he managed to do with his life ever since.

In compiling this book, first and foremost, I interviewed Roberto regarding his experiences in the Andes and later as a doctor. Then I spoke to members of his family, as well as various individuals involved in the rescue. Finally, I interviewed many of his patients and their families, for what better way to explain his career as a pediatric cardiologist than by talking to some of the people whose lives he has touched over the years? Roberto never attended any of these interviews, to avoid having his presence influence their recollections.

Throughout the process, I sought genuine testimony from the heart, in order to explore just how this man was forged by his ordeal on that mountain so many years ago, and how that experience in turn forged the extraordinary doctor he would become.

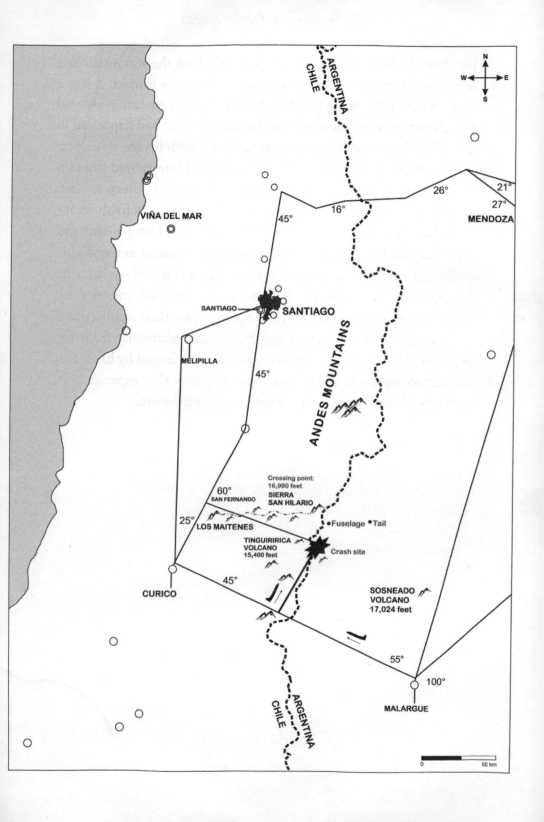